ZION
Our Origin and Our Destiny

LARRY BARKDULL

Pillars of Zion Series Titles

Introduction: *Portrait of a Zion Person*

Book 1: *Zion—Our Origin and Our Destiny*

Book 2: *The First Pillar of Zion—The New and Everlasting Covenant*

Book 3: *The Second Pillar of Zion—The Oath and Covenant of the Priesthood*

Book 4: *The Third Pillar of Zion—The Law of Consecration*

Book 5: *The Pure in Heart*

Book 6: *No Poor among Them*

Pillars of Zion Publishing
Orem, Utah

Copyright and Permission

Copyright © 2009, 2013 Barkdull Marketing, Inc

Publishing Imprint: Pillars of Zion Publishing, a division of Barkdull Marketing, Inc. Licensed for publication and distributed by BestBooks Publishing and Distribution, Spanish Fork, Utah. Phone: 801.815.5349.

All Rights Reserved. No part of this book may be reproduced in any format or in any medium without the written permision from the publisher, BestBooks Publishing and Distribution.

Contact

Contact us at info@pillarsofzion.com
Visit our Website at www.PillarsOfZion.com

Disclaimer

This series is heavily documented with some 5,000 references and 400 works cited. Every effort has been made to achieve accuracy. This work is not an official publication of the Church of Jesus Christ of Latter-day Saints, and the views expressed within this work are the sole responsibility of the author and do not necessarily reflect the position of The Church of Jesus Christ of Latter-day Saints or any other entity.

LICENSE USE

1) If you received the free PDF version of the introduction to t he series *Portrait of a Zion Person,* you have the right to store it on your computer. You also have the right to share the PDF with as many people as you please, provided that neither they nor you use part or all of the content to disparage The Church of Jesus Christ of Latter-day Saints in any manner. Neither you nor anyone with whom you share the PDF has the right to change the content of the PDF.

2) If you purchased the printed book or a version of the book for an electronic reader, you do not have the right to share those versions of the book.

Refer all copyright and permissions issues to the contact above.

Library of Congress Cataloging Publication Data is on file at the Library of Congress.
ISBN: 978-1-937399-02-3

Dedication
To Elizabeth Barkdull
Ron and Bonnie McMillan
David and Lorelea Anderson
Paul and Sharon Meyers

Acknowledgments
My wife, Elizabeth, and I would like to acknowledge a number of people, who, in one way or another, lent their support for the creation of this project.

- Lawrence and Georgia Shaw
- Lance and Jozet Richardson
- Blaine and Kathy Yorgason
- Scot and Maurine Proctor
- Clay Gorton
- Ted Gibbons
- Grover Cardon
- Gary and Bonnie Leavitt
- Bud and Barbara Poduska
- Dee Jay Bawden
- Steve Glenn
- Gavon and Tanya Barkdull

Production Staff
Thanks to Eschler Editing for editorial and design work.

- Editors—Jay A. Parry and Michele Preisendorf
- Graphic Artist—Douglass Cole
- Typesetter—Sean Graham

Note about The Three Pillars of Zion
The complete Zion series contains seven books. The full bibliography, and index are included in each of the books for ease of referencing and navigation. Each volume includes its own table of contents except for the Introduction book, *Portrait of a Zion Person*, includes the table of contents for each volume in order to introduce the entire series.

Table of Contents

Book 1
Zion—Our Origin and Our Destiny

Introduction 1
    Parallels between the 3 Nephi Saints and the Latter-day Saints   1
    An Important Key to Establishing Zion   2
    Enoch's Dispensation Is a Pattern   3
    The Three Pillars of Zion   3

Section 1
Zion—What Do We Know of It? 5
    Zion Is Our Ideal   6
    The Celestial Order   7
    Zion and Babylon—Exact Opposites   7
    Becoming a Zion Person   8

Section 2
Overview of Zion Peoples 9
    Fall from Zion   9
    The Way Back to Zion Revealed   10
    Zion—A New Way of Life   12
    Surety of a Better World   12
    Adam's Zion   13
    Enos's Zion   13
    Enoch's Zion   13
    Methuselah and Noah's Zion   14
    Melchizedek's Zion   15
    Abraham's Zion   16
    Moses' Attempt at Zion   18
    Alma the Elder's Zion   19
    King Benjamin's Zion   20
    Alma the Younger's Zion   26
    The Apostles' Zion   28
    The Nephites' Zion   28
    Joseph Smith's Zion   31
    Latter-day Zion   36
    Summary and Conclusion   37

Section 3
We Were Prepared to Become Latter-day Zion People 39
    Divine Appointment   40
    Special Spirits of the Royal Generation   42
    Perspective on the Cosmic War   43
    Preparation in the "First Place"   44
    Summary and Conclusion   46

Section 4
Babylon the Great 49
    Anti-Christ Philosophy   50
    Cain   51
    Nimrod   52
    Sodom and Gomorrah   55
    Descriptions of Babylon   57
    Babylon As a Religion   60
    The "Great Church" of the Devil   61
    Babylon As a Temple   63
    Nephi's Description of Babylon   64
    Spiritual Babylon   74
    Competition   77
    Hypocrites   80
    False Philosophies   81
    Popularity   84
    Latter-day Babylon—Prophetic Description of Our Time   84
    Babylon Today Compared to the Days of Noah   86
    Paul's Prophecy   88
    Inverting the Truth   89
    Moroni's Prophecy   90
    The Fall of Babylon   92
    Samuel the Lamanite's Parallel Denunciation of Babylon   95
    Go Ye Out from Babylon   99
    Summary and Conclusion   100
    Postlude   103

Bibliography 105
Index and Concordance 115
About the Author 141

Book 1
Zion—Our Origin and Our Destiny

Introduction

In the beginning of the thirty-fourth year of the Nephite calendar,[1] a remarkable event occurred, one that is of critical importance to us today. According to Mormon, on the fourth day of the first month of the year, the Nephite nation collapsed under the weight of its own depravity. The fall was on the scale of the cataclysms of the Flood and Sodom and Gomorrah. Only a small group of Christians survived. Suddenly, above the darkness that had choked out any semblance of light, the voice of Christ was heard announcing his identity and the fulfillment of his mission; he declared the destruction of the wicked, lamented the evils of his people, and invited the remnant to come unto him with full purpose of heart.

Then the record goes silent. Mormon picks up the account "in the *ending of the thirty and fourth year*,"[2] nearly twelve months later. What happened in the lives of the surviving Nephites during that year? Mormon only hints at what the people did with Jesus' message, but when we piece together the account, we discover one of the great sermons of the Book of Mormon—a sermon that is of utmost importance to those of us who would become Zion-like.

Parallels between the 3 Nephi Saints and the Latter-day Saints

We should keep in mind that these people were not unlike many of us: either they were new members or they were good people who were trying to live the gospel as best they could. Perhaps some were lukewarm; maybe others were sitting atop spiritual plateaus and lacking the motivation to keep climbing. Whatever their condition, we do know this: The Lord declared that they had escaped the destructions only because they were "more righteous" than those who had perished. We are left to speculate as to their degree of righteousness, but, as we shall see, they needed time to change some things. The Savior was also quick to point out that they needed to change. Therefore, he called them to repentance and bade them strive to become truly converted so he could heal them.[3]

Why is this account important to us? To answer that question, we must first remember that from the outset of the Book of Mormon, Moroni testifies that the book was

---

1   3 Nephi 8:5.
2   3 Nephi 10:18; emphasis added.
3   3 Nephi 9:13.

written for us.[4] Then, within the first pages of the Book of Mormon, Nephi instructs us to read the book by *likening* the scriptures unto ourselves.[5] Armed with those two pieces of information, we might envision ourselves as members of that small group of Nephite survivors. Somehow these people, who had escaped the annihilation, had taken to heart his commandment and invitation and had changed their lives so that within twelve months they achieved Zion.

How did they do it? How can we do it?

Mormon seems to have wanted us to dig for the answer as one would mine for a pearl of great price. A careful reading of the books of 3 and 4 Nephi, which include the Savior's directives and Mormon's description of the achievement of Zion by the Nephite people, helps us to fill in the twelve-month gap and shows us what we must do to rise to such a lofty ideal. This book explores the Lord's call to us to likewise repent, become converted, and come to Jesus with full purpose of heart so that he might heal us, too, and establish us as a Zion people.

An Important Key to Establishing Zion

In the latter days, a key to establishing Zion in our lives is found in Doctrine and Covenants 42, the revelation called, the law of the Church,[6] which comprises the law of Zion. In one sentence, the Lord prophesied that he would give us three significant covenants that had the power to make us Zion individuals: "And ye shall hereafter receive church covenants, such as shall be sufficient to establish you, both here and in the New Jerusalem."[7] The references in this scripture lead to what we are calling in this series, The Three Pillars of Zion:

1. The New and Everlasting Covenant. (D&C 132:4–7)
2. The Oath and Covenant of the Priesthood. (D&C 84:33–44)
3. The Law of Consecration. (D&C 82:11–15)

These three covenants (pillars) are sufficient to establish Zion-like qualities in our individual lives and in our marriages, families, and other groups under the direction of the priesthood. Understanding that this is the Lord's way of establishing Zion, we are left without excuse. Clearly, we have been given all that we need. To become the pure in heart, which is the definition of Zion people,[8] we simply must better understand our covenants and then live up to our privileges.

This book explores the contrast between Zion and Babylon; the three covenants, or pillars, upon which Zion lives are built; the elements of the journey to achieve a Zion-like life; and a portrait of the pure in heart.

---

4 Book of Mormon title page.
5 1 Nephi 19:24; 2 Nephi 11:8.
6 D&C 42, section heading.
7 D&C 42:67.
8 D&C 97:21.

Introduction

Enoch's Dispensation Is a Pattern

The scriptures that describe Enoch's Zion provide us a model for establishing Zion in our lives. For example, both Enoch and Joseph Smith were commanded to:
- Preach the gospel of Jesus Christ (Moses 6:37; 7:19; D&C 19:21, 31; 38:41)
- Gather the Saints to places of safety (Moses 7:17–19; D&C 33:6; 45:69, 71; 115:6)
- Attain unity and righteousness (Moses 7:18; D&C 21:4–7; 38:27)
- Become "pure in heart" (Moses 7:18; D&C 97:21)
- Care for the poor and needy (Moses 7:18; D&C 38:35; 42:30)
- Build a "City of Holiness" (Moses 7:19; D&C 45:66–70)[9]

"Zion is the ensign to the nations. 'I intend to lay a foundation,' Joseph Smith boldly declared, 'that will revolutionize the whole world.' And then, emphasizing the source of this revolutionary movement, he added, 'It will not be by sword or gun that this kingdom will roll on: the power of truth is such that all nations will be under the necessity of obeying the Gospel.'"[10]

The Three Pillars of Zion

With very few exceptions, this series does *not* attempt to describe what the latter-day "priesthood society"[11] of Zion will look like. That is the prerogative of the President of the Church. What this series does attempt to describe is Zion people, those individuals who become Zion-like now and who will one day make up the latter-day Zion priesthood society. Therefore, when the word *Zion* is used in this set, it is almost exclusively meant to refer to a Zion-like person.

We must keep in mind that the term *Zion* is described in the scriptures and by prophets in a variety of ways. Zion is a location, a group of followers, a journey, and a destination.[12] It is always a condition of the heart.[13] Zion can be manifested in a telestial setting and an Edenic terrestrial setting—and, of course, its ultimate manifestation is in a celestial setting.

Despite our best efforts, without divine help we cannot establish Zion in our lives, marriages, families, or in a priesthood society. Only the Lord can establish Zion.[14] The Saints in 3 Nephi are a case in point. They did all that they could do, but in the end the ideal of Zion was created because the Lord came to help them complete their journey. Were they Zion people before his appearance? Of course; but they had not yet achieved the ideal. That step required the Lord's intervention. Can we similarly qualify as Zion people without having achieved the ideal? Most assuredly. As we journey toward Zion

---

9   "Enoch and His Message for Latter Days," *LDS Church News*, Feb. 5, 1994.
10 "Enoch and His Message for Latter Days," *LDS Church News*, Feb. 5, 1994, quoting Smith, *Teachings of the Prophet Joseph Smith*, 366.
11 President Spencer W. Kimball called Zion a "priesthood society" in his address, "Welfare Services: The Gospel in Action," 77–78.
12 *Encyclopedia of Mormonism*, 1624–26.
13 Young, *Discourses of Brigham Young*, 118.
14 Nibley, *Approaching Zion*, 6–7.

and earnestly strive to assimilate Zion-like attributes in our lives, we are Zion. We simply must keep our eye single to the ideal of Zion and move forward with the Lord's grace compensating for those attributes that we have not yet acquired. Thus, in these books, when we discuss Zion and its various manifestations, we will typically be describing the ideal that should be our goal.

Striving to become Zion people is as important as arriving. Enoch's people achieved their ideal of Zion "in the process of time."[15] Neither Enoch's people nor Melchizedek's people nor the Nephites who were visited by Christ achieved the ideal of Zion overnight. As far as we can tell, they were much like us—people who made covenants with the Lord and did their best to understand and live those covenants. Their prophets, like ours, held the ideal of Zion before them, and they rose to the occasion. According to prophecy, we will do likewise in the latter-days. In writing these books, my only desire is to promote the cause of Zion and to urge us to gain a greater appreciation of our covenants, which have the power to make us the pure in heart.

In these books, I made every effort to research and document my ideas and statements. Combined, the set includes more than 3,800 references. When I present an opinion, I attempt to use qualifying language so as not to advance a doctrine or interpretation of that doctrine. I've tried to assume the position of *guide*, allowing prophets and well-respected gospel writers to state or clarify doctrine, offer explanations, or paint descriptions. In the end, however, this work is uniquely mine and not an official statement of The Church of Jesus Christ of Latter-day Saints.

---

15 JST, Genesis 7:27.

Section 1
Zion—What Do We Know of It?

We speak of Zion, sing of Zion, covenant to promote the establishment of Zion, and long for Zion—but what *is* Zion? Latter-day Saints ought to know. We have more scriptures and prophets' statements about it than any other people. One could hardly read a page from the Book of Mormon, Doctrine and Covenants, or Pearl of Great Price and not bump into the term or its principles. Why? Because we have the singular charge to become Zion individually, and we have the charge to prepare for the collective establishment of the Lord's Zion. Consequently, we—all of us—are (or should be) more identified with Zion than any other generation.

Moreover, the fact that we have the additional responsibility to call God's children to Zion suggests that we, individually, must first become Zion people: "Verily I say unto you all: Arise and shine forth, that thy light may be a standard for the nations."[16] Hugh Nibley reminded us that a primary purpose of the Church [the kingdom of God] is to prepare a people to become Zion: "[We] work for the building up the Kingdom of God on earth and the establishment of Zion. *The first step makes the second possible.*"[17] At the outset of this last dispensation—the dispensation of Zion—Joseph Smith said, "We ought to have the building up of Zion as our greatest object."[18] If we were to conduct a survey, would the building up of Zion be our greatest object? Regardless of how we might answer, we nevertheless are fond of defending Zion as uniquely *us*, and we are not timid about claiming the blessings of Zion as our birthright. Nevertheless, many of us are hard-pressed to describe or envision Zion, let alone live its principles.

What can we do about this dilemma?

Brigham Young had the answer: "[Zion] commences in the heart of each person."[19] That is, Zion, the priesthood society, is made up of Zion—individual people. Beyond the

---
16 D&C 115:5.
17 Nibley, *Approaching Zion*, 25; emphasis added.
18 Smith, *Teachings of the Prophet Joseph Smith*, 160.
19 Young, *Discourses of Brigham Young*, 118.

typical uses of the word *Zion*—as a location or a society—Zion is a person whose heart is pure; therefore, that person "shall see God"[20]—in other words, to stand in and regain his presence. President John Taylor said, "The Zion of God. What does it mean? The pure in heart in the first place. In the second place . . . the pure in heart who are governed by the law of God."[21] Elder Matthew Cowley added, "And to you whose lives are committed to righteousness, I say unto you, You are Zion."[22] If we will fully embrace these statements, a vast library of Zion material will open to our view. We suddenly realize that by *likening* the scriptures concerning Zion to ourselves,[23] many of the descriptions of that ideal priesthood society are also descriptions of individual Zion-like people who are comprised of the same attributes. Therefore, none of us is exempt. Zion is a vibrant, current idea that we must embrace. Zion is now; we are Zion!

Zion Is Our Ideal

Although there are a number of usages of the word *Zion*, we will examine it in its ultimate sense—a person who is striving to become pure in heart and who is in the process of qualifying to stand in the presence of God. As we stated in the introduction, the term *Zion* is described in the scriptures and by prophets in a variety of ways. Zion is a process, a people, and a place.[24] It is always a condition of the heart.[25] Zion can be manifested in a variety of settings, from telestial to terrestrial to, ultimately, celestial. We qualify as Zion people by remaining on the path to Zion. As we journey toward the ideal of Zion and strive to assimilate Zion-like attributes in our lives, we are Zion. We simply must keep our eye single to this purpose and move forward with the Lord's grace compensating for those Zion-like attributes we have not yet acquired.

The ideal of Zion, we will learn, is the end purpose of the new and everlasting covenant, the oath and covenant of the priesthood, and every saving covenant and ordinance of the gospel. Therefore, if we do not have becoming Zion-like in mind, the gospel plan has little meaning or power in our lives. To become a Zion person or to have a Zion marriage or a Zion family should be our *only* aims in the gospel of Jesus Christ. Every program, every function, every activity is (or ought to be) designed with Zion in mind. We can become distracted and caught up in extraneous details, but in the end we will only postpone or forfeit our blessings. Because the celestial world and law are the ultimate manifestations of Zion, our origin is Zion, Zion is our earthly birthright,[26] and it can be our destiny. Very literally, we are children of Zion.

Zion people take their covenants seriously and literally. They have a feeling of urgency and a longing that drives them to establish Zion in their hearts. The day will come when Zion individuals will receive their inheritance in the priesthood society of Zion.

---

20 JST, Matthew 5:10; 3 Nephi 12:8.
21 Taylor, *The Gospel Kingdom*, 245.
22 Cowley, *Matthew Cowley Speaks*, 30.
23 1 Nephi 19:23–24.
24 *Encyclopedia of Mormonism*, 1624–26.
25 Young, *Discourses of Brigham Young*, 118.
26 Every person descends from Enoch, and a high percentage of the world descends from Abraham.

Section 1   Zion—What Do We Know of It?

But until that day, each of us is commanded to become Zion individually. President Benson handed each covenant person the responsibility for becoming Zion-like. Zion, the priesthood society, he said, can be brought about only by Zion people. As more and more of us decide to embrace the principles of Zion, the celestial order will finally exist among us and we, individually and collectively, will be prepared to receive the Lord.[27] We recall that Enoch built his city of Zion *after* his people had individually qualified as Zion people (notice the sequence); just so, we will gather to build latter-day Zion when our hearts are pure, and then only under the direction of the prophet.[28] President Spencer W. Kimball was another prophet who laid the responsibility for becoming and establishing Zion squarely upon our shoulders. How well we incorporate the new and everlasting covenant (the Covenant[29]) in our lives directly determines the time required to "accomplish all things pertaining to Zion."[30]

The Celestial Order

Zion is the standard among celestial and celestial-seeking beings.[31] We can measure substantially any situation, institution, person, group, philosophy, theory, or motivation against the standard of Zion. Hugh Nibley explained that three orders exist on the earth, just as they exist in the universe: The order of Zion is celestial; the order of Eden is terrestrial; and the order of Babylon is telestial.[32] Discernment is a gift of the Spirit,[33] and freedom of choice is inherent in the spirit of man.[34] How we choose among these orders determines where our hearts are now and where they will be in eternity.[35] This life is uniquely and strategically designed so that the three orders are ever before us. We must learn to discern between them and make our choices consistent with our eternal desires.

Zion and Babylon—Exact Opposites

Wherever there exists anything or anyone that is celestial, there exists Zion. It is in every way the exact opposite of the telestial order of Babylon,[36] making the two as incompatible and mutually resistant as positive and negative poles. President Gordon B. Hinckley said that compromising the revealed doctrines of the Covenant is never an option.[37] Like Jesus and Satan, celestial and telestial things cannot compromise in any degree. When a person attempts to straddle Babylon and Zion, he will eventually be pulled into Babylon. It is unavoidable.

---

27   Benson, "Jesus Christ—Gifts and Expectations," 16.
28   Moses 7:19.
29   Note: In this book we will refer to the new and everlasting covenant as the *Covenant*.
30   Kimball, "Becoming the Pure in Heart," quoting D&C 105:37.
31   D&C 105:5.
32   Nibley, *Approaching Zion*, xv.
33   D&C 50:23–24; 1 Corinthians 2:11.
34   McKay, *Gospel Ideals*, 299.
35   Matthew 6:21; Luke 12:34; 3 Nephi 13:21.
36   Nibley, *Approaching Zion*, 30.
37   Hinckley, "The Dawning of a Brighter Day," 81.

When we attempt to mix celestial Zion with telestial Babylon (often called the world), Zion simply flees to its eternal lofty location. Thus the saying, "Zion is fled."[38] Why? Because Zion is a constant that never changes despite the inconsistency of her children: "Zion shall not be moved out of her place, notwithstanding her children are scattered." Our covenantal responsibility, then, is to conform to Zion rather than insisting that Zion conform to us: "They that remain, and are pure in heart, shall return, and come to their inheritances, they and their children, with songs of everlasting joy, to build up the waste places of Zion."[39] If we choose otherwise or if we lack courage and commitment, we will be left to ourselves to languish in this telestial world and its order. Referencing Elder John A. Widtsoe, Elder Ezra Taft Benson said, "The troubles of the world may largely be laid at the doors of those who are neither hot nor cold; who always follow the line of least resistance; whose timid hearts flutter at taking sides for truth. As in the great Council in the heavens, so in the Church of Christ on earth, there can be no neutrality."[40] Therefore, either we are Zion or we are not. There is no compromising or mingling of Zion and Babylon. Hugh Nibley explained: "Zion is pure, which means 'not mixed with any impurities, unalloyed'; it is all Zion and nothing else."[41]

Becoming a Zion Person

If we truly long for Zion, to become that kind of person and to enjoy Zion's unique privileges, we must first make and keep the foundational covenant of Zion—*The New and Everlasting Covenant*. This Covenant is *not* the covenant that will someday be required of Zion people when they are invited into that order; that future covenant will be an appendage to the new and everlasting covenant, which is the totality of all saving covenants, ordinances, and commandments. The new and everlasting covenant prepares us to become Zion in our hearts and to someday gain an inheritance in the heavenly society of Zion. The new and everlasting covenant that we embrace with all our hearts walls out Babylon and welds us irrevocably to Zion and her King. The pure in heart become "all Zion and nothing else."

This, then, is what we know of Zion. She is our origin, our birthright, and our destiny. She is our ideal. Her establishment should be our greatest desire. As part of the latter-day dispensation, we are under[42] covenant to build up the kingdom of God for the purpose of establishing Zion. To accomplish that feat and to ensure our salvation and exaltation, we enter into the new and everlasting covenant. By this act, we specify that we have made a choice between Zion and Babylon and that forevermore we will not attempt to mix the two. We will follow the Covenant to its perfect conclusion: to snatch us from Babylon, to single us out, to purify our hearts, to prepare us in e every way to regain the presence of God, and to obtain our inheritance and our crown. "This is Zion: THE PURE IN HEART."

---

38   Moses 7:69.
39   D&C 101:17–18.
40   Benson, *God, Family, Country*, 359.
41   Nibley, *Approaching Zion*, 26.
42   D&C 97:21.

Section 2
Overview of Zion Peoples

When God completed the creation of the earth, he looked upon his work and pronounced it "good."[43] Then when he placed Adam and Eve in the garden of the earth, he pronounced the creation "very good."[44] The term seems more than a convenient modifier. Once a young man saluted Jesus as "Good Master." Jesus quickly challenged him: "Why callest thou me good? There is none good but one, that is, God."[45] That Jesus would equate good with God is telling. Moreover, that God would pronounce his creation with Adam and Eve on it as "very good" seems to suggest that he considered the end result Godlike. Why would that be? Perhaps the answer lies in the fact that Heavenly Father patterned this creation after our heavenly home—Zion.[46] Certainly heaven is a "very good" and Godlike place. Could we expect anything less from a perfect being?

Interestingly, "the word *Zion* may derive from the Hebrew root *tsayan*, meaning 'perfection,' which is also a meaning of the former city name Salem or Shalem, 'city of perfection.'"[47] Therefore, from the outset of human history, Adam and Eve were placed in a condition that was preeminently *good*—that "very good" Zion-like place that pointed our first parents and all of humanity toward the ideal of Zion.

Fall from Zion

Adam and Eve's *fall* from Eden's Zion-like state shot cataclysmic changes through their bodies and all creation. This earth has likely never before nor since experienced such a violent change. Where there had been unity, equality, peace, abundant health, eternal life, spontaneously growing fruits and flowers, incorruption, and the presence of God,

---

43 Genesis 1:25.
44 Genesis 1:31.
45 Mark 10:17–18.
46 D&C 77:2; Moses 6:63.
47 Galbraith, Ogden, and Skinner, *Jerusalem: The Eternal City,* 41.

there now existed discord, competition, enmity, illness, death, tormenting thorns, briars, and noxious weeds, and, worst of all, separation from God. Adam and Eve had just entered the telestial world, which would be corrupted by Lucifer and become Babylon! The profound differences between Zion and Babylon were as opposite as day and night. Adam and Eve's immediate reaction was to find a way out, and they knew that there was only one Person who knew the way. Therefore, they built an altar and prayed. The answer that they received became the universal answer for all of us who came after them; that answer was and is the Covenant—*The New and Everlasting Covenant.*

> And after many days an angel of the Lord appeared unto Adam, saying: Why dost thou offer sacrifices unto the Lord?
>
> And Adam said unto him: I know not, save the Lord commanded me. And then the angel spake, saying: This thing is a similitude of the sacrifice of the Only Begotten of the Father, which is full of grace and truth. *Wherefore, thou shalt do all that thou doest in the name of the Son, and thou shalt repent and call upon God in the name of the Son forevermore.*
>
> And in that day the Holy Ghost fell upon Adam, which beareth record of the Father and the Son, saying: I am the Only Begotten of the Father from the beginning, henceforth and forever, that as thou hast fallen thou mayest be redeemed, and all mankind, even as many as will.
>
> And in that day Adam blessed God and was filled, and began to prophesy concerning all the families of the earth, saying: Blessed be the name of God, for because of my transgression my eyes are opened, *and in this life I shall have joy, and again in the flesh I shall see God.*
>
> And Eve, his wife, heard all these things and was glad, saying: Were it not for our transgression we never should have had seed, and never should have known good and evil, and the joy of our redemption, and the eternal life which God giveth unto all the obedient.[48]

The Way Back to Zion Revealed

Adam and Eve were going home! By entering into the Covenant that God offered them, they could once again enjoy the happiness of heaven and experience the presence of God—*in this life!* That was *good* news—*God's* news.

---

[48] Moses 5:6–12; emphasis added.

The new and everlasting covenant is "the fulness of the gospel (D&C 39:11; 45:9; 66:2; 133:57)," said Elder Bruce R. McConkie. "When men accept the gospel, they thereby agree or covenant to keep the commandments of God, and he promises or covenants to give them salvation in his kingdom. The gospel is the *everlasting* covenant because it is ordained by Him who is Everlasting and also because it is everlastingly the same. . . . Each time this everlasting covenant is revealed it is *new* to those of that dispensation. Hence the gospel is the *new and everlasting covenant*."[49] Immediately, Adam and Eve entered into the new and everlasting covenant by accepting the ordinance of baptism and receiving the gift of the Holy Ghost. Upon Adam's doing so, God declared that those ordinances had been simultaneously recorded in heaven; thus they were valid "henceforth and forever."[50] Clearly, if our desire is to become Zion-like, as were our first parents, we must likewise enter into the new and everlasting covenant.

But there is more. No one can make the journey to Zion alone; we must take others with us. Hence, Adam received the authority of God to administer the Covenant to his children, that they might also escape Babylon and come home to Zion. That is the pattern: the redeemed of Zion are sent back into the world to bring others to the redemption of Zion. Something marvelous happened when Adam was ordained to the priesthood: He was inducted into the order of Jesus Christ, receiving from him the authority to administer the Covenant and thus become a savior in the similitude of the Savior. The Lord said to Adam, "And thou art after the order [priesthood] of him who was without beginning of days or end of years, from all eternity to all eternity. Behold, thou art one in me, a son of God; and thus [by receiving the holy priesthood] may all become my sons. Amen."[51] Again, we see the pattern; we become sons of God in the order of Jesus Christ in the same way Adam became a son of God in the order of Jesus Christ.

How grand is the Covenant! Fallen Adam could become a redeemed, saved, and exalted Adam. Doomed Adam could be rescued and reconciled with God. He could become one with God in knowledge, might, dominion, and lifestyle, and he could become heir to all that the Father has. Furthermore, Adam received God's authority and thereby became a son of God[52] in the similitude of *the* Son of God.[53] He was empowered to become a savior to his family[54] like *the* Savior was to the family of God.

Only the Atonement of Jesus Christ makes the Covenant possible; and we accept the Atonement by means of the Covenant. By our accepting the terms of the Atonement and enduring in the Covenant to the end, we are delivered from Babylon (redeemed), we are provided the Savior's grace to become Zion people and return home to Zion (saved), and we are blessed to become like God (exalted).

---

49   McConkie, *Mormon Doctrine*, 529.
50   Moses 6:64–66.
51   Moses 6:68.
52   D&C 45:8; Abraham 1:18.
53   Moses 1:6, 13, 16.
54   Petersen, Conference Report, Oct. 1959, 14.

Zion—A New Way of Life

Of course, the Fall brought with it a new set of realities. For one thing, Adam had to work for his support. Nevertheless, even his definition of work changed when he received the Covenant and the priesthood. Now he would redefine his work as the work of God. That mindset and reprioritization is essential to becoming a Zion person. Although Adam would continue to work to support his family, he would adopt as his real work the teaching, preaching, and administering of the Covenant to all the souls of men. And Eve was his helpmeet in all his labors: "And Adam and Eve blessed the name of God, and they made all things known unto their sons and their daughters."[55] How, then, do we, the children of Adam and Eve, likewise flee Babylon and find our way back to Zion? Follow the example of our first parents: receive and keep the Covenant, and bring others to Zion with us.

If the definition of Zion is "perfection," as well as "reaching for perfection," as we have said, then the definition of a Zion person is someone who receives the Covenant for the purpose of becoming perfect and entering into a perfect priesthood society. A Zion person will strive to become pure in heart and become one with God. Such a person will certainly find his or her way home.

Surety of a Better World

Making and keeping the Covenant are worth the effort. The Book of Mormon prophet Ether said, "Wherefore, whoso believeth in God might with surety hope for a better world."[56] That better world is Zion, a place devoid of pettiness, selfishness, and wickedness, a place of abundance and no lack, a place of oneness, equality, and righteousness—a place described by Mormon as consummately happy: "And surely there could not be a happier people among all the people who had been created by the hand of God."[57] In this better world, the Savior reigns as the King of Zion.[58] The scriptures state that Zion is his habitation.[59] But that better world begins in each person's heart,[60] which also is ruled by the Lord as his holy habitation. Such a heart, then, must be changed, purified, and prepared for Zion by the Atonement of Jesus Christ, and that process occurs by entering and abiding in the Covenant.

The better world of Zion has always been the goal of people of the Covenant, and many have achieved it. Certainly achieving Zion is possible for us as well. Elder Neal A. Maxwell said, "Those who look forward to a next and better world are usually 'anxiously engaged' in improving this one, for they 'always abound in good works' (D&C 58:27; Alma 7:24)."[61]

The following is a brief overview of people who responded to the Covenant and became Zion people. This is not an exhaustive list. We expect that other groups, such as

---

55 Moses 5:12.
56 Ether 12:4.
57 4 Nephi 1:16; see Moses 7:18.
58 Moses 7:53.
59 Psalms 132:13.
60 Young, *Discourses of Brigham Young*, 118.
61 Maxwell, *The Neal A. Maxwell Quote Book*, 265.

the brother of Jared and his people, and the Ten Tribes, who were visited by the resurrected Savior, also achieved Zion.

Adam's Zion

Beginning with Adam, the Lord, "the Holy One of Zion . . . established the foundations of Adam-ondi-Ahman."[62] In the hymn, "Glorious Things Are Sung of Zion," William W. Phelps preserved the doctrine: "In Adam-ondi-Ahman, Zion rose where Eden was."[63] In another hymn, "Adam-ondi-Ahman," Phelps wrote, "This earth was once a garden place, / With all her glories common, / And men did live a holy race, / And worship Jesus face to face, / In Adam-ondi-Ahman."[64]

When Adam and Eve lost the Garden of Eden, the first Zion, the Lord again established Zion in the hearts of the people, who gathered to Adam-ondi-Ahman. This new Zion society became the model for all subsequent Zion societies, and Adam and Eve became the models for all Zion people. Having experienced "the joy of [their] redemption and the eternal life which God giveth unto all the obedient," they "blessed the name of God, and they made all things known unto their sons and daughters."[65] Thus, beginning at Adam-ondi-Ahman, Zion was established in the hearts of the righteous.

Enos's Zion

At the rebellion of Cain, who created spiritual Babylon under the direction of Satan, a crisis arose in the earth. In response, a group of people under the leadership of Adam's grandson, Enos, fled the wicked land of Shulon and established Cainan,[66] named after Enos's son. The land of Cainan became a new Zion with a new Zion people.

Cainan may have been the longest-lived Zion in history, perhaps even longer than Enoch's Zion. Four generations later, Enoch was born there. His father, Jared, "taught Enoch in all the ways of God,"[67] which is a significant key to establishing Zion in a family. From the land of Cainan, Enoch and other righteous priesthood brethren went out into the world to teach the Covenant and draw people to Zion. "They were preachers of righteousness, and spake and prophesied, and called upon all men, everywhere, to repent; and faith was taught unto the children of men."[68]

Enoch's Zion

Enoch experienced amazing success. Many received the Covenant under his hands. Wherever they lived, "upon the mountains and upon the high places, [Zion] did

---

62 D&C 78:15.
63 "Glorious Things Are Sung of Zion," *Hymns*, no. 48.
64 "Adam-ondi-Ahman," *Hymns*, no. 40.
65 Moses 5:11–12.
66 Moses 6:17.
67 Moses 6:21.
68 Moses 6:23.

flourish."[69] In these pockets of Christianity, "the glory of the Lord . . . was upon his people. And the Lord blessed the land, and they were blessed. . . . And the Lord called his people Zion, because they were of one heart and one mind, and dwelt in righteousness; and there was no poor among them."[70] Of significance, "the Lord came and dwelt with his people, and they dwelt in righteousness."[71]

Eventually, when the world was filled with violence and wickedness, Enoch's pure-hearted people gathered to build a "city that was called the City of Holiness, even Zion,"[72] which, "in process of time, was taken up into heaven."[73]

We see a pattern here. Zion people precede the Zion priesthood society. They gather into local groups; in our day, these groups are called wards and stakes. Then, when the world grows incredibly wicked and dangerous, Zion people gather to one or more central locations for protection and unity. If we knew more about the gathering of Enoch's people, we would likely discover that they gathered to build a temple. That is always the reason why Zion people gather together. They desire to worship God and come into his presence, and the temple is the only way.

Methuselah and Noah's Zion

After Enoch's Zion had "fled,"[74] Enoch's son, Methuselah remained to perpetuate the chosen bloodline and to continue the missionary effort.[75] When Methuselah was 269 years old, his grandson, Noah, was born.[76] Together, as suggested by Joseph Fielding Smith,[77] Methuselah and Noah, and possibly three of Noah's sons, declared the "Gospel unto the children of men, even as it was given unto Enoch."[78] Contrary to popular opinion, these men had tremendous success in teaching and preaching the Covenant and perpetuating the cause of Zion. Enoch foresaw their success. In vision, he noted that, before the Flood, "many would be caught up by the powers of heaven into Zion."[79] We can't know for certain, but it seems reasonable that the converts of Noah and his family formed a Zion society before they were caught up to the heavenly Zion.

Noah received a promise from the Lord regarding latter-day Zion. This promise was a renewal of the promise the Lord had made earlier to Enoch. The sign of that promise, or covenant, was the rainbow. The promise was twofold: (1) God promised never again to destroy the wicked with a universal flood, and (2) Zion would be established in the last days and be joined by Enoch's Zion: "When men should keep all my commandments, Zion should again come on the earth, the city of Enoch which I have caught up unto

---

69 Moses 7:16.
70 Moses 7:17–18.
71 Moses 7:16.
72 Moses 7:19.
73 Moses 7:21.
74 Moses 7:69.
75 Moses 8:2.
76 Moses 8:8–9.
77 Smith, *Doctrines of Salvation*, 3:204.
78 Moses 8:19; see Moses 8:27.
79 Moses 7:27.

myself. And this is mine everlasting covenant, that when thy [Noah's] posterity shall embrace the truth, and look upward, then shall Zion look downward, and all the heavens shall shake with gladness, and the earth shall tremble with joy; and the general assembly of the church of the firstborn shall come down out of heaven, and possess the earth, and shall have place until the end come. And this is mine everlasting covenant, which I made with thy father Enoch."[80]

Regarding the rainbow as the physical sign of this promise made to Enoch and Noah, Joseph Smith said, "The Lord hath set the bow in the cloud for a sign that while it shall be seen, seed time and harvest, summer and winter shall not fail; but when it shall disappear, woe to that generation, for behold the end cometh quickly."[81] Commenting, gospel writers Jay A. Parry and Donald W. Parry stated: "The rainbow . . . also suggests the Lord's covenant with Noah, signified by a rainbow, that He would again bring Zion to the earth (JST, Gen. 9:21–23)."[82]

The absence of the rainbow in a coming year will be bad news for the wicked and good news for the pure in heart. For the righteous, an event rivaled only by the coming of the Lord will occur. Heavenly Zion will descend to meet earthly Zion. The Lord prophesied: "I shall prepare an Holy City that my people may gird up their loins, and be looking forth for the time of my coming; for there shall be my tabernacle, and it shall be called Zion, a New Jerusalem. And the Lord said unto Enoch: Then shalt thou and all thy city meet them there, and we will receive them into our bosom, and they shall see us; and we will fall upon their necks, and they shall fall upon our necks, and we will kiss each other; and there shall be mine abode, and it shall be Zion, which shall come forth out of all the creations which I have made; and for the space of a thousand years the earth shall rest."[83]

Melchizedek's Zion

The next Zion people of record were those to whom Melchizedek preached and administered the Covenant. This man's name is also actually a title. In Hebrew, *Melchizedek* is a combination of "king" and "righteousness." Therefore, Melchizedek was the *King of Righteousness*, a fitting title for those who would receive the priesthood after him.[84] Melchizedek "represents the scriptural ideal of one who obtains the power of God through faith, repentance, and sacred ordinances, for the purpose of inspiring and blessing his fellow beings."[85]

Alma gave us insight into Melchizedek's ministry: "Now this Melchizedek was a king over the land of Salem [meaning "city of perfection"[86] or "righteousness and peace,"[87]

---

80   JST, Genesis 9:21–23.
81   Smith, *Teachings of the Prophet Joseph Smith*, 305.
82   Parry and Parry, *Understanding the Book of Revelation*, 126.
83   Moses 7:62–64; emphasis added.
84   D&C 107:2–4.
85   *Encyclopedia of Mormonism*, 879–80.
86   Galbraith, Ogden, and Skinner, *Jerusalem: The Eternal City*, 41.
87   Smith, *Teachings of the Prophet Joseph Smith*, 321.

the forerunner of Jerusalem[88]]; and his people had waxed strong in iniquity and abomination; yea, they had all gone astray; they were full of all manner of wickedness; but Melchizedek having exercised mighty faith, and received the office of the high priesthood according to the holy order of God, did preach repentance unto his people. And behold, they did repent; and Melchizedek did establish peace in the land in his days; therefore he was called the prince of peace, for he was the king of Salem; and he did reign under his father."[89]

Melchizedek, like Enoch, was enormously successful in establishing Zion in the hearts of his people: "And his people wrought righteousness, and obtained heaven, and sought for the city of Enoch [they were likewise translated]."[90] Of note, Melchizedek became Abraham's spiritual tutor,[91] the one who ordained Abraham to the Holy Priesthood,[92] and the one, we assume, who "blessed" or administered the Covenant to Abraham.[93] None of these blessings could have been possible without the higher ordinances, of course. We thank the Jewish historian, Josephus, for preserving the fact that Melchizedek built in Salem a temple,[94] around which such edifices Zion people always gather.

Abraham's Zion

When Melchizedek and his Zion people were translated and taken into heaven to join with the city of Enoch, Abraham remained on the earth, the only man who held "all the priesthood and authority of his predecessors," and the remaining Zion person.[95] Like Methuselah and Noah, Abraham became the primal father of the covenant people, and for the remainder of his days, Abraham sought to reestablish Zion. In his monumental work, *The Blessings of Abraham—Becoming a Zion People*, E. Douglas Clark writes, "It was Abraham's right [by lineage] . . . to be ordained to the patriarchal priesthood to establish and preside over Zion for the benefit of all mankind."[96]

The Lord, through his servant Melchizedek, gave Abraham the fulness of the new and everlasting covenant, and he blessed Abraham to be associated with the Covenant eternally. From that point forward the Covenant would also be known as the Abrahamic covenant, and, as mentioned above, Abraham would be known as the father of the covenant people. The Abrahamic covenant emphasizes several important promises that flow to each person who chooses to receive it: (1) a covenant person's posterity has the right by lineage to receive all the blessings of the gospel and priesthood; (2) a covenant person will have an inheritance in the promised land of Zion both now and in eternity; (3) a covenant person will be blessed with "eternal lives,"[97] meaning eternal marriage and infinite and endless posterity.

---

88 McConkie, *Mormon Doctrine*, 531.
89 Alma 13:17–18.
90 JST, Genesis 14:34.
91 Alma 13:15; JST, Genesis 14:37–40.
92 D&C 84:14.
93 JST, Genesis 14:40.
94 Josephus, "The Wars," *Complete Works*, 6.10.1.
95 Clark, *The Blessings of Abraham*, 140.
96 Clark, *The Blessings of Abraham*, 79.
97 D&C 132:24.

Abraham received the Melchizedek Priesthood from the man Melchizedek,[98] and we assume that he received from Melchizedek the keys of the priesthood as well. When Melchizedek and his people were translated, Abraham was left as the sole administrator.

The advent of Abraham marked a new gospel dispensation. From that point forward, as is evidenced in the scriptures, priesthood keys would be held by a prophet, a high priest in the Melchizedek Priesthood, a worthy man called of God and not necessarily entitled to presidency because of his lineage, a man who would have the right to preside over the covenant people, administer the Covenant to God's children, and ordain worthy men to the priesthood, regardless of their bloodline.[99] These priesthood keys are highly important. Only by them can the ordinances of salvation and exaltation be bound or validated for eternity.[100]

Abraham's family was given the responsibility to teach and bless all other families of the earth with the Covenant.[101] Thus, authorized with the Melchizedek Priesthood, Abraham set out to establish Zion by preaching the Covenant to all the world. According to E. Douglas Clark, Abraham's success was legendary. Everywhere he went, from Ur to Haran to Canaan to Egypt and back to Canaan, he taught and administered the Covenant and introduced many souls to the principles of Zion.[102]

Abraham set the example of Zion for all who would follow him. For example, we read that he paid tithes to Melchizedek because Melchizedek was "the high priest, and the keeper of the storehouse of God."[103] Additionally, he paid generous offerings of 'all the riches which he possessed, which God had given him *more than that which he had need.*"[104] That is, he lived the law of consecration and paid offerings of his excess. The result of Abraham's being true to the Covenant and living the law of Zion was the Lord's pouring out upon him unimaginable riches: "And it came to pass, that God blessed Abram, *and gave unto him riches, and lands* for an everlasting possession, *according to the covenant which he had made,* and according to the blessing wherewith Melchizedek had blessed him."[105]

We see in Abraham's example Zion's celestial law of prosperity in contrast to Babylon's telestial law of wealth building. For Zion people such as Abraham, God himself becomes the paymaster. How many times, especially in the Book of Mormon, do we read that the Lord rewards obedience to the Covenant with great prosperity and a multitude of blessings? Like Abraham, Zion people pay tithing on their increase, and additionally, they pay generous offerings of "more than that which [they have] need." As a reward for their obedience and sacrifice, God gives unto them "riches . . . and lands for an everlasting possession: according to the covenant which [they have] made, and according to the blessing wherewith [they have been blessed in the temple of God by the Melchizedek Priesthood]."[106]

---

98 D&C 84:14.
99 D&C 81:2; 107:8–9.
100 Packer, "Restoration," 2.
101 Abraham 2:11.
102 Abraham 2:4, 15; Clark, *The Blessings of Abraham,* 85–87.
103 JST, Genesis 14:37.
104 JST, Genesis 14:39; emphasis added.
105 JST, Genesis 14:40; emphasis added.
106 JST, Genesis 14:40; emphasis added.

If Father Abraham had written a book called *How to Become Rich*, he might have recommended that we have faith in the Covenant we have made and give our surplus to the bishop, "the keeper of the storehouse," who shoulders the responsibility to care for the poor. It is by means of consecrating who we are and what we have to the Lord that abundance flows. Abraham might have reminded us that whereas tithing is a defined sum, offerings are not. The faith required to pay generous offerings is greater than the faith required to pay tithing, and the greater the faith and sacrifice, the greater the blessings. Therefore, our opportunity for growth and blessings lies in our paying offerings.

Abraham's Zion set the stage for latter-day Zion. Because the latter-day Church is either made up of Abraham's children or people who are adopted into the family of Abraham, we all share the responsibility of extending the blessings of Abraham, including the blessings of Zion, to all people.

Moses' Attempt at Zion

Moses led the children of Israel out of Egypt—which has represented Babylon, the wicked world, ever since[107]—with an overwhelming display of power. The Israelites experienced the power of Jehovah and the grandeur of his Covenant with unmistakable signs, wonders, and symbolic representations such as deliverance by the blood of a lamb, escaping their life of captivity, entering their new life by passing through the water, and so forth. By the power of the priesthood, six hundred thousand men, plus women and children,[108] united as one and left behind the fleshpots of Egypt to go forth into an unknown wilderness with the purpose of becoming "a holy community, a nation of priests, God's own people (see Exodus 19:6)."[109] Moses had one intention: to return Israel to its inheritance—Zion. To that end he built a tabernacle wherein the ordinances of the priesthood could be administered and where the Lord could visit his people.

Moses wore out his life teaching and administering the Covenant of the fathers to the children of Israel. This covenant was the Abrahamic covenant, the same covenant that Adam, Enos, Enoch, Methuselah, Noah, and Melchizedek had embraced to establish their Zions. Moses taught his people that the Melchizedek Priesthood "administereth the gospel and holdeth the key of the mysteries of the kingdom, even the key of the knowledge of God." Moreover, he taught them that in the ordinances of the Melchizedek Priesthood, "the power of godliness is manifest," and by means of these ordinances a "man can see the face of God, even the Father, and live."[110] Tragically, of the millions of Israelites, only "Moses, and Aaron, Nadab, and Abihu, and seventy of the elders of Israel"[111] accepted Moses' invitation to become Zion-like and receive Zion's blessings. This failing was a terrible indictment of the children of Abraham, Isaac, and Jacob. Moses had done his best to "plainly" teach the principles of Zion "to the children of Israel in the wilderness, and [he]

---

107 "The 'Hymn of the Pearl,'" 129–31.
108 Exodus 12:37.
109 Smith, *Church History and Modern Revelation*, 1:58.
110 D&C 84:19–22.
111 Exodus 24:9–10.

sought diligently to sanctify his people that they might behold the face of God; but they hardened their hearts and could not endure his presence; therefore, the Lord in his wrath, for his anger was kindled against them, swore that they should not enter into his rest while in the wilderness, which rest is the fulness of his glory."[112]

Substantially all of the Israelites rejected their heritage—Zion! The disappointing result recalls the impact of the fall of Adam and Eve: "Therefore, he took Moses out of their midst, and the Holy Priesthood also."[113] Or in an Enochian term, "Zion is fled!"[114] Moses was removed, and the balance of the people remained. When people reject the Covenant and the invitation to establish Zion, the pure in heart are separated and either taken into heaven or a heavenly setting. Those who are left behind are the weak and the rebellious, who continue to struggle in Babylon. In that situation, depending on the hearts of the remaining people, the Lord does one of two things: either he destroys the people because of their wickedness, or he reaches out to them with a preparatory gospel. In the case of the ancient Israelites, the Lord provided the lesser priesthood to administer the preparatory gospel, because the higher priesthood is the priesthood of Zion. Now angels would minister to them, while Zion people enjoy the presence of God. Their preparatory gospel was limited to faith, repentance, baptism, the remission of sins, and the law of carnal commandments,[115] while the higher commandments and ordinances, which pertain to Zion, are administered by the Melchizedek Priesthood and received in the temple.

This preparatory gospel, called the law of Moses, was intended to point the hearts of the Israelites toward Zion, and, in fact, it succeeded in its purpose among the people of Alma the Elder,[116] the people of King Benjamin,[117] and the people of Alma the Younger.[118] But the full realization of the law of Moses[119] was not complete until the Savior established Zion after his Resurrection among the Jews and the Nephites.[120]

Alma the Elder's Zion

Upon organizing the Church among the Nephites, Alma the Elder administered the Covenant to his people and immediately encouraged them to adopt the principles of Zion: no contention, true unity, love of God and neighbor, equality, consecration, free-will offerings, obedience, sacrifice, and blessedness.

> And he commanded them that there should be no contention one with another, but that they should look forward with one eye, having one faith and one baptism, having their hearts knit together in unity and in love one

---

112 D&C 84:23–24.
113 D&C 84:25.
114 Moses 7:69.
115 D&C 84:26–27.
116 Mosiah 18:21, 27–30.
117 Mosiah 2–5; see Mosiah 5:5–12.
118 Alma 1:25–32.
119 Matthew 5:17–18.
120 Acts 4:32–35; 4 Nephi 1:2–3, 15–18.

towards another. . . . And thus they became the children of God. . . . And again Alma commanded that the people of the church should impart of their substance, every one according to that which he had; if he have more abundantly he should impart more abundantly; and of him that he had but little, but little should be required; and to him that had not should be given. And thus they should impart of their substance of their own free will and good desires towards God, and to those priests that stood in need, yea, and to every needy, naked soul. And this he said unto them, having been commanded of God; and they did walk uprightly before God, imparting to one another both temporally and spiritually according to their needs and their wants. And . . . how beautiful are they to the eyes of them who there came to the knowledge of their Redeemer; yea, and how blessed are they, for they shall sing to his praise forever.[121]

King Benjamin's Zion

In an event that defined the Nephite nation ever after, the prophet-king Benjamin taught his people the Covenant and introduced them to the principles of Zion. In doing so, he applied the principle of gathering "to raise up a committed society of 'pure people' who will 'serve [God] in righteousness.'"[122] Gathering always is associated with Zion. When Benjamin, who had been called and consecrated to his holy office[123] and whose right it was to call such a gathering, had assembled his people, he stood before them and taught one of the greatest sermons on Zion ever delivered. He began by explaining that he had never exacted money for his service, a restatement of Nephi's principle: "The laborer in Zion shall labor for Zion; for if they labor for money they shall perish."[124] Furthermore, Benjamin said that he had always sought to maintain a people free from sin.[125] He also had tried to set an example of service—service to God and to God's children, which is the essence of "the law and the prophets."[126] Service was the sermon of his life, and he exhorted his people to follow his example.[127] Remarkably, giving service to one of God's children is counted as giving service to God.[128]

King Benjamin bid them to be grateful for their blessings[129] and to become profoundly aware of their continual dependence on the Lord. This doctrine stands in stark

---

121 Mosiah 18:21–30.
122 *Encyclopedia of Mormonism*, 1625; D&C 100:13, 16.
123 Mosiah 2:11–12.
124 2 Nephi 26:31.
125 Mosiah 2:13.
126 Matthew 22:40.
127 Mosiah 2:16–19.
128 Mosiah 2:17.
129 Mosiah 2:19–21.

Section 2   Overview of Zion Peoples

contrast to Babylon's anti-Christ doctrine of self-dependency: "every man fared in this life according to the management of the creature . . . prospered according to his genius, and . . . every man conquered according to his strength."[130] Benjamin explained that pride claims that we, without God, are independently "profitable," a satanic notion. When we take into account that our very creation, including our "every breath,"[131] comes from God, we realize that we consume more than we produce—unprofitable indeed! Therefore, Benjamin explained, we are ever in debt to God, implying that he is never in debt to anyone.[132] As an example of the ledger of indebtedness, when we obey him, he "doth immediately bless you; and therefore he hath paid you. And ye are still indebted unto him, and are, and will be, forever and ever."[133]

King Benjamin taught his people the Zion principle of equality: "And I, even I, whom ye call your king, am no better than ye yourselves are."[134] Equality and service allow us to walk "with a clear conscience before God . . . [and] be found blameless . . . when [we] shall stand to be judged of God."[135] He reminded his people that prosperity and protection follow obedience to God's commandments: "Ye shall prosper in the land, and your enemies shall have no power over you."[136]

King Benjamin singled out the danger of contention, which is a condition of Babylon and therefore a device of the devil.[137] Contention results from listening to and obeying "the evil spirit,"[138] he said. Moreover, contention draws from God a "wo" upon the contender. A wo (woe) is a condition of "calamity, wretchedness, deep distress, misery and grief."[139] That person who listens to and obeys Satan, "and remaineth and dieth in his sins, the same drinketh damnation to his own soul."[140] Where Zion exists, contention does not.[141]

King Benjamin taught his people the law of consecration: a person must render all that he has and is to God.[142]

King Benjamin spoke of our obligation regarding the revealed word of God. Because we are the covenant people, we are under covenant to study and obey the word of God or face severe and eternal consequences.[143] If a person lives contrary to the scriptures and thereby rejects the Covenant, he has abandoned Zion and defected to Babylon. He has come "out in open rebellion against God . . . and [become] an enemy to all righteousness; therefore, the Lord has no place in him, for he dwelleth not in unholy temples. Therefore, if that man repenteth not, and remaineth and dieth an enemy to God, the

---

130 Alma 30:17.
131 Mosiah 2:21, 23.
132 Mosiah 2:23.
133 Mosiah 2:24.
134 Mosiah 2:26.
135 Mosiah 2:27.
136 Mosiah 2:31.
137 3 Nephi 11:29.
138 Mosiah 2:32.
139 *American Heritage Dictionary*, s.v. "woe."
140 Mosiah 2:33.
141 4 Nephi 1:2, 15.
142 Mosiah 2:34.
143 Mosiah 2:9, 36.

demands of divine justice do awaken his immortal soul to a lively sense of his own guilt, which doth cause him to shrink from the presence of the Lord, and doth fill his breast with guilt, and pain, and anguish, which is like an unquenchable fire, whose flame ascendeth up forever and ever."[144] Then the words of the prophets and the scriptures "shall stand as a bright testimony against this people, at the judgment day; whereof they shall be judged, every man according to his works, whether they be good, or whether they be evil."[145] On the other hand, embracing the word of God and abiding in the Covenant result in safety, prosperity, and eternal happiness.[146]

King Benjamin explained the mission of the Savior and how we must embrace the Atonement if we ever hope to escape Babylon. Otherwise our path leads to eternal damnation.[147] Benjamin explained that this message corresponds with the universal message of all the prophets sent to "every kindred, nation, and tongue, that thereby whosoever should believe that Christ should come, the same might receive remission of their sins, and rejoice with exceedingly great joy."[148] The Atonement of Jesus Christ is far-reaching, King Benjamin said; little children who die before the age of accountability will be saved and exalted.[149]

With reference to the atoning Savior, the name *Jesus Christ* is both the identity of the great atoning God and the name of salvational power. King Benjamin explained that only *by* Jesus Christ and *in the name of* Jesus Christ can salvation "come unto the children of men."[150] Furthermore, an unavoidable reality lies in every person's future; that reality is the Judgment, when each of us must stand before Jesus Christ, the Lord Omnipotent, to be judged by him. Then we will have no excuse, for the Lord's judgment will be just.[151] King Benjamin prophesied that "the time shall come when the knowledge of a Savior shall spread throughout every nation, kindred, tongue, and people,"[152] and when that time comes, everyone will be held accountable for his actions.[153] Judgment can be just only on the principles of total knowledge and unrestricted agency. Neither will we be condemned for another's actions, nor will we be convicted if we are victims of deception.

King Benjamin drew a stark contrast between Babylon's "natural man," who "is an enemy to God," and Zion's "saint," who embraces "the Atonement of Christ the Lord." A sign of this transformation is our willingness to "[yield] to the enticings of the Holy Spirit, and [put] off the natural man . . . [becoming] as a child, submissive, meek, humble, patient, full of love, willing to submit to all things which the Lord seeth fit to inflict upon him, even as a child doth submit to his father."[154]

King Benjamin successfully laid out two universal philosophies: Zion and Babylon, or Christ and Satan. He showed his people that one philosophy leads to immeasurable

---

144 Mosiah 2:37–38.
145 Mosiah 3:24.
146 Mosiah 2:41.
147 Mosiah 3:1–12.
148 Mosiah 3:13.
149 Mosiah 3:16, 18.
150 Mosiah 3:17, 18.
151 Mosiah 3:18.
152 Mosiah 3:20.
153 Mosiah 3:21.
154 Mosiah 3:19.

blessings while the other leads to immeasurable misery. The people could no longer "halt between two opinions."[155] Having received their prophet/king's words, which he had borne "down in pure testimony,"[156] he constrained them to choose immediately. Either they were for Zion or they were for Babylon, but they could no longer straddle the two.

King Benjamin's people were shocked. These were good people, members of the Church who by and large obeyed the commandments and were trying to do what was right. Yet Babylon had crept in among them. Now their astonishment overwhelmed them. They may have thought that they had been Zion people, but they were not. Not yet. They may have thought that all was well in Zion and that Zion was prospering, but now they saw themselves as lacking. Their reaction was immediate: they collapsed "to the earth, for the fear of the Lord had come upon them. And they had viewed themselves in their own carnal state, even less than the dust of the earth."[157] What could they do to shed Babylon and fully embrace Zion?

King Benjamin had given them the answer: the Atonement. "And they all cried aloud with one voice, saying: O have mercy, and apply the atoning blood of Christ that we may receive forgiveness of our sins, and our hearts may be purified; for we believe in Jesus Christ, the Son of God."[158] Their declaration had the effect of renewing their Covenant, which they had made at baptism, and renewing their allegiance to Christ and his Zion. Such renewal brought them joy, remission of sins, and peace of conscience,[159] all attributes of Zion people.

Now that they had made a choice, King Benjamin was able to teach them the foundational points of the law of Zion. First, he said, we must always remember that we are wholly dependent upon and beholden to God, who is infinitely good, and matchless in his power, wisdom, patience, and long-suffering. Because of his love for us, he provided the Atonement to rescue us from Babylon, reconcile us to him, and bring us back to his presence—Zion. The journey to Zion is made possible by believing that God exists, that he is a being comprised of a perfection of attributes, and that therefore we can trust him. Zion is achieved by repenting and forsaking sin, humbling ourselves, asking for forgiveness, diligently keeping the commandments, and abiding in the Covenant to the end. Such a person "receiveth salvation."[160] There is no other way.[161]

King Benjamin taught that our prayers must be continual and humble, so that they might anchor us to Jesus Christ and his Atonement. If we do this, we shall: (1) "always rejoice," (2) be "filled with the love of God," (3) "always retain a remission of [our] sins," and (4) "grow in the knowledge of" God and "that which is just and true."[162] The benefits of humble prayer are many, he said. We abandon Babylon's disposition to injure other people, and we embrace Zion's disposition to live peaceably and to treat people fairly

---

155   1 Kings 18:21.
156   Alma 4:19.
157   Mosiah 4:1–2.
158   Mosiah 4:2.
159   Mosiah 4:3.
160   Mosiah 4:5–10.
161   Mosiah 4:8.
162   Mosiah 4:11–12.

and as equals.[163] Through humble prayer our families become Zion-like. Parents labor to support their children, as is required by the law of God. They teach their children the commandments and correct them when they transgress. They check contention when it enters into the family, so that the devil can never gain a foothold. They teach their children "to walk in the ways of truth and soberness . . . to love one another, and to serve one another."[164] Clearly, Zion principles must be learned first in the home.

A hallmark of Zion is to have no poor of any kind among us.[165] Reminding his people that all of us are poor and therefore in a constant state of begging for the Lord's assistance, King Benjamin commanded his people to succor (help) "those that stand in need of your succor; . . . to administer of your substance unto him that standeth in need; and . . . to respond to "the beggar [who] putteth up his petition to you."[166] And they were required do all of this without judgment or prejudice! For "whosoever doeth this the same hath great cause to repent; and except he repenteth of that which he hath done *he perisheth forever, and hath no interest in the kingdom of God.*"[167] Therefore, we are left without excuse. If God is willing to respond to our pleas for help, if he has blessed us with resources and abundance, which the Covenant defines as belonging to him, how can we, the Lord's stewards, withhold the Lord's goods from one of his needy children? What right do we have to judge harshly, treat the beggar as an inferior, or consider our property as our own? If we claim to desire to become like God, should we not strive to act as unselfishly as he does? King Benjamin thought so.[168] He could not abide the Babylonian attitude of selfishness. He said, "Wo be unto that man, for his substance shall perish with him."[169]

The mindset of a Zion people is opposite that of the people of Babylon. Zion pivots on the absence or existence of pride. Neither the rich nor the poor are exempt from pride, Benjamin said. President Ezra Taft Benson concurred, warning that pride retards the establishment of Zion.[170] The rich are under covenant not to withhold, and the poor are under covenant not to covet. Neither attribute is Zion-like. The antidote for pride is humility. Even the poor Zion-like person humbly assumes a giving attitude: "I give not because I have not, but if I had I would give."[171] King Benjamin stated a powerful principle that forms the foundation of selfless giving and service: obtaining a remission of sins and retaining a guiltless life are dependent upon charity: "For the sake of retaining a remission of your sins from day to day, that ye may walk guiltless before God—I would that ye should impart of your substance to the poor, every man according to that which he hath, such as feeding the hungry, clothing the naked, visiting the sick and administering to their relief, both spiritually and temporally, according to their wants." As we extend charitable service, we should follow Benjamin's counsel to do so with wisdom, order, and temperance: "for it is not requisite that a man should run faster than he has strength."

---

163 Mosiah 4:13.
164 Mosiah 4:14–15.
165 Moses 7:18.
166 Mosiah 4:16.
167 Mosiah 4:18; emphasis added.
168 Mosiah 4:19–22.
169 Mosiah 4:23.
170 Benson, "Beware of Pride," 4.
171 Mosiah 4:24.

But this counsel is not to be an excuse for noncompliance. Diligence, he said, enables us to "win the prize; therefore, all things must be done in order."[172]

Finally, a Zion person is fair and honest in his dealings.

Now that King Benjamin had clearly described a Zion person, his people recognized that despite their perception, they had allied themselves with various philosophies of Babylon. Evidently they were horrified and cried out for deliverance. Then the compassionate Lord responded, and the "Spirit of the Lord came upon them, and they were filled with joy, having received a remission of their sins, and having peace of conscience."[173] Now they were ready to be presented with the Covenant,[174] which would formalize their commitment and give them power to become Zion. But first King Benjamin needed to ascertain their level of belief and judge the condition of their hearts, for Zion is the pure in heart.[175] "And now, it came to pass that when king Benjamin had thus spoken to his people, he sent among them, desiring to know of his people if they believed the words which he had spoken unto them. And they all cried with one voice, saying: Yea, we believe all the words which thou hast spoken unto us; and also, we know of their surety and truth, because of the Spirit of the Lord Omnipotent, which has wrought a mighty change in us, or in our hearts, that we have no more disposition to do evil, but to do good continually."[176]

Note that the state of a changed heart is defined as "no more disposition to do evil, but to do good continually." That the people bore testimony of the miracle of a changed heart is significant. Sincere testimony becomes part of the record of heaven; it is "recorded in heaven for the angels to look upon; and they rejoice over you, *and your sins are forgiven you.*"[177] Bearing testimony purifies the heart!

Suddenly the people began to enjoy Zion's abundance: "the infinite goodness of God, and the manifestations of his Spirit." Revelation poured into their minds and hearts. With astonishment, they cried, "[We] have great views of that which is to come; and were it expedient, we could prophesy of all things."[178] Their faith increased exponentially, resulting in extraordinary knowledge, rejoicing, and "exceedingly great joy."[179] What did they want then? The Covenant! They wanted to enter into an agreement with God that he would bring them out of Babylon and back into Zion. "And we are willing to enter into a covenant with our God to do his will, and to be obedient to his commandments in all things that he shall command us, all the remainder of our days, that we may not bring upon ourselves a never-ending torment, as has been spoken by the angel, that we may not drink out of the cup of the wrath of God."[180]

King Benjamin, because he had the keys of authority, was in a position to administer this Covenant to the people: "And now, these are the words which king Benjamin de-

---

172 Mosiah 4:26–27.
173 Mosiah 4:3.
174 Note: This occasion may have been one of renewing the Covenant.
175 D&C 97:21.
176 Mosiah 5:1–2.
177 D&C 62:3.
178 Mosiah 5:3.
179 Mosiah 5:4.
180 Mosiah 5:5.

sired of them; and therefore he said unto them: Ye have spoken the words that I desired; and the covenant which ye have made is a righteous covenant. And now, because of the covenant which ye have made ye shall be called the children of Christ, his sons, and his daughters; for behold, this day he hath spiritually begotten you; for ye say that your hearts are changed through faith on his name; therefore, ye are born of him and have become his sons and his daughters."[181]

A Zion person receives a new family and a new name; that name is *Jesus Christ*. Suddenly empowered with the name of Jesus Christ and armed with the Covenant, we are free—free from Babylon, its sins, its philosophies, its trappings, its enticements and follies. We can leave Babylon with the full assurance that we will be safe in Christ's Zion—safe, because we are holding fast to the Covenant in the family of Christ and because we are bearing the Lord's name with dignity. Now we are in a position to receive an inheritance in Zion in this life and in eternity.[182] Ultimately, the Lord will seal us his, which is the Lord's absolute guarantee of eternal life.[183] There are no greater blessings than those associated with the Covenant. Hence, King Benjamin admonished his people to stay put in the Covenant: "Therefore, I would that ye should be steadfast and immovable, always abounding in good works, that Christ, the Lord God Omnipotent, may seal you his, that you may be brought to heaven, that ye may have everlasting salvation and eternal life, through the wisdom, and power, and justice, and mercy of him who created all things, in heaven and in earth, who is God above all. Amen."[184]

Alma the Younger's Zion

Under King Mosiah, King Benjamin's son, a major shift in the Nephite government occurred. The people adopted a constitution of elected representation, and Alma the Younger became the nation's first chief judge. To compound his responsibilities, he also had been called of God to lead the Church as its presiding high priest.[185]

In the first year of the constitution, a wicked man named Nehor introduced priestcraft to the people, challenging both the laws of the land and of the Church. Because priestcraft makes "merchandise" of men's souls,[186] it stands opposite to charity.

"Priestcrafts are that men preach and set themselves up for a light unto the world, that they may get gain and the praise of the world; *but they seek not the welfare of Zion*. Behold, the Lord hath forbidden this thing; wherefore, the Lord God hath given a commandment that *all men should have charity*, which charity is love."[187]

The introduction of priestcraft set off a series of events that sent both the country and the Church into a freefall. Alma did all he could to check the downslide, but after several years, he realized that he could no longer occupy both positions effectively. His

---

181 Mosiah 5:6–7.
182 Mosiah 5:8–12.
183 Smith, *Teachings of the Prophet Joseph Smith*, 149–51; see D&C 131:5.
184 Mosiah 5:15.
185 Mosiah 29:42.
186 2 Peter 2:3.
187 2 Nephi 26:29–30.

choice between his two occupations is an indication of Zion principles in action: the work of God trumps every other labor. Understanding the greater work, Alma, a Zion person, resigned as chief judge, the most powerful political position in the land; he gave up all of the job's benefits, prestige, and protection, and he became a servant, devoting himself fully to the work of God. For the rest of his life, his labor would focus on teaching, preaching, and administering the Covenant. We are forever grateful for his choice.

Under Alma's leadership, and in response to the threat of ongoing priestcrafts, the Saints gathered around the Covenant and Zion principles, and found safety and prosperity amid the storms of apostasy and persecution that raged about them. Consider the descriptive language that reminds us of Zion:

> They were *steadfast and immovable* in keeping the commandments of God.
> They bore with *patience* the persecution which was heaped upon them.
> They were all *equal*.
> They did all *labor*, every man according to his strength.
> They did *impart of their substance*, every man according to that which he had, to the poor, and the needy, and the sick, and the afflicted.
> They did not wear *costly apparel*, yet they were neat and comely.
> They began to have *continual peace* again, notwithstanding all their persecutions.
> And now, because of the *steadiness* of the church they began to be *exceedingly rich, having abundance of all things whatsoever they stood in need*—an abundance of flocks and herds, and fatlings of every kind, and also abundance of grain, and of gold, and of silver, and of precious things, and abundance of silk and fine-twined linen, and all manner of good homely cloth.[188]

Abundance and wealth always describe Zion people. Because Alma's people were willing to abide in the Covenant, the Lord prospered them.

Central to the Covenant is the law of consecration, which makes a Zion person the Lord's conduit through which he can funnel resources to bless the poor: "And thus, in their prosperous circumstances, they did not send away any who were naked, or that were hungry, or that were athirst, or that were sick, or that had not been nourished; and they did not set their hearts upon riches; therefore they were liberal to all, both old and young, both bond and free, both male and female, whether out of the church or in the church, having no respect to persons as to those who stood in need."[189]

The result drew a stark contrast between Zion and Babylon: "And thus they did prosper and become *far more wealthy* than those who did not belong to their church."[190] To drive home the point, Mormon, who is recounting the story, painted a frightening picture of the condition of the people remaining in Babylon: "For those who did not belong to their church did indulge themselves in sorceries, and in idolatry or idleness, and in babblings, and in envyings and strife; wearing costly apparel; being lifted up in

---

188 Adapted from Alma 1:25–29.
189 Alma 1:30.
190 Alma 1:31; emphasis added.

the pride of their own eyes; persecuting, lying, thieving, robbing, committing whoredoms, and murdering, and all manner of wickedness."[191] With such a clear portrayal of the two ways of life, we are left to wonder why people would choose Babylon over Zion.

The Apostles' Zion

After the Resurrection and Ascension of Christ, the Apostles assumed the leadership of the Church and began to experience great success. As they administered the Covenant, they implemented the principles of Zion.

> And the multitude of them that believed were of one heart and of one soul: neither said any that [any] of the things which he possessed was his own; but they had all things common. And with great power gave the apostles witness of the resurrection of the Lord Jesus: and great grace was upon them all. Neither was there any among them that lacked: for as many as were possessors of lands or houses sold them, and brought the prices of the things that were sold, and laid them down at the apostles' feet: and distribution was made unto every man according as he had need.[192]

As mentioned, the Apostles' mission was to fulfill the law of Moses,[193] which had been given to the Israelites to prepare them for the fulness of the gospel and the law of Zion, which their fathers had rejected.[194] Therefore, when the Lord finally established Zion among the Jews, the law of Moses had completely fulfilled its purpose and was dismantled. Now the Apostles, clothed in the authority of the Melchizedek Priesthood, administered the fulness of the new and everlasting covenant and advanced the cause of Zion.

The Nephites' Zion

To fulfill the law of Moses among the Nephites in the western hemisphere, the resurrected Savior administered to them the Covenant and taught them the principles of Zion. The account is found in the book of 3 Nephi, and the occasion was the sermon at the temple. Remarkably, the principles taught in this sermon are so universal and weighty that he repeated to the Nephites almost word for word what he had originally given to the Jews in what we call the Sermon on the Mount. According to President Harold B. Lee, this sermon contains "the constitution for a perfect life,"[195] specifying the Zion principles of *blessedness*, which we call the *Beatitudes*.

---

191 Alma 1:32.
192 Acts 4:32–35.
193 Matthew 5:17–18.
194 D&C 84:23–26.
195 Lee, *Decisions for Successful Living*, 56–57.

Section 2 Overview of Zion Peoples

Jesus began by gathering the Nephites together. The process of gathering, we have learned, always precedes the establishment of Zion.[196] A year earlier, when he had spoken to them through the mist of darkness, he had chastised them for their historical unwillingness to gather to him "with full purpose of heart."[197] Now they gathered without reservation. He taught the Nephites precepts that echoed principles associated with Zion. For instance:

- avoid contention[198]
- become selfless[199]
- love our neighbor[200]
- give to the poor for the right reasons[201]
- establish our treasure according to Zion standards[202]
- become an ambassador of Zion[203]
- choose between mammon and God (Babylon and Zion)[204]
- embrace the Lord's offer of safety and security[205]
- set in order our priorities: first, the kingdom of God, *then* all things will be added[206]
- drawing upon the resources of heaven by asking for what we need, seeking for knowledge, and knocking to come into the presence of God.[207]

Jesus expounded the reciprocal law of service: We receive in proportion to how well we serve.[208] He promised the people that their latter-day posterity would be blessed with Zion.[209] He taught them to selflessly draw others into their circle and strive for equality.[210]

Amazingly, the Savior's visitation seems to have suspended telestial laws. Apparently, time was no longer a factor. In the period of one earth day, he managed to invite some 2,500 people to come and touch his wounds; he organized the Quorum of Twelve Apostles; he taught major sermons; he instructed the people on prayer, explained his mission pertaining to the house of Israel and prophesied of critical future events; he invited all 2,500 to bring their sick to him to be healed; he prayed for the people; he blessed their children with angelic ministrations; he instituted the sacrament; he gave the Apostles power to confer the Holy Ghost—all in a time frame that would seem impossible in a telestial setting.[211] Perhaps only in the celestial condition of Zion could an abundance of love, resources, spiritual gifts, and *time* be possible.

---

196 3 Nephi 11:1.
197 3 Nephi 10:6.
198 3 Nephi 12:23–24, 39–40; 13:14–15.
199 3 Nephi 12:42.
200 3 Nephi 12:43–45.
201 3 Nephi 13:1–4.
202 3 Nephi 13:19–21.
203 3 Nephi 12:13–16; 18:24–24.
204 3 Nephi 13:24.
205 3 Nephi 13:25–34.
206 3 Nephi 13:33.
207 3 Nephi 14:7–11.
208 3 Nephi 14:12.
209 3 Nephi 16:17–18.
210 3 Nephi 18:22–23, 25, 32.
211 3 Nephi 12–17.

Within the pages of 3 Nephi, we glimpse the wonders of Zion: angels ascending and blessing spontaneously, children prophesying, protective fire from heaven, widespread healings, transfigurations, Christ himself ministering to his people, the books of heaven open so that revelation flows freely, and boundless and unequalled miracles.

Throughout the course of his visitation, Jesus continually taught of Zion, particularly when he quoted Isaiah concerning the latter-day redemption and glory of Zion.[212] The result was immediate and dramatic. Individually and collectively, the people embraced this new culture: "And they taught, and did minister one to another; and they had all things common among them, every man dealing justly, one with another."[213]

They became unified, as is required by Zion.[214]

With Christ's visit, the definition of labor changed. Without interrupting the command to work for their support, Jesus focused the Nephites' attention on the need to reprioritize their efforts by adopting Christ's work as their own and placing it first, with the promise that all else would be added unto them.[215]

The results of Christ's teachings and the people's implementing them were amazing. Within two years of intense missionary effort, all people in the land were converted and became Zion people.[216] Mormon gives a description: No contentions or disputations; every man dealing justly one with another; all things in common; no rich or poor; no one in bondage; peace in the land; prosperity enjoyed by all; a love of God in the hearts of the people; no envyings, strifes, tumults, whoredoms, lyings, murders, or lasciviousness; no robbers, murderers, or any "-ites."[217] Widespread healings and mighty miracles abounded.[218] "The Lord did prosper them exceedingly,"[219] and "the people of Nephi did wax strong, and did multiply exceedingly fast, and became an exceedingly fair and delightsome people."[220] "There could not have been a happier people among all the people who had been created by the hand of God. . . . And how blessed were they! For the Lord did bless them in all their doings."[221]

All of these blessings were preceded by a decision to once and for all receive and live the new and everlasting covenant. In the course of his sermon, the Lord warned the people about refusing to make or choosing to break this Covenant: "Wo unto him that spurneth at the doings of the Lord; yea, wo unto him that shall deny the Christ and his works! Yea, wo unto him that shall deny the revelations of the Lord, and that shall say the Lord no longer worketh by revelation, or by prophecy, or by gifts, or by tongues, or by healings, or by the power of the Holy Ghost! Yea, and wo unto him that shall say at that day, to get gain, that there can be no miracle wrought by Jesus Christ; for he that doeth this shall become like unto the son of perdition, for whom there was no mercy, according

---

212 3 Nephi 20–23.
213 3 Nephi 26:19.
214 3 Nephi 27:1.
215 3 Nephi 27:21; 13:3.
216 4 Nephi 1:2.
217 4 Nephi 1:15–17.
218 4 Nephi 1:5.
219 4 Nephi 1:7.
220 4 Nephi 1:10.
221 4 Nephi 1:16, 18.

to the word of Christ!"²²² One need only read the remainder of the Book of Mormon to realize the tragedy of rejecting the Covenant.

Joseph Smith's Zion

The subject of Zion was ever on the Prophet's mind. One of the first recorded commandments in this dispensation regarded Zion: "Seek to bring forth and establish the cause of Zion." Then followed the sister commandment, which set in place the foundation upon which all subsequent Zion relationships would arise: "Seek not for riches but for wisdom."²²³ Clearly, the Restoration was establishing a culture diverse from Babylon.

A year later, on the day the Church was organized, the subject of Zion once again was advanced as the predominant goal of the Restoration. The Lord announced, '[Joseph Smith] have I inspired to move the cause of Zion in mighty power for good, and his diligence I know, and his prayers I have heard. Yea, his weeping for Zion I have seen, and I will cause that he shall mourn for her no longer; for his days of rejoicing are come."²²⁴ The time for the glorious latter-day Zion had come at last!

On April 6, 1830, much of the new and everlasting covenant had already been restored, including the Melchizedek Priesthood, but an essential element was missing for Zion to be built up "by the principles of the law of the Celestial Kingdom."²²⁵ That missing element was the "revelation of the priesthood," that is, the temple covenants and ordinances. Those who would call themselves Zion people needed to be endowed with "power from on high,"²²⁶ for the purpose "that they themselves may be prepared, and that my people may be taught more perfectly, and have experience, and know more perfectly concerning their duty, and the things which I require at their hands."²²⁷

This endowment of knowledge and power had been promised years earlier, when Moroni had first appeared to the young Prophet. On the night of September 21, 1823, Moroni announced that the day would soon come when Elijah the prophet would come to *reveal* the Priesthood.²²⁸ (Note: When *Priesthood* is capitalized in this work, it refers to the patriarchal order of the Melchizedek Priesthood, which is entered into by husbands and wives when they are sealed by the keys of Elijah in the temple.) The *revelation* of the Priesthood would complete the *restoration* of the priesthood, which included the visitations of John the Baptist and Peter, James, and John.

The revelation of the Priesthood—the initiatory ordinances, the endowment covenants and ordinances, and the sealing covenant and ordinance—is central to the establishment of Zion. Zion people must receive this revelation in a most holy place: a temple, "the earthly type of Zion."²²⁹ Therefore, for the purpose of establishing Zion and exalting

---

222 3 Nephi 29:5–7.
223 D&C 6:6–7.
224 D&C 21:7–8.
225 D&C 105:5.
226 D&C 38:32, 38; 95:8; 105:11.
227 D&C 105:10.
228 D&C 2:1.
229 Nibley, *Approaching Zion*, 27.

his people, the Lord commanded the Saints to build a house of God to endow them with power from on high.[230] This endowment of knowledge and power would include the sacred ordinances of the Melchizedek Priesthood by which "the power of godliness is manifest. And without the ordinances thereof, and the authority of the priesthood, the power of godliness is not manifest unto men in the flesh; for without this [the ordinances and authority of the priesthood and the power of godliness] no man can see the face of God, even the Father, and live."[231]

We recall that Moses had attempted to endow his people with the revelation of the Priesthood, to make of them a Zion people, and to bring them into the presence God, but they refused.[232] Now Joseph Smith, the latter-day Moses,[233] whose code name, interestingly, was *Enoch*,[234] shouldered the same responsibility to administer the Covenant to his people that thereby we might be cleansed, sanctified, endowed with knowledge and power, sealed into the patriarchal chain, and prepared in every way to become Zion people. In preparation for the revelation of the Priesthood, the Lord had earlier revealed the law of Zion,[235] and shortly thereafter, he had revealed the oath and covenant of the priesthood.[236] Now, the new and everlasting covenant was nearly complete, lacking only the revelation on eternal marriage, which had been revealed to the Prophet as early as 1831 but had not been made public.[237] When that revelation was finally recorded in 1843, the Covenant now embodied all the principles, laws, covenants, and ordinances for the individual and collective building up of the kingdom of God on the earth and the establishment of Zion. Now, to become Zion individuals, marriages, families, and a Zion church, all the Saints had to do was implement the Covenant. That single act had the power to purify their hearts and make them Zion individually .

Would they live up to their privileges? Or would they, like the children of Israel, reject Zion and be relegated to a lesser, preparatory law that would merely point them toward Zion?

Blaine M. Yorgason writes:

> With the dedication of the Kirtland Temple, Joseph's lofty desire of establishing a Zion for this priesthood generation of the last days had begun its fulfillment. Truly had the Lord blessed His people as they struggled and sacrificed to expand their city, construct a temple to the Most High God, and become a holy people like the ancient Saints of Enoch. Like Enoch's people, these Latter-day Saints were led by a mighty prophet to whom the Lord revealed

---

[230] D&C 95:8; emphasis added.
[231] D&C 84:20–22.
[232] D&C 84:23–24.
[233] D&C 28:2.
[234] Note: In earlier versions of the Doctrine and Covenants, Joseph Smith and other brethren occasionally used code names for their protection. For example, see D&C 78:1 in the 1969 edition of the Doctrine and Covenants.
[235] D&C 42.
[236] D&C 84:33–44.
[237] D&C 132, preface.

> His will and who had also been given keys . . . powerful enough to open the heavens. These keys Joseph freely passed on to the Lord's people through what the Lord termed the "endowment," thus giving all, who were so blessed, power to bring themselves back into His presence. And like Enoch's people, a remarkable number in this generation did so, seeing and hearing glorious heavenly manifestations during that season of rejoicing.[238]

The spiritual manifestations surrounding the dedication of the Kirtland Temple were reminiscent of Christ's visit to the Nephites in America and the day of Pentecost in Jerusalem. On all three occasions, the people experienced great spiritual outpourings of the magnitude that we might expect of Zion.[239] "For a period of weeks," Elder McConkie writes, "the visions of eternity were opened to many, angels visited in the congregations of the saints, the Lord himself was seen by many, and tongues and prophecy were multiplied."[240] In Kirtland, many of the pure in heart truly achieved and experienced the condition of Zion. But sadly, many of the Latter-day Saints, like the Nephites, could not contend with the subsequent opposition, and, worse, they could not contain their desire for the things of this world. They looked back longingly at Babylon, as did Lot's wife,[241] and when they chose Babylon over Zion, they quickly lost their privileges.

> Sadly, a period of great apostasy followed immediately thereafter, and many of the Saints succumbed to the enticements of Satan and the cares of the world. . . . Between November 1837 and June 1838, possibly two or three hundred Saints withdrew from the Church in Kirtland, and a significant number also left the Church in Missouri. In that nine-month period, the Three Witnesses, a member of the First Presidency (Frederick G. Williams), four members of the Twelve Apostles, and several members of the First Quorum of Seventy left the Church. . . . On both continents Jesus taught: "No man can serve two masters: for either he will hate the one, and love the other; or else he will hold to the one, and despise the other. Ye cannot serve God and mammon" (Matthew 6:24; 3 Nephi 13:24). And Hugh Nibley adds: "The first commandment given to the Saints . . . was an ominous warning: 'Seek not for riches but for wisdom' (D&C 6:7)—all in one brief mandate that does not allow compromise. Why start out on

---

238 Yorgason, *I Need Thee Every Hour*, 49–50.
239 Acts 2:1–17.
240 McConkie, *Mormon Doctrine*, 181–82.
241 Genesis 19:26.

such a negative note? The Lord knew well that the great obstacle to the work would be what it always had been in the past. The warning is repeated throughout the Doctrine and Covenants and the Book of Mormon again and again. The positive and negative are here side by side and back to back, making it clear, as the scriptures often do, that the two quests are mutually exclusive—you cannot go after both, you cannot serve both God and Mammon, even if you should be foolish enough to try" (Hugh Nibley, *Approaching Zion* [Provo and Salt Lake City: Foundation for Ancient Research and Mormon Studies and Deseret Book Company, 1989], 343)."[242]

Like the Israelites in the days of Moses, the Latter-day Saints rejected Zion and shifted "their allegiance from God to mammon, or the things of the world. Eliza R. Snow apparently understood the cause of the spiritual decline of the Saints perfectly, for she said that many members felt that 'prosperity was dawning upon them . . . and many who had been humble and faithful . . . were getting haughty in their spirits, and lifted up in the pride of their hearts. As the Saints drank in the love and spirit of the world, the Spirit of the Lord withdrew from their hearts, and they were filled with pride and hatred toward those who maintained their integrity' (*History of the Church*, 2:487–88, footnotes)."[243]

Hugh Nibley wrote,

> Then came the crash of 1837, brought on by those same shrewd, hardheaded businessmen. "During this time," [Heber C.] Kimball recalled, "I had many days of sorrow and mourning, for my heart sickened to see the awful extent that things were getting to." Many apostatized and "also entered into combinations to obtain wealth by fraud and every means that was evil." Later, Kimball returned to Kirtland again after a mission to England: "The Church had suffered terribly from the ravages of apostasy." Looking back over many years, he recalled that "the Ohio mobbings, the Missouri persecutions, the martyrdom, the exodus, nor all that Zion's cause has suffered since, have imperiled it half so much as when mammon and the love of God strove for supremacy in the hearts of His people." Note that they were torn between God and Mammon, and "no man can serve both!"[244]

---

242 Yorgason, *I Need Thee Every Hour*, 49–52.
243 Yorgason, *I Need Thee Every Hour*, 52.
244 Nibley, *Approaching Zion*, 347.

Continuing, Nibley wrote, "Every step in the direction of increasing one's personal holdings is a step away from Zion, which is another way of saying, as the Lord has proclaimed in various ways, that one cannot serve two masters: to the degree in which he loves the one he will hate the other, and so it is with God and business, for mammon is simply the standard Hebrew word for any kind of financial dealing."[245]

The result? Beautiful Zion returned to its heavenly home, so to speak, and the Saints in Kirtland and Missouri, like their fathers of old, were left in Babylon to live a preparatory law, which financially was marked by *tithing*.[246] We should note here that the law of tithing was not a step down; tithing is an essential part of the law of consecration and a "standing law . . . forever."[247] Nevertheless, tithing is not the fulness of consecration, and therefore, as magnificent as is tithing, it does not offer the Saints the same weight of blessings as does consecration. Gratefully, the Lord left in place the law of *offerings*, which allowed the Saints the individual choice to better live the law of consecration and receive its blessings. But because many of the Saints in Kirtland and Missouri rejected the Covenant, they forfeited the supernal blessings of Zion.

They had recently tasted the wonderful fruit of Zion—how could they have fallen so far in such a short period of time? Blaine Yorgason describes the tragedy of the Saints' abandoning their covenant to establish Zion in their hearts and as a people.

Once the Saints were no longer sacrificing their all for the building of the temple in Kirtland, many of them bowed down to the god of mammon. They began looking to themselves, and soon their personal religion was no longer a religion of spiritual power and progression. . . . [It became] a gospel of convenience, [and as it] increased its hold in the hearts and minds of Latter-day Saints, fewer and fewer of them had power to bring to pass and enjoy such spiritual experiences as had occurred in Kirtland—and this despite the fact that they had been endowed with that power from on high. Truly, had their spiritual progression been slowed or in some cases even stopped altogether. The next step, of course, was that angelic ministrations and other manifestations of the Lord's Spirit quite literally went out of fashion. Those who continued to seek and enjoy such rich spiritual blessings hesitated to discuss them or bear witness of them for fear of ridicule and outright scorn, and so their numbers grew fewer and fewer. And the scorners? Besides the apostates and the anti-Christs, they grew to include good, well-meaning people, especially members of the Church, who had never sought such transcendent experiences, had never sacrificed the things of the world in order to experience them, and who doubted that ordinary people such as themselves could ever see, hear, feel, and know such things. And so they mocked and scorned or shook their heads in sorrow and pity that so-and-so could be so deluded as to think he or she had actually seen and spoken with an angel.[248]

---

245 Nibley, *Approaching Zion*, 37.
246 *Encyclopedia of Mormonism*, 313; see 1481–82.
247 D&C 119:4.
248 Yorgason, *I Need Thee Every Hour*, 54–55.

Latter-day Zion

The Lord told Noah, "When men should keep all my commandments, Zion should again come on the earth, the city of Enoch which I have caught up unto myself. And this is mine everlasting covenant, that when thy posterity shall embrace the truth, and look upward, then shall Zion look downward, and all the heavens shall shake with gladness, and the earth shall tremble with joy; and the general assembly of the church of the firstborn shall come down out of heaven, and possess the earth, and shall have place until the end come. And this is mine everlasting covenant, which I made with thy father Enoch."[249]

Zion has always been our destiny!

Zion's day of redemption shall come with power. Quoting the revelation, Elder McConkie wrote: "'Behold, I do not require at their hands'—the hands of mine elders—'to fight the battles of Zion; for, as I said in a former commandment, even so will I fulfill—I will fight your battles.' [D&C 105:14.] We need not suppose our swords must slay the enemies of God or that any mortal power must cleanse the land and make it available for the Saints. The building of the New Jerusalem is the Lord's work, and he will prepare the way for his people when that people have prepared themselves to perform the heaven-given labors."[250]

How will the Lord do this? Again, quoting the revelation, Elder McConkie stated: "'Behold, the destroyer I have sent forth to destroy and lay waste mine enemies.' [D&C 105:15.] Destructions, wars, calamities, the violence of nature—those things that men call 'acts of God'—shall sweep over the land. 'And not many years hence'—the 'little season' shall last for years—'they shall not be left to pollute mine heritage, and to blaspheme my name upon the lands which I have consecrated for the gathering together of my saints.' [D&C 105:15.] We are thus left to conclude that the wicked will slay the wicked, and the God of Nature will loose the forces of nature to destroy those who oppose the manifest destiny of his saints."[251]

The redemption of Zion is a sacred subject not to be discussed with the world: "The Lord then counsels his people to be wise and discreet and not stir up opposition as they gather together. 'Talk not of judgments, neither boast of faith nor of mighty works,' they are commanded, 'but carefully gather together, as much in one region as can be, consistently with the feelings of the people.' [D&C 105:24.] They are to seek 'favor in the eyes of the people, until the army of Israel becomes very great.' [D&C 105:26.]"[252] Zion is not a threat to the world; rather, Zion is the world's salvation. To become so, Zion's "army"—its people—must become holy, a pure-hearted people who are capable of living the celestial law: "And let it [the army of the Lord] be sanctified before me, that it may become fair as the sun, and clear as the moon, and that her banners may be terrible unto all nations; that the kingdoms of this world may be constrained to acknowledge that the kingdom of Zion is in very deed the kingdom of our God and his Christ; therefore, let us become subject unto her laws."[253]

---

249   JST, Genesis 9:21–23.
250   McConkie, *A New Witness for the Articles of Faith*, 616.
251   McConkie, *A New Witness for the Articles of Faith*, 617.
252   McConkie, *A New Witness for the Articles of Faith*, 617.
253   D&C 105:31–32.

Each of us must individually become Zion. Elder McConkie wrote: "Again the word is this: The worthiness of the Lord's people, their sanctified state, their purity and uprightness before him—these are the things that will enable them to build the New Jerusalem, for Zion is the City of Holiness. When it is built, as it was in Enoch's day, its grandeur and glory and power must be such that those in all nations, from one end of the earth to the other, standing in awe, will feel inclined to be subject to such a mighty city, whence comes such a perfect law. The day in which the latter-day Zion will have such renown and be held in such unlimited awe is clearly Millennial."[254]

Summary and Conclusion

Today, we still are awaiting the promised redemption of Zion.[255] But if we are waiting to become Zion individuals in response to a Zion program issued from Church headquarters, we are being deceived and irresponsible. *Zion is who we are!*[256] Right now—today! Every person who has entered into the new and everlasting covenant has the immediate responsibility to live the Covenant—*all of it!*

We might ask ourselves what part of the Covenant has ever required a program? Baptism? Sabbath-day observance? Temple worship? Eternal marriage? Why, then, should we consider parts of the Covenant futuristic, including consecration? If we have accepted the Covenant, which is intended to make of us Zion people, what stops us from becoming such? If the answer is lack of understanding and fear, we might be served by striving for a clearer comprehension of the Covenant, so that we might gain the courage to break loose from Babylon's hold on us.

Gratefully, the Lord has given us the law of tithes and offerings to prepare our minds and hearts to live the higher manifestation of the Covenant. No one who has faithfully lived the preparatory law of tithes and offerings can deny that the law foreshadows Zion's power, safety, security, and prosperity. No one has ended up with less by living the law. Therefore, armed with that knowledge, we might, with confidence, press past our fears and embrace Zion's principles entirely, as we covenanted to do.

Perhaps in the spirit of allaying our fears, the Lord encouraged us to consider the fowls in the air and the lilies of the field.[257] Most certainly, if he is willing to take care of them that have made no covenant, he will take care of us, his covenant children. To the end that we become such, the Lord gave us the Book of Mormon, the textbook on becoming Zion people. We are without excuse. President Spencer W. Kimball laid the responsibility for becoming and establishing Zion squarely on our shoulders.[258] How well we incorporate the Covenant in our lives, he said, will determine the required time to "accomplish all things pertaining to Zion."[259]

---

254 McConkie, *A New Witness for the Articles of Faith,* 618; emphasis added.
255 D&C section 101; 103:15, 18; 105:9, 13.
256 Taylor, *The Gospel Kingdom,* 245.
257 Matthew 6:28–29; 3 Nephi 13:28–29.
258 Kimball, "Becoming the Pure in Heart," 79. D&C 105:37
259 D&C 105:37.

Section 3
We Were Prepared to Become Latter-day Zion People

Neither the telestial world nor Babylon is our home. They are as foreign to us as would be slavery to a free person. We are strangers here.[260] We have fallen into a state that is completely alien to us. We cannot comprehend the Fall's depth and distance. We fell physically, spiritually, and emotionally into a condition described by President Joseph F. Smith as "below all things,"[261] and Babylon compounds the circumstances of the Fall. Nevertheless, this experience is evidently essential to our eventually achieving the condition of the heart called *Zion*.

The Savior is our Exemplar: as he descended below all things so that he could ascend above all things, so we, in like manner, must "follow him below." "If with our Lord, we would be heirs," we sing, we must "in his footsteps tread."[262] The universal law of opposites[263] states that rising above depends on descending below, to the end that we might comprehend all things and thereby gain the ability to become as the gods, who are above and in and through all things.[264] Brigham Young said, "It seems to be absolutely necessary in the providence of him who created us, and who organized and fashioned all things according to his wisdom, that man must descend below all things. It is written of the Savior in the Bible that he descended below all things that he might ascend above all. Is it not so with every man? Certainly it is. It is fit, then, that we should descend below all things and come up gradually, and learn a little now and again, receive 'line upon line, precept upon precept, here a little and there a little.'"[265] For reasons that we do not completely understand, this process is the only way to become Zion-like and achieve exaltation.

---

260 Cook, "Home and Family: A Divine Eternal Pattern," 30.
261 Smith, *Gospel Doctrine*, 13.
262 "Come Follow Me," *Hymns*, no. 116.
263 2 Nephi 2:10.
264 D&C 88:6.
265 Young, *Discourses of Brigham Young*, 60.

We cannot fathom the range of emotions that must have barraged us as we contemplated our descent from the celestial condition of the Zion of premortality into the telestial condition of the Babylon of the world. Nevertheless, this mortal experience was what we had fought for. Mortality would provide us at least three essential blessings that we could not obtain in any other environment: a physical body, experience with good and evil, and the establishment of our own eternal kingdom: *marriage and family*. We vigorously defended the Father's plan for the possibility of receiving those blessings—and to sustain God and his Son—and we shouted for joy at the expectation.[266] In that premortal setting, we dedicated our lives to Jesus Christ, who was to become our Savior and the central figure of the plan. But despite the glorious possibilities, we must have been horrified at the prospects of living in Babylon and most assuredly succumbing to sin.

Brigham Young University professor M. Catherine Thomas wrote: "The period of descent was surely seen by the righteous premortal spirits as a great sacrifice. The most righteous did not want to sin. They knew the truth about sin. A veil was necessary so that they would make the descent . . . into spiritual darkness."[267] Only profound faith in Christ could have persuaded us to step off the celestial ledge and, by choice—for agency demands that no one is forced—fall into this dark telestial world, armed only with the Light of Christ. Our hope lay in the transcendent possibilities of eternal life. We knew that everything depended on keeping our second estate,[268] and that feat required our having experience with Babylon, completely rejecting it, and rediscovering and embracing Zion. Therefore, it was "trailing clouds of glory"[269] and commissioned with a divine purpose that we willingly fell into this benighted orb to finally, after untold eons of preparing, claim our eternal inheritance in Zion by working out our salvation with "fear and trembling."[270]

Divine Appointment

We are not here by accident; rather, we qualified in the premortal life.[271] With humble acknowledgment, we concede that, as those who've embraced the gospel here on earth, we were among the most capable and qualified spirits in the premortal life. That we have emerged at this place and time signals that Zion is at hand. President Wilford Woodruff said, "I want to say to my brethren and sisters, that we are placed upon the earth to build up Zion."[272] Our specific commission could not be clearer: we Latter-day Saints have the mandate to build up the kingdom of God on the earth for the establishment of Zion.

Elder Neal A. Maxwell taught that we were placed here by *divine appointment* according to God's intimate knowledge our unique abilities.[273] Heavenly Father's house is a house of order;[274] we are not here by a cosmic roll of the dice. In the premortal world we

---

266 Job 38:7.
267 Thomas, "Alma the Younger, Part 1," n.p.
268 Abraham 3:26.
269 Wordsworth, "Ode on Intimations of Immortality," in *Narcissism and the Text*, 116–29.
270 Mormon 9:27.
271 Larsen, "A Royal Generation," 33.
272 Woodruff, *Journal of Discourses*, 22:334.
273 Maxwell, "These Are Your Days," 4.
274 D&C 132:8.

certainly had proven ourselves by consecrating our all to the Lord. Evidently, the Lord extended to us the call to come in this generation to become Zion people and help to establish latter-day Zion. By our choice, we must have accepted the call and perhaps even requested to come in this day of both wickedness and promise. Therefore, we assume, the Lord strategically positioned us to combat Babylon, champion Zion, and prepare the world for the Savior's Second Coming.

Our importance to the Lord and the magnitude of our missions cannot be overstated. President Ezra Taft Benson referred to us as a generation marked for greatness, with more expected of us than any other generation. And we have very little time to accomplish our work.[275] There is no boasting here, only a humble owning of truth and our recognizing that we have been "given much," so "much is required"; and if we sin "against the greater light," we "shall receive the greater condemnation."[276] Clearly, our responsibilities are equal to our privileges. We must rise to the level of our true character and special commission by accomplishing our mission or face the eternal consequences for our disregard.

To be purposely and divinely placed at this crucial time and place, each person of the Covenant must have proven exceedingly righteous. Joseph Smith taught, "There is a time appointed for every man, according as his works shall be."[277] Paul explained that this "time appointed" would be especially true of the Latter-day Saints; we would be specifically singled out and strategically placed because premortally we had "to be conformed [made similar] to the image of [God's] Son."[278] Therefore, God had taken careful note of our potential to do good and deigned to position us in an era and circumstance that was best suited to our abilities. Elder Erastus Snow explained that the premortal ministry of God's "peculiar people," destined us to assume important mortal assignments and obtain our exaltation:

> For he has had his eye upon the chosen spirits that have come upon the earth in the various ages from the beginning of the world up to this time. . . . The Lord has sent those noble spirits into the world to perform a special work, and appointed their times . . . , *and their future glory and exaltation is secured unto them;* and that is what I understand by the doctrine of election spoken of by the Apostle Paul and other sacred writers: "For whom he did foreknow, he also did predestinate to be conformed to the image of His Son, that he might be the first-born among many brethren." Such were called and chosen and elected of God to perform a certain work at a certain time of the world's history and in due time he fitted them for that work.[279]

---

275 Benson, "In His Steps," 2.
276 D&C 82:3.
277 D&C 121:25.
278 Romans 8:29.
279 Erastus Snow, *Journal of Discourses*, 23:186–87; emphasis added.

This is an amazing promise, one that should give us humble pause as we consider our true identity. Only by embracing the Covenant can we rise to the stature of our premortal greatness and accomplish the latter-day work of Zion.

Special Spirits of the Royal Generation

Pursuant to the perfect foreknowledge of God, we may well have been assigned family placement, birth time, location, and mortal opportunities according to our strengths and weaknesses. We—*all of us*[280]—are part of the group that the prophets have referred as the "royal generation" of very special spirits.[281]

Clearly, we were "good," and that goodness needed expression at the right time and place. Our divine positioning allowed us to continue our premortal work—advancing the Atonement of Jesus Christ and offering the Covenant to God's children. We had adopted God's work as our eternal work. In the celestial world, the work of redemption is not *a* work of God, it is *the* work of God, and therefore it is the preeminent work of all celestial beings. M. Catherine Thomas wrote:

> Out of all of Heavenly Father's spirit children, a smaller group distinguished itself by its exceeding faith in the Lord Jesus Christ during the conflicts that occurred incident to the war in heaven. Those who were valiant in these conflicts, and in other ways also, demonstrated both their abilities and their desires to become actively involved in the cosmic work of redemption through the great Atonement of the Lord Jesus Christ. The thing that characterizes the Gods and those who aspire to godhood is the love of the work of redemption; that is, nurturing spirit children through the first estate of premortality, then leading them through a mortal probation, and finally raising them to the level of their parent gods. . . . The great work of the gods is family work—the raising and nurturing of children and the redemption of families to be sealed together for all eternity. We cannot comprehend the cosmic proportions of the love and the infinite investment of labor and grace that go into this magnificent work. You and I, as members of the literal house of Israel and of the Church of Jesus Christ, were called in the premortal world to participate in that work, everything else being trivial in comparison. Redemption is not just one of the things going on in the universe; it is *the* thing. That work of redemption

---

280 Peterson, "Your Special Purpose," 34.
281 Kimball, "In Love and Power and without Fear," 8.

> is *the* work to which the premortal covenant people, the house of Israel, were called, and it was to take precedence over all other work and to subordinate all other work to itself.[282]

Because we tried in every way to become like the Savior, we had the potential to become *saviorlike*—saviors on Mount Zion.[283] In vision, Nephi saw that our numbers would be few.[284] In proportion to the world's present population, each Latter-day Saint represents 1 in 508.[285] In proportion to all the people who have ever lived, each Latter-day Saint is 1 in 7,692.[286] Because we have always been in the minority, our accomplishing our premortal calling is highly important. As we have mentioned, our latter-day charge is singular: to offer the Covenant to all of God's children since the world began, and to gather those who will, to Zion.[287] We are the heralds of Zion, the Lord's "very great" army,[288] the might of which is unparalleled in the earth's history. Our influence will circumscribe the globe, and the amount of good that we will accomplish will be incalculable.[289]

Because the redemptive work of Zion is so essential, and because the laborers who can effectively do the work are few, God, in order to save his children, in the beginning divided his family according to the number of the "special spirits," whom he called "Israel."[290] These are faithful individuals who are *becoming like God* or *prevailing with God*.[291] When we consider the proportionately small number of Israelites who have been born or adopted into the Church, we wonder at our apparent premortal stature and our weighty responsibility. Clearly, without becoming egotistical, each of us is one covenant person among thousands of noncovenant people.

Perspective on the Cosmic War

We have come to earth at this time and place to fight for Zion and to vanquish Babylon. We can neither fathom the length of time that we were engaged in the work of redemption nor imagine our potential to bring other people to Christ. To gain perspective, let us review some truths.

We have been told that we are ancient souls who practiced righteousness and did the work of redemption over vast eons in the premortal life. For how long, we do not know. The scriptures indicate that we existed as spirits before the world was created.[292] If the current scientific estimate of the earth's age—4.55 billion years[293]—is accurate,

---

282 Thomas, "Alma the Younger, Part 1," n.p.
283 Petersen, Conference Report, Oct. 1959, 14.
284 1 Nephi 14:12.
285 Church membership at the end of 2008 was about 13 million, and world population was 6.6 billion.
286 Estimated human population across history is about 100 billion.
287 D&C 128:22–24.
288 D&C 105:31.
289 Cook, "The Seat Next to You," 4.
290 McConkie, *A New Witness for the Articles of Faith*, 510.
291 Brickey, BYU Education Week address, 2006; see Genesis 32:28.
292 Job 38:7; Alma 13:3; Abraham 3:22.
293 Dalrymple, *The Age of the Earth*, 492.

our spirits have existed for a long time. During that enormous duration, we lived in the celestial atmosphere of Zion. The focus of our attention was to become like our heavenly parents; therefore, we needed to come to earth and gain a body, experience mortality, choose good over evil, enter into the new and everlasting covenant and follow it to its perfect conclusion, die and achieve a glorious resurrection, and earn exaltation.

We brought with us mature gospel knowledge. For the moment, it might be buried deep in our souls, but it is there just the same. The Fall might have caused us temporary amnesia, but God has not forgotten who we are or what we did.

Of course, neither has Satan forgotten us. We are the ones who helped Michael cast out the devil and his angels from heaven, causing Satan to swear in his wrath that he would attempt to destroy us in the flesh. And for good reason. Satan knew if we were allowed to continue our premortal work, we would conquer him again and help to cast him into outer darkness forever. Therefore, we are and have been enemies. The war in heaven goes on, and this earth is its frontline. The adversary treats us differently. While he merely tempts the people of Babylon,[294] he viciously attacks us.[295] Why are we so ruthlessly confronted? Brigham Young had the answer: "God never bestows upon his people, or upon an individual, superior blessings without a severe trial to prove them, to prove that individual, or that people, to see whether they will keep their covenants with him, and keep in remembrance what he has shown them. Then the greater the vision [or blessings], the greater the display of the power of the enemy. So when individuals are blessed with visions, revelations, and great manifestations, look out, then the Devil is nigh you, and you will be tempted in proportion to the visions, revelations, or manifestations you have received."[296]

Our premortal nobility, righteousness, and exceedingly good works surely warranted extraordinary blessings and opportunities in this life—royal birth, immediate access to gospel blessings, the privileges of Zion, and so forth. But these blessings carry a price. The adversary attacks us in proportion to our blessings, and our seemingly invincible premortal souls, now weakened by the Fall, are more susceptible to Satan's attacks.

Nevertheless, we were prepared.

Preparation in the "First Place"

The Prophet Joseph said: "Every man who has a calling—*every man or woman*—to minister to the inhabitants of the world was ordained to that very purpose in the grand council of heaven before this world was."[297] Virtually every prophet has echoed these words. In the premortal world, reasoned President J. Reuben Clark Jr., we accepted placement in the last days and were empowered and trained for our individual assignments to build up God's kingdom for the establishment of Zion.[298]

---

294 D&C 29:39.
295 D&C 76:28–29.
296 Young, *Discourses of Brigham Young*, 338.
297 Smith, *Teachings of the Prophet Joseph Smith*, 365.
298 Clark, Conference Report, Oct. 1950, 169–71.

Alma spoke in depth about our stature and preparation in the premortal world or the "first place."[299] In that setting, as Catherine Thomas explained, a select group of people received a special calling into the *holy order*[300] because they were "conformed to the image of [God's] Son."[301] That premortal holy order was comprised of righteous men who were ordained to the priesthood as well as righteous women who were worthy of the blessings of the priesthood. We who now hold the priesthood and enjoy the blessings of the temple were likely included in that select group. We had "demonstrated [our] abilities and desires to become actively involved in the cosmic work of redemption through the Atonement of Jesus Christ,"[302] which is that "mighty power that can take a lost and fallen person and work a miraculous transformation."[303] In other words, in the premortal world we loved Zion and the work of redemption so much that we dedicated ourselves to the cause by nurturing the weaker spirits and bringing them to Christ. In the process we became Christlike, or "types of Christ,"[304] "that thereby [other premortal spirits] might look forward on the Son of God, . . . that they might look forward to him for a remission of their sins, that they might enter into the rest of the Lord."[305]

There, in that "first place," we of the holy order "elected to become gods," to "come to earth and learn the work of redemption in apprenticeship to the Lord Jesus Christ." The Lord promised us that if we continued to embrace the principles of Zion and do the work of redemption on the earth, we would someday "qualify to live with the Gods in the eternal worlds"[306] and be blessed to live in Zion and do the work of redemption forever. Here in mortality we would be called "Saviors on Mount Zion"[307] because we would try to emulate the Lord in every way,[308] as we had done in the premortal world. Such emulation transcends admiring Jesus' teachings and striving to adopt his attributes; true emulation includes doing his work—the work of redemption. Elder John A. Widtsoe gave us an important insight into our premortal preparation for our life's missions. He said that we made a contractual agreement with God concerning the eternal welfare of all of his children. Each of us, whether we are weak or strong, became partners with the Lord to become saviors for the entire family of Adam to bless them with the Covenant and bring them to Zion.[309]

As mentioned, we who formed the holy order in premortality became known by the family name *Israel*. In mortality, our founding fathers would be Abraham, Isaac, and Jacob (or *Israel*). Elder Bruce R. McConkie wrote: "Israel is an eternal people. She came into being as a chosen and separate congregation before the foundations of the earth were laid; she was a distinct and a peculiar people in preexistence, even as she is in this

---

299 Alma 13:3.
300 Alma 13:1.
301 Romans 8:29.
302 Thomas, "Alma the Younger, Part 1," n.p.
303 Thomas, "Alma the Younger, Part 2," n.p.
304 Thomas, "Alma the Younger, Part 1," n.p.
305 Alma 13:16.
306 Thomas, "Alma the Younger, Part 1," n.p.
307 JST, Obadiah 1:21.
308 3 Nephi 27:27.
309 Widtsoe, *Utah Genealogical and Historical Magazine*, Oct. 1934, 189.

sphere."[310] As Israelites, by blood or by adoption, we, like our father Abraham, desired to come to earth and teach the gospel, administer the ordinances of salvation, and become a "father [or mother] of many nations and a prince [or princess[311]] of peace."[312] This is the desire and attitude of Zion people. Moreover, righteous men who were premortally ordained "High Priests of God,"[313] having proved themselves by choosing good over evil and endorsing Zion in the conflict in heaven, had "undoubtedly labored among the spirits in the premortal world and were ordained and prepared to descend to earth and be leaders in the Lord's redeeming work here."[314] Additionally, said President Kimball, righteous women were given special assignments and prepared for those responsibilities.[315]

The power to redeem, bless, heal, and save is possibly "the most coveted power among enlightened beings."[316] Those who will persist in learning and perfecting that power will be exalted to the stature of their parent Gods. Is it any wonder, then, that God places so much weight on our learning the principles of redemption? Clearly, we who lived in Zion in the "first place" were pure hearted, and apparently we were assigned missions, trained, and strategically positioned to come to earth at this time to become the pure in heart again and do the work of redemption among God's children for the establishment of latter-day Zion. We are, perhaps, the greatest army of Zion people to ever have inhabited the globe.

Summary and Conclusion

We began this book by quoting the Prophet Joseph Smith: "We ought to have the building up of Zion as our greatest object."[317] Brigham Young laid the responsibility of Zion upon each of us individually, saying, "[Zion] commences in the heart of each person,"[318] and Elder Matthew Cowley stated unequivocally that individually, we are Zion.[319] We cannot read the scriptures, especially latter-day scriptures, and avoid personal responsibility for becoming Zion people. Without reservation, our obligation is to accept every revealed Zion principle and put it into practice. To that end, President Benson laid the responsibility of becoming Zion squarely on our shoulders. Zion, the priesthood society, he said, can be brought about only by Zion people. As more and more of us decide to embrace the principles of Zion, the celestial order will finally exist among us; then we, individually and collectively, will be prepared to receive the Lord.[320]

In the "first place," or the premortal world, we lived in the celestial atmosphere of Zion. We, who were among a select group called *Israel* fully internalized the principles of

---

310   McConkie, *A New Witness for the Articles of Faith*, 510.
311   Note: Jacob or Israel was called a "prince" (Genesis 32:28), and the name Sarah means "princess" (Genesis 17:15, footnote).
312   Abraham 1:2.
313   Alma 13:1–2, 10.
314   Thomas, "Alma the Younger, Part 1," n.p.
315   Kimball, "The Role of Righteous Women," 102.
316   Thomas, "Alma the Younger, Part 1," n.p.
317   Smith, *Teachings of the Prophet Joseph Smith*, 60.
318   Young, *Discourses of Brigham Young*, 118.
319   Cowley, *Matthew Cowley Speaks*, 30.
320   Benson, "Jesus Christ—Gifts and Expectations," 16.

Section 3   We Were Prepared to Become Latter-day Zion People

Zion and became ambassadors for the virtues of Zion to weaker spirits. We took as our example the Lord Jesus Christ and desired to become, like him, saviors to our fellow beings. To further our work, we entered into the *holy order* of the priesthood, which gave us the power of redemption under the direction of Jesus Christ. His work became our work: to preach and teach the virtue of the new and everlasting covenant for the purpose of establishing Zion. By *divine appointment*, and with intense preparation, we qualified for the blessings of Abraham, Isaac, and Jacob, and were assigned mortal missions to come into this life and continue with our premortal work. Here, we were to receive the Covenant, fully incorporate it into our lives, and then take it to family, friends, and the children of God within our influence. As heirs of Zion, we were to become Zion, and then invite all people to likewise become Zion.

Mortality is the testing ground that determines our genuine desires and the quality of our hearts; therefore, embracing Zion principles in this life ensures our inheritance in Zion in the eternal world. If we truly seek Zion, we must choose Zion here and now. The scriptures are filled with tragic examples of people who made the Covenant, then became lukewarm to it or rejected it altogether. That the latter-day Church is prospering does not necessarily mean that all is well in the lives of the people who call themselves Zion. Nephi clearly warned that adopting this philosophy is a one-way ticket to hell.[321]

For Latter-day Saints, the subject of Zion should be familiar and delightsome. Zion is our heritage, and it will be our destiny. Zion was and is heaven, the habitation of Deity, the presence of God. Zion was introduced to Adam and Eve in the Garden, a place that was preeminently *good*, or "perfect," for one meaning of the word Zion is "perfection."[322] Our first parents' subsequent *fall* from Zion created cataclysmic changes in their bodies that effected all of creation. Suddenly everything became mortal and telestial, and eventually that situation opened the door for a fallen condition of the heart called *Babylon*. Adam and Eve's immediate reaction to discovering themselves in the lone and dreary world[323] was to find a way out and return to Zion, which represented a return to the presence of God. Theirs is an example for all of us. God the Father provided the answer for their return: His Beloved Son would atone for every sin they committed and break down every obstacle that stood between them and the celestial state of Zion. The vehicle by which Adam and Eve could embrace the Atonement and reap its benefits was the new and everlasting covenant. This Covenant is an agreement of salvation, which Jesus Christ offers to each of us. We simply need to agree to the Covenant's stipulations and abide in it to the end.[324] The Covenant is a product of the Atonement, with power to rescue us from Babylon and return us to Zion.

The new and everlasting covenant is the most glorious doctrine ever revealed. It comprises the totality of the gospel of Jesus Christ, the authority and power of the priesthood, and all of the covenants and ordinances of salvation and exaltation.[325] When we

---

321   2 Nephi 28:21.
322   Galbraith, Ogden, and Skinner, *Jerusalem: The Eternal City*, 41.
323   Holland and Holland, *On Earth As It Is in Heaven*, 62.
324   D&C 98:14–15; 132:4.
325   D&C 132:5–7.

fully receive and live the Covenant, we can escape the captivity and misery of Babylon and enter the embrace and glory of Zion. Our obedience to the Covenant has the power to bind the Lord and guarantee eternal blessings.[326] The Covenant cleanses us and sets us apart for a holy purpose; it endows us with knowledge and power to think, feel, see, hear, and act like and become like God in every way. It empowers us to do work that only God can do. When we enter into the Covenant, we are immediately separated for salvation; that is, we are "called" and become candidates for celestial glory. Then, by abiding (staying put) in the Covenant, we qualify for "election" in the celestial kingdom. That is, we are *selected*[327] for eternal life. If we receive the Covenant with full purpose of heart and follow it through to its perfect conclusion, we will become pure in heart and, in every way, like God.

The more deeply we delve into scriptures, the more we learn that the Covenant has everything to do with our relationship with God. Our journey to Zion, therefore, involves discovering that relationship and following it until we come face-to-face with our Maker. All of the prophets, from Adam to Joseph Smith, including the latter-day prophets, set the example by making the Covenant and then embracing the resulting relationship with the Lord. When they understood and laid hold of the benefits of the Covenant, they wore out their lives preaching, teaching, and offering the Covenant to all the children of God. Some of the greatest moments in history were when they succeeded in administering the Covenant to people who responded. Those people became Zion. They escaped Babylon and entered into the rest of the Lord.

That is the destiny of every person who will forsake Babylon and come to and become Zion.

---

[326] D&C 82:10.
[327] Bible Dictionary, "Election," 662–63.

Section 4
Babylon the Great

The antithesis of Zion is Babylon. The two systems are reverse orders, contrary programs, opposed and inverse in every way. They are like day and night or opposite poles on a compass. The king of Zion is Jesus Christ;[328] the king of Babylon is the anti-Christ, Satan. The work of the king of Zion is "to bring to pass the immortality and eternal life of man,"[329] that we might have "fulness of joy."[330] The work of the king of Babylon is captivity and death, that we might become miserable like him.[331]

There can be no greater fall than from Zion to Babylon. An example is the Nephites. Within two hundred years of the coming of Christ, they plummeted from Zion (described as a condition with no contentions or disputations; every man dealing justly one with another; having all things common among them; no rich or poor; widespread freedom; great and marvelous spiritual outpourings and miracles; incredible prosperity; the love of God felt in the hearts of the people; no envyings, strifes, tumults, whoredoms, lyings, murders, or any manner of lasciviousness; no robbers or murderers; no separate classes of people; true equality and oneness; all people qualifying as the children of Christ and heirs to the kingdom of God; the happiest people ever created by God, and blessed in all their doings[332]) to Babylon (described as being lifted up in pride, with hearts set upon costly apparel, expensive jewelry, and the fine things of the world; the people ceased to have all things in common, divided into classes, built up churches and manmade philosophies to get gain, denied the true church of Christ and the more parts of his gospel, participated in all manner of wickedness, exercised power and authority over each other, hardened their hearts against God, willfully rebelled against the gospel, taught their children to not believe, reestablished secret combinations, sought after and

---

328   Moses 7:53.
329   Moses 1:39.
330   3 Nephi 28:10.
331   2 Nephi 2:27.
332   4 Nephi 1:1–18.

horded gold and silver, and trafficked in all manner of merchandising—the economy became their preoccupation and their god[333]).

The downfall of the Nephite nation can be traced back to their abandoning Zion and embracing Babylon.

Anti-Christ Philosophy

According to Blaine Yorgason, Satan's first two articles of faith are that "we can buy anything in this world with money, and . . . we can buy it now and pay for it later on."[334] The philosophy of Babylon is anti-Christ. Godlessness, selfishness, and competition are its hallmarks.[335] The anti-Christ doctrine states that people fare "according to the management of the creature," prosper according to their genius, and conquer according to their strength. Because they assume no accountability to God, they believe that they can act without moral consequences. In Babylon, people succeed or fail on their own merits; they are totally alone. They pretend a form of godliness, but deny the power that comes from and makes godliness possible. They eschew hope in and dependency upon Jesus Christ; they trample the plan of salvation and reject the holy priesthood and the gifts of the Spirit; they judge the humble followers of Christ as having frenzied minds and being held captive by what they call the false traditions of the gospel.[336]

In a general conference address, Elder Mark E. Petersen said, "Every force now corrupting America is a form of anti-Christ. Criminality is anti-Christ. Immorality is anti-Christ. Drunkenness is anti-Christ. Rioting, pillaging, and anarchy likewise are anti-Christ. Robbery, assault, and murder are all anti-Christ. Deception, duplicity, perjury, and covetousness are anti-Christ. The distribution of pornographic material that corrupts the morals of young and old alike is anti-Christ. And so is every other force destructive of the high principles that have made America great. . . . Oh, America—wake up to the peril that confronts you. Arouse yourself from this delirium in which you find yourself. Realize that this Christian nation can never survive on the principles of anti-Christ."[337]

Frighteningly, the anti-Christ philosophy forms a type of sinister worship. Hugh Nibley wrote: "This is the great voice of the economy of Babylon. It does not renounce its religious pretensions for a minute. Many in it think they are identical with a pious life."[338] We shall discuss Babylon as a religion hereafter. Suffice it to say that the anti-Christ philosophy always results in the downfall of those who subscribe to any part of it. We recall the dismal demises of Sherem and Korihor,[339] and we have the testimonies of the once-mighty Jaredite and Nephite nations. Clearly, there is no safety in Babylon. Satan will not support his children;[340] his only aim is to captivate them, make them miserable, and destroy them.[341]

---

333 4 Nephi 1:24–46.
334 Yorgason, *I Need Thee Every Hour*, 200.
335 Alma 30:12.
336 Alma 30:12–18.
337 Petersen, Conference Report, Oct. 1967, 67–68.
338 Nibley, *Approaching Zion*, 334.
339 Jacob 7:13–20; Alma 30:49–60.
340 Alma 30:60.
341 2 Nephi 2:27.

Cain

We can thank Cain and his descendant Nimrod for creating Babylon and perpetuating the anti-Christ philosophy that has enslaved the world and engulfed it in incarcerating misery.

From the dawn of history, Satan, the "father of lies"[342] and the would-be usurper of the Father and the Son's power, glory, and missions,[343] endeavored to gain a foothold in this world and build a kingdom here. He devised a "cunning plan" to make men miserable by means of deceptions and false revelations, which things would be "particularly effective against those who struggle with vanity and pride (2 Nephi 9:28). . . . His goal is to destroy the world (Moses 4:6) . . . [and] to separate what God has joined together and unite what God has separated."[344]

Failing to indoctrinate Adam and Eve with the anti-Christ doctrine, he found a willing apprentice in Cain. The two became inseparable, literally the inverse of the Father and the Son. Moses reports: "And Cain loved Satan more than God." This perverted affection allowed Satan to drive a wedge between Cain and God. To bring Cain to the point of decision, he told him to "make an offering unto the Lord." Of course, offerings ordered by Satan are rejected out of hand by God. It is God alone who mandates offerings; such offerings must be accomplished by proper priesthood authority through a specific ordinance. No wonder, then, that the Lord had no respect for Cain's offering. "Now Satan knew this, and it pleased him. And Cain was very wroth, and his countenance fell." We know the result. The Lord warned Cain of the consequences of following his course of action, but Cain had made his choice.[345] Thereafter, the Lord would call him "Perdition," which means entirely lost or ruined.[346]

On the other hand, Satan called Cain "Master Mahan," which suggests that Satan had given Cain a "new name"[347] within the order of his priestcraft (not *priesthood*), which name suggests a high level of authority in the demonic craft and extraordinary expertise. Now fully willing to establish the foundation of Satan's benighted kingdom, which would become known as Babylon, Cain learned from Satan the signs, tokens, and oaths of the devil's priestcraft, which were calculated to deliver power into his hands so that he could gain control and dominate the people of the earth.[348] The success of this diabolical father-and-son team was so great that their *religion* soon enslaved and degraded the whole world until the Lord had no choice except to destroy it by flood.

Hugh Nibley explained:

> [Satan] boasts just how he plans to put the world under his bloody and horrible misrule: He will control the world economy by claiming possession of the earth's

---

342 2 Nephi 9:9.
343 Moses 4:3; Isaiah 14:12–17.
344 Yorgason, *I Need Thee Every Hour*, 326.
345 Moses 5:18, 21–26.
346 *Webster's New World Dictionary* s.v. "perdition."
347 D&C 130:11.
348 Moses 5:16–34.

resources; and by manipulation of its currency—gold and silver—he will buy up the political, military, and ecclesiastical complex and run everything his way. We see him putting his plan into operation when he lays legal claim to the whole earth as his estate, accusing others of trespass, but putting everything up for sale to anyone who has the money. And how will they get the money? By going to work for him. He not only offers employment but a course of instruction in how the whole thing works, teaching the ultimate secret: "That great secret" (Moses 5:49–50) of converting life into property. Cain got the degree of Master Mahan, tried the system out on his brother, and gloried in its brilliant success, declaring that at last he could be free, as only property makes free, and that Abel had been a loser in a free competition.

The discipline was handed down through Lamech and finally became the pattern of the world's economy (Moses 5:55–56). . . Cain slew "his brother Abel for the sake of getting gain" (Moses 5:50)—not in a fit of pique but by careful business planning, "by the conspiracy" (D&C 84:16). The great secret he learned from Satan was the art of converting life into property—all life, even eternal life! The exchange of eternal life for worldly success is in fact the essence of the classic Pact with the Devil, in which the hero (Faust, Jabez Stone, even Jesus) is offered everything that the wealth of the earth can buy in return for subjection to Satan hereafter. There is no question of having some of both—"You cannot serve two masters" (see Matthew 6:24), the one being Mammon; if you try to have it both ways by putting off the final settlement, says Amulek, "the Spirit of the Lord hath withdrawn from you, and has no place in you, and the devil hath all power over you" (Alma 34:35).[349]

Nimrod

The Flood decimated the followers of Cain, but Satan was not to be denied. The principles of Babylon are as eternal as the principles of Zion; they only need revealing to a new Babylonian "prophet" in a new Babylonian "dispensation." Satan's new prophet was

---

349 Nibley, *Approaching Zion*, 166–67.

Section 4   Babylon the Great   53

Nimrod, a descendant of Cain through Ham's son, Cush. The irony that Nimrod was Cain's direct descendant and therefore that he possessed the right by bloodline to Cain's *priestcraft* cannot be overlooked. Nimrod, Cain's legal heir, who is also identified with Pharaoh,[350] was the one who tried to take the life of Abraham, the rightful heir to the legitimate *priesthood*.[351] David H. Yarn wrote:

> One of the earliest and most influential apostates in the dispensation of Noah was named Nimrod, who was the son of Cush, who was the son of Ham. He was a mighty hunter and hero. He began a kingdom in Babel, Erech, and Accad (Shinar). Josephus tells us Nimrod excited the people to a contempt of God. He persuaded the people to ascribe their well-being to himself instead of God. "He also changed the government into tyranny, seeing no other way of turning man from the fear of God, but to bring them into a constant dependence on his power." He also said ". . . he would avenge himself on God for destroying their forefathers." Furthermore, Josephus reports that Nimrod established his kingdom through rapine, murder, and tyranny. (Josephus, *Antiquities of the Jews*, Book I, chap. 4.) He urged the people to depart from the religion of Shem and cleave to the institutes of Nimrod. (Clarke, *Bible Commentary*, Vol. I, p. 84.) He tried to get men to worship great conquerors and in time the deification of humans became a chief characteristic of heathen religions in Egypt, Babylon, Greece, Rome, China, and India. He also introduced animal worship. Idolatry and adultery ("institutionalized immorality") became common religious rites. Even human sacrifices were instituted.[352]

The philosophies of Babylon were championed by Cain, but Babylon became an institution under Nimrod. Adjacent to the Euphrates River, Nimrod built a city (*Babel*), which over time became "one of the wonders of the ancient world, with its ziggurat and many miles of hanging (terraced) gardens."[353] Babel (later Babylon) became known for supplying its citizens every luxury the world had to offer. Later, under Nebuchadnezzar, Babylon grew into an enormous city, spreading fifty-six miles in circumference; it had massive walls and elegant parks and gardens.[354] We can immediately see the trappings and dan-

---
350 Nibley, *Abraham in Egypt*, 61–66.
351 Clark, *The Blessings of Abraham*, 35.
352 Yarn, *The Gospel: God, Man, and Truth*, 127–28.
353 Galbraith, Ogden, and Skinner, *Jerusalem: The Eternal City*, 103–4.
354 Bible Dictionary, "Babylon or Babel," 618.

gers of Babylon. From Cain to Nimrod to Nebuchadnezzar to Caesar to the latter days, Babylon has been a place or state of mind defined by excesses, self-indulgence, wanton sin, and contempt of God. Babylon has always been the nemesis of Zion.

Elder McConkie wrote: "As the seat of world empire, Babylon was the persistent persecutor and enemy of the Lord's people. . . . To the Lord's people anciently, Babylon was known as the center of iniquity, carnality, and worldliness. Everything connected with it was in opposition to all righteousness and had the effect of leading men downward to the destruction of their souls. It was natural, therefore, for the apostles and inspired men of New Testament times to apply the name Babylon to the forces organized to spread confusion and darkness in the realm of spiritual things. (Rev. 17; 18; D&C 29:21; Ezek. 38; 39.) In a general sense, the wickedness of the world generally is Babylon. (D&C 1:16; 35:11; 64:24; 133:14)."[355]

Nimrod sought to dominate the world from his capital city, Babel, and, according to M. Catherine Thomas, Nimrod, like his spiritual father, Satan, "sought to dethrone God by bringing men into constant dependence on his, Nimrod's, power." Nimrod was very successful. "A multitude followed Nimrod, persuaded that it was cowardice to submit to God. The people began to build the tower, apparently some type of temple, as their objective was to reach heaven by means of the tower. God's response was to break up their evil combination by scrambling their languages, thus depriving them of the powerful Adamic language. The name *babel* means, in Akkadian, 'gate of God' and is a play on the Hebrew *balal*, meaning 'to mix or confound.' It is apparent then that the tower of Babel was a counterfeit gate of God, or temple, that Ham's priesthood-deprived descendants built in rebellion against God. Jared and his family and friends rejected this temple and were spared the Lord's punishments."[356]

Nimrod's Babel became Babylon, the world order, philosophy, and religion that would dominate the hearts of people throughout millennia. Elder McConkie explained: "The name Babylon means many things to many people. The Hebrew word (*bbel*) goes back to a kingdom Nimrod founded, where the ancients built the tower of Babel, or Babylon (Genesis 10:9–10; 11:1–9). This kingdom evolved into an idolatrous materialistic civilization that reached a zenith in the powerful neo-Babylonian empire of Nebuchadnezzar (cf. Daniel 2:37–38). The prophet Isaiah identifies Babylon typologically as both a people and a place: the sinners and the wicked; the earth and the world (Isaiah 13:1, 9, 11). He predicts latter-day Babylon will suffer the fate of Sodom and Gomorrah, thus likening the world's desolation to a fiery cataclysm falling upon the wicked (Isaiah 13:4–19)."[357]

Nimrod and his people rebelled against God, and their religion of choice became idolatry, the worship of nature, images, or false gods—all defined by covetousness.[358] E. Douglas Clark writes: "An early Christian source reported . . . , 'The whole world was again overspread with errors, and . . . for the hideousness of its crimes destruction was ready for it, this time not by water, but fire, and . . . already the scourge was hanging over

---

355 McConkie, *Mormon Doctrine*, 69.
356 Parry, *Temples of the Ancient World*, 389–90.
357 Lundquist and Ricks, *By Study and Also by Faith*, 2:384.
358 Colossians 3:5; Ephesians 5:5; Philippians 3:19; see also Bible Dictionary, "Idol," 706.

the whole earth.' Never in the troubled history of mankind had there been greater darkness and depravity. It was a world as far from Zion as possible."

Clark continues by quoting from the book of Jubilees:

> Noah's children began to fight one another, to take captive, and to kill one another; to shed human blood on the earth, to consume blood; to build fortified cities, walls, and towers; men to elevate themselves over peoples, to set up the first kingdoms; to go to war—people against people, nations against nations, city against city; and everyone to do evil, to acquire weapons, and to teach warfare to their sons. City began to capture city and to sell male and female slaves. . . . They made molten images for themselves. Each one would worship the idol which he had made as his own molten image. They began to make statues, images, and unclean things; the spirits of the savage ones were helping and misleading them so that they would commit sins, impurities, and transgressions. Prince Mastema [Satan] was exerting his power in effecting all these actions and, by means of the spirits, he was sending to those who were placed in his control the ability to commit every kind of error and sin and every kind of transgression; to corrupt, to destroy, and to shed blood on the earth.[359]

This description reads like a how-to book for Babylon—or the morning newspaper.

Nimrod succeeded in contaminating the entire world with his Babylonian practices. Thereafter, Satan's great chain once again veiled the earth in darkness, as it had in the days preceding the Flood. "And he looked up and laughed, and his angels rejoiced."[360] That same chain binds down the people of the latter days. Enoch foresaw our day and recorded that "a veil of darkness shall cover the earth."[361]

Sodom and Gomorrah

President Spencer W. Kimball spoke of "the rise and fall of great civilizations, such as Babylon, Ninevah, Jerusalem, Egypt, Greece, Rome, and numerous others which have flared like an arc-light, then dimmed even to candlelight proportions, or to be extinguished."[362] Sodom and Gomorrah, too, had their day and likewise perished. These cities, now covered by the Dead Sea, were in the image of Babylon. Because the latter

---

359 Clark, *The Blessings of Abraham*, 31, quoting Jubilees 11:2–5.
360 Moses 7:26.
361 Moses 7:61.
362 Kimball, *Faith Precedes the Miracle*, 51.

days have been compared to Sodom and Gomorrah, we would do well to examine the characteristics that brought about their downfall.

Quoting Rabbi Eliezer, Hugh Nibley wrote:

> The men of Sodom were the wealthy men of prosperity, on account of the good and fruitful land whereon they dwelt. For every need which the world requires, they obtained therefrom.... But they did not trust in the shadow of their Creator, but [they trusted] in the multitude of their wealth, for wealth thrusts aside its owners from the fear of Heaven.... The men of Sodom had no consideration for the honour of their Owner by (not) distributing food to the wayfarer and the stranger.... They [even] fenced in all their trees on top above their fruit so that they should not be seized; [not] even by the bird of heaven.... These were the crimes of Sodom and Gomorrah. At the time of Abraham, the people elected leaders "of falsehood and wickedness, who mocked justice and equity and committed evil deeds"... the wicked oppressed the weak and gave power to the strong. Inside the city was tyranny and the receiving of bribes. Every day, without fail, they plundered each others' goods. The son cursed his father in the streets, the slave his master. They put an end to the offerings and entered into conspiracy.... It's not surprising, the records tell, that travelers and birds alike learned to avoid the rich cities of the plain, while the poor emigrated to other parts. "If a stranger merchant passed through their territory, he was besieged by them all, big and little alike, and robbed of whatever he possessed."... This was a world in which every man was for himself. What a terrible state of things.[363]

Elsewhere, Ezekiel and Jude describe Sodom and Gomorrah's sins as:
1. pride
2. "fulness of bread" (luxuriant living)
3. abundant idleness
4. failure to care for poor and needy
5. idolatry (worshipping anything else instead of God)
6. contempt for others
7. fornication
8. "going after strange flesh" (homosexuality)[364]

---
363 Nibley, *Approaching Zion*, 322–23.
364 Ezekiel 16:49–50; Jude 1:7.

Section 4   Babylon the Great

We know the fate of these offshoots of Babylon. The Lord obliterated them with fire from heaven;[365] then he hid Sodom and Gomorrah from his face by covering them with the waters of the Dead Sea.[366]

Our leaders have compared the conditions of the last days to the evils of Sodom and Gomorrah. They have stated that they know of no time in the history of the earth when there was greater spiritual danger from evil that permeates the world in epidemic proportions, not even in the time of Sodom and Gomorrah. At no time has wickedness been so widely accepted. Whereas evil was localized in Sodom and Gomorrah, our leaders have pointed out, now it has spread across the world.[367]

Descriptions of Babylon

When we read the descriptions of Babylon, we wonder why anyone would want to live there, and yet all of us, to one degree or another, shop in her stores, partake of her delicacies, and participate in her wickedness. Raising a voice of warning, Jesus prophesied that even the very elect of the latter-day Church would be deceived.[368] Babylon is simply so pervasive in our world that avoiding her requires divine intervention and dogged determination.

Paul explained that Babylon focuses on "the works of the flesh," which are "adultery, fornication, uncleanness [pursuing that which is unholy], lasciviousness [an unseemly focus on sex], idolatry [worshipping anything other than the true God], witchcraft, hatred, variance [disputations], emulations [trying to equal or surpass someone else], wrath [anger and revenge], strife [bitter conflict], seditions [to incite rebellion], heresies [contradicting the truth], envying [covetousness], murders, drunkenness, revellings [uproarious partying], and such like." Then, in damning language, he informs us, "They which do such things shall not inherit the kingdom of God."[369]

Satan is the founder of Babylon. From the beginning, Hugh Nibley said, Satan "taught men how to make knives, weapons, shields, and breastplates, the trade secrets, and showed them the various metals and how to work them, and bracelets, jewelry, makeup, and eyepaint, and all kind of precious stones and hairdos." Then, quoting from another ancient document, he says Satan's primary weapon was "all the treasures of the earth. And there were great wickedness and whoredoms [sexual perversions], and they all became perverted and lost in all their ways. And he taught them spells, drugs and quackery." How similar this sounds to Satan's attacks on our youth. Over the millennia, his strategy has not changed much. To the ancients, Satan introduced the science of astrology, a counterfeit for seeking the words of true prophets, which science contributed in a major way to the people's downfall: "And Araqil [Satan] taught them astrology, the interpretation of signs, the observations of signs, and the series of the moon. They

---

365   Genesis 19:24.
366   "Map: Old Testament Stories: Part Two," *LDS Church News,* Jan. 8, 1994.
367   Packer, "One Pure Defense," Feb. 5, 2004.
368   Matthew 24:24.
369   Galatians 5:19–21.

maliciously brought them gold and silver and copper and all manner of metals; and this was what finally completed their ruin, and established their perennial earthly order of human society, which persists to this day."[370] Once Satan can get a person to buy into the philosophy of Babylon, he can have a heyday. He is capable of taking our fears, insecurities, appetites, and passions and transforming them to his advantage. Continuing, Nibley wrote:

> The Abraham literature includes the Old Testament, which also makes it clear that the people he dealt with were scoundrels—mean and inhospitable. The nature of their economy is fully set forth: their one guiding principle was the maximizing of profits. After the flood, the Jewish writings explain, the people were haunted by an understandable feeling of insecurity. To overcome it, they undertook tremendous engineering projects and became very knowledgeable in fire, flood, earthquake, and other potential disasters. A great economic boom and commercial expansion enabled them to undertake all kinds of engineering projects for controlling a dangerous nature. . . . And the Nimrod legends are full of the great scientific understanding of Abraham's day of which a good deal is made in the time of Enoch. The people had a great deal of sophistication and know-how. It was a world of unrest and insecurity, and the people were mean and short-tempered. . . . The fabulous prosperity of the cities of the plain turned them into little Babylons. The record describes their ways of doing things, how they dealt with all strangers, taking away possessions by force; then the wrath of the Lord came upon them. . . . [Abraham] found the same hostility elsewhere. There was world-wide cruelty, inhospitality, insecurity, suspicion wherever he went.[371]

Do we not see the same in our day?

John the Revelator described Babylon as "the great whore that sitteth upon many waters: With whom the kings of the earth have committed fornication, and the inhabitants of the earth have been made drunk with the wine of her fornication."[372] The reference to universal domination is terrifying. Perhaps worse is the mention of sexual intercourse with a whore; that is, intimacy that is unlawful and unholy; selfish, lustful, wanton, immoral gratification with no accountability to one's spouse or to the Lord; the

---

370 Nibley, *Approaching Zion*, 321–22.
371 Nibley, *Approaching Zion*, 321–22.
372 Revelation 17:1–2.

Section 4   Babylon the Great   59

buying and selling for money of the power of creation given by God to man. Who is this whore, who lures us in with her charms, who is "full of names of blasphemy" and "arrayed in purple and scarlet colour, and decked with gold and precious stones and pearls, having a golden cup in her hand full of abominations and filthiness of her fornication"? John identifies her: "MYSTERY, BABYLON THE GREAT, THE MOTHER OF HARLOTS AND ABOMINATIONS OF THE EARTH." Babylon is the great seducer of the world and the persecutor of the Saints: "And I saw the woman drunken with the blood of the saints, and with the blood of the martyrs of Jesus: and when I saw her, I wondered with great admiration."[373] Nephi's brother, Jacob, adds that the whore of all the earth is anyone who "fighteth against Zion, both Jew and Gentile, both bond and free, both male and female, [and they] shall perish; for they are they who are the whore of all the earth; for they who are not for me are against me, saith our God."[374]

In section 1 of the Doctrine and Covenants, the Lord describes Babylon as the world itself and the people who in any degree worship or partake of the things of the world: "They seek not the Lord to establish his righteousness, but every man walketh in his own way, and after the image of his own god, whose image is in the likeness of the world, and whose substance is that of an idol, which waxeth old and shall perish in Babylon, even Babylon the great, which shall fall."[375] Such people define their priorities and relationships in terms of money and property, "preach[ing] up unto themselves their own wisdom and their own learning, that they might get gain and grind upon the face of the poor."[376] This attitude of idolatry, pride, wealth-seeking, and selfishness is not exempted from the Latter-day Saints.

The fact that mortal men are by nature carnal, sensual, and devilish[377] plays to Satan's advantage in establishing Babylon among them. Carnal, sensual, and devilish seems to form a downward, spiraling cycle. To be carnal is to be of the flesh; that is, we naturally pamper the physical body and are inclined to succumb to its passions and appetites. Both the apostle Paul and Nephi's brother, Jacob, state that "to be carnally-minded is death."[378] That is, if we give in to carnality, we will eventually submit to sensuality by seeking more and more physical and sexual pleasures. As we seek these pleasures, we become more inclined to lie to cover up those things that our conscience would have us change. Before long, our testimony is damaged. As the carnal takes precedence, we become confused, stop believing, and begin seeking physical evidence and signs to bolster their faith.[379] This is death. Such behavior weakens us to the point that Satan can take control of our bodies and we become devilish. Our behavior begins to mirror that of Satan; we become sexually perverted, sinister, cruel, scheming, deceitful, mischievous, and in every way like the demons who prod us to be like them. The carnal, sensual, and

---

373   Revelation 17:1–6.
374   2 Nephi 10:16.
375   D&C 1:16.
376   2 Nephi 26:20.
377   Alma 42:10.
378   Romans 8:6; 2 Nephi 9:39.
379   Matthew 12:39; 16:4.

devilish cycle inevitably leads to apostasy. Breaking the new and everlasting covenant[380] is inevitable, and that tragedy summons the judgment of God and the damnation of the soul.[381]

Clearly, Babylon is designed to make us miserable and to destroy us. It waves the flag of safety and security, but when hard times come—and they always do in this benighted condition—Babylon will leave us flat. Thus, we read, there is a natural curse placed upon those who place their trust in the "arm of flesh" rather than in the arm of the Lord.[382] There is neither safety nor security in Babylon.

Babylon As a Religion

Nephi speaks of a false religion that shall be set up among the latter-day Gentiles. That he casts Babylon in terms of a church is chilling. At once we see Satan declaring himself as the god of this world and advancing philosophies that his followers worship, as if they were holy.

Because this religion's founder is the devil, it can neither endure nor remain unified. Therefore, Nephi describes this false religion as "many churches," whose goal is to destroy the one true Church of God. In the process, this demonic religion will strive to cause as much misery as possible, especially among the weak and vulnerable. Here is Nephi's description of Babylon as a false religion:

> And the Gentiles are lifted up in the pride of their eyes, and have stumbled, because of the greatness of their stumbling block, that they have built up many churches; nevertheless, they put down the power and miracles of God, and preach up unto themselves their own wisdom and their own learning, that they may get gain and grind upon the face of the poor.
>
> And there are many churches built up which cause envyings, and strifes, and malice.
>
> And there are also secret combinations, even as in times of old, according to the combinations of the devil, for he is the founder of all these things; yea, the founder of murder, and works of darkness; yea, and he leadeth them by the neck with a flaxen cord, until he bindeth them with his strong cords forever.[383]

Note that this religion consists of doctrines that run counter to the doctrines of Zion. In fact, they discount God, his power and miracles, and replace them with intellectualism,

---

380 D&C 1:15; Isaiah 24:5.
381 D&C 76:101; 132:5, 15–27; see 41:1; 82:2; 132:27.
382 2 Nephi 4:34; 28:31.
383 2 Nephi 26:20–22.

which is a powerful counterfeit philosophy promoted by Babylon. "I act, succeed, dominate, influence, and conquer because of my superior intellect, which I protect, nurture and worship above all else." Intellectualism and other false doctrines cause envy, strife, malice, and poverty. Interestingly, because Nephi describes Babylon in religious terms, he seems to suggest that the false religion's precepts are preached as if they were holy principles; he states categorically that they "put down the power and miracles of God." The people of Babylon worship these doctrines as if they had issued from the mouth of their god. Nevertheless, however one wishes to define it, Babylon as a religion is, pure and simple, idolatry and anti-Christ.

Moroni ends the Book of Mormon with an ominous warning to us who live in the latter days: "Wherefore I would exhort you that ye deny not the power of God; for he worketh by power, according to the faith of the children of men, the same today and tomorrow, and forever."[384] Both Moroni and Nephi foresaw the formation of this false religion that would limit or outright deny the power of God and his miracles and replace them with intellectualism, wealth-building, oppressive selfishness, and other counter-doctrines to Zion. Our adherence to these Babylonian philosophies in any degree makes us proponents of that false religion. Moreover, our adopting these doctrines in any degree serves to increase our pride and paves the way for envy, strife, and malice, and ultimately we will persecute and withhold our substance from the poor.

The "Great Church" of the Devil

The false religion is also described as a false church or the "great church" of the devil.[385] In every way, Satan seeks to duplicate and counterfeit God and his works. If God has a beloved Son, Satan will have a beloved son (Cain, and later Nimrod); if God has a church, Satan will have a church; if God has priesthood power, Satan will have priestcraft power; if God has a religion with saving covenants and ordinances, Satan will have a religion with damning covenants and ordinances (secret combinations); if God has *mysteries* that can be learned only by revelation from God, Satan will have *secrets* that can be learned only by revelation from Satan; if God has a capital city (Jerusalem and New Jerusalem), Satan will have a capital city (Babylon); if God has a temple, Satan will have a temple (Tower of Babel, great and spacious building, etc.).

Nephi was shown in vision that "there are save two churches only; the one is the church of the Lamb of God, and the other is the church of the devil; wherefore, whoso belongeth not to the church of the Lamb of God belongeth to that great church, which is the mother of abominations; and she is the whore of all the earth."[386] There are only two ways, two religions, two churches, and they are exact opposites that take us in conflicting directions. We are incapable of standing still. We are either going one way or the other; we believe one philosophy or the other; we belong to one church or the other. There is no neutrality. Quoting Elder John A. Widtsoe, Elder Ezra Taft Benson wrote:

---
384 Moroni 10:7.
385 1 Nephi 14:10.
386 1 Nephi 14:10.

"'The troubles of the world may largely be laid at the doors of those who are neither hot nor cold; who always follow the line of least resistance; whose timid hearts flutter at taking sides for truth. As in the great Council in the heavens, so in the Church of Christ on earth, there can be no neutrality.'"[387]

We are presented with the two churches and we must choose, but we cannot choose both. The purpose of the Church of the Lamb of God is to preserve agency and save souls; the purpose of the church of the devil is to dominate and destroy souls.[388] Which we claim membership in is our choice.

Nephi casts the church of the devil as an unfaithful woman, reminiscent of Hosea's imagery of the unfaithful wife who becomes a prostitute.[389] Nephi's term, "mother of abominations," summons the image of a mother giving birth to wicked children. Clearly, the devil's church spawns evil of every variety. Nephi also uses the term "whore" to describe this church. The suggestion seems to be one of an illegitimate relationship, broken covenants, and carnal gratification. In another place, Nephi describes the members of the church of the devil as those who commit "whoredoms,"[390] that is, sexual sins of every kind. He calls such people "harlots,"[391] a genderless term suggesting those who engage in illicit sexual activity, which is a central doctrine of the church of the devil.

According to Nephi, the devil's church is the "most abominable" institution on the earth. It "slayeth the saints of God, yea, and tortureth them and bindeth them down, and yoketh them with a yoke of iron, and bringeth them down into captivity."[392] Nephi's adopting the language of war should strike horror in our hearts. Beyond enslaving the people of the earth and causing widespread misery, the church of the devil specifically singles out the Saints of God to inflict upon them intense pain and anguish by twisting and contorting us to the boundaries of endurance. The devil's ultimate intent is to murder us both physically and spiritually. To that end, he employs every evil device to load us with heavy burdens and to subjugate and press us into his servitude. What is the devil's strategy? Nephi says it is fourfold:

1. The pursuit of wealth—"gold and silver"
2. Fashion and materialism—"silks and scarlets and fine-twined linen, and all manner of precious clothing"
3. Sexual sin of every variety—"many harlots"
4. Peer acceptance and popularity or recognition—"praise of the world."

According to the angel who instructed Nephi, these four things are the primary "desires of this great and abominable church."[393] One need only survey the membership of the Latter-day Saints to observe the devil's success in luring us away from the true Church and into his church with these four strategies. As the angel predicted, the result is always

---

387 Benson, *God, Family, Country,* 359.
388 1 Nephi 14:9–13.
389 Hosea 1–3.
390 2 Nephi 28:14.
391 1 Nephi 13:8.
392 1 Nephi 13:5.
393 1 Nephi 13:8.

Section 4   Babylon the Great

heavy burdens, loss of freedom, confinement, torment, suffering, and death. And with every success, Satan and his followers rejoice. Their triumph in destroying the Saints of God and bringing them down into captivity garners them and their adherents "the praise of the world,"[394] the perfect prize for the great and abominable church of the devil.

Satan's strategy to deceive and destroy even the very elect[395] is working. He has made us to "bow down with grief, sorrow, and care, under the most damning hand of murder, tyranny, and oppression." He has "strongly riveted the creeds of the fathers, who have inherited lies, upon the hearts of the children, and filled the world with confusion." This multigenerational oppression forms the foundation of our culture, and we are hard-pressed to imagine life any other way. Frighteningly, this deep-seated culture of wickedness and confusion has been "growing stronger and stronger, and is now the very mainspring of all corruption, and the whole earth groans under the weight of its iniquity." As a society, we live in a condition of bondage to the church of the devil. "It is an iron yoke, it is a strong band; they are the very handcuffs, and chains, and shackles, and fetters of hell." Satan has been so successful in establishing his church that even he is horrified. His "dark and blackening deeds are enough to make hell itself shudder, and to stand aghast and pale, and the hands of the very devil to tremble and palsy."[396]

To establish his diabolical church, Satan must have a set of scriptures. To accomplish this feat, he simply wrested troublesome doctrines from the true scriptures and reassembled the remaining parts so that they could seem mystifying. Yes, the Bible has beautiful language and contains much important truth—but some of the most vital truths have been removed. Nephi says, "[He has] taken away from the gospel of the Lamb many parts which are plain and most precious; and also many covenants of the Lord [has he] taken away. And all this [has he] done that [he] might pervert the right ways of the Lord, that [he] might blind the eyes and harden the hearts of the children of men."[397] It is a sinister plot to tamper with the words of God and make that which was once "plain and precious" mystifying and dangerous.

To further deceive the Latter-day Saints, Satan will resort to such strategies as intellectualism, rumor, apathy, conjecture, criticism of the Lord's anointed, seeking counsel from external sources that are separate from and nonsupportive of those with keys, pursuing gospel hobbies, and the "private interpretation" of the scriptures.[398] It all has the same effect. The true scriptures are displaced or whittled down by these philosophies or practices, and our attention shifts to the doctrines of the great church of the devil.

Babylon As a Temple

Perhaps one of the most detailed descriptions of latter-day Babylon comes from the father-son team of Lehi and Nephi. Lehi began his description by viewing a "great and spacious

---
394   1 Nephi 13:9.
395   Matthew 24:24.
396   D&C 123:7–10.
397   1 Nephi 13:26–27.
398   1 Peter 1:20.

building" that "stood as it were in the air, high above the earth." Immediately, we note that the building has no foundation and it is elevated high in the air by its pride. Lehi observed that multitudes of people of every age, gender, and class occupied this building. These people had two identifying characteristics: "their manner of dress was exceedingly fine, and they were in the attitude of mocking." Commenting, Nephi described this building as "strange," that is, unnatural, difficult to understand, something that Nephi was not acquainted with. Those who migrated to this building after they had tasted of the fruit of the tree of life (and thus by definition were members of the true Church), then fell away from the love of God and departed from the truth because they felt shame.[399]

We might assume that this building was indeed Babylon's temple, where the malevolent doctrines, covenants, and ordinances of the false religion are disseminated. These doctrines are pursuit of wealth, fashion, materialism, and sexual sin of every variety; seeking peer acceptance, recognition, and popularity; embracing priestcrafts and combinations; and delving into secrets. Nephi described this false temple and its doctrines as "the world and the wisdom thereof," "the pride of the world," and the "vain imaginations and pride of the children of men." The purpose of this false temple was to "fight against the twelve apostles of the Lamb." When the false temple finally fell, "the fall thereof was exceedingly great."[400] Speaking futuristically, Nephi says Babylon will be destroyed "speedily . . . : It shall be at an instant, suddenly."[401]

Nephi's Description of Babylon

We can thank Nephi for detecting and detailing the characteristics of Babylon. He portrays Babylon so plainly that we are left without excuse if we fail to distinguish her. In plain language, Nephi gives us the keys that expose Babylon. For example, anytime we perceive people seeking material wealth for their own purposes, when we observe people dominating or manipulating others, when we see people striving for recognition and popularity or indulging in the lusts of the flesh, we see Babylon. Nephi warns that such people "need fear, and tremble, and quake; they are those who must be brought low in the dust; they are those who must be consumed as stubble."[402]

In an effort to help us detect and steer clear of Babylon, Nephi lists at least ten indicators:

1. **Contention.** Foremost, is contention.[403] The trouble with contention is one of the predominant themes of the Book of Mormon. The resurrected Savior told the Nephites: "For verily, verily I say unto you, he that hath the spirit of contention is not of me, but is of the devil, who is the father of contention, and he stirreth up the hearts of men to contend with anger, one with another."[404] Where there is contention and anger, there is Babylon.

---

399 1 Nephi 8:25–28, 31–34.
400 1 Nephi 11:35–36; 12:18.
401 2 Nephi 26:18.
402 1 Nephi 22:23.
403 2 Nephi 28:4.
404 3 Nephi 11:29.

2. **Man's wisdom.** People who espouse the doctrine of Babylon "teach with their learning and deny the Holy Ghost, which giveth utterance."[405] This statement hearkens to one of the first things Jesus told young Joseph Smith about the despicable condition of the last days: "I was answered that I must join none of [the churches], for they were all wrong; and the Personage who addressed me said that all their creeds were an abomination in his sight; that those professors were all corrupt; that: 'they draw near to me with their lips, but their hearts are far from me, they teach for doctrines the commandments of men, having a form of godliness, but they deny the power thereof.'"[406]

   The creeds of Babylon rely on the learning of man, but Nephi pronounces a wo on those who depend on man's wisdom. The Holy Ghost is the source of the power of God for man and the conveyor of pure knowledge. Whereas Zion people look to God for intelligence, Babylon people look to man while simultaneously limiting or discounting God's words to safeguard Babylon's position: "Yea, wo be unto him that saith: We have received, and we need no more!" The foundation of man's knowledge is at best a "sandy foundation," says Nephi. Nevertheless, Babylonians tenaciously build their foundation upon the sand and tremble when their precepts are threatened by the word of God; they even react violently toward the truth in order to protect the precepts of men: "Wo unto all those who tremble, and are angry because of the truth of God!" To maintain some semblance of piety, Babylonians will tolerate a smattering of the word of God, carefully extracted from the whole to bolster their position—but they will only put up with so much: "Wo be unto him that shall say: We have received the word of God, and we need no more of the word of God, for we have enough!" What will be the fate of the people of Babylon? "From them shall be taken away even that which they have."[407] Satan intends to keep the people of Babylon off balance and in the dark.

3. **Denying the power of God.** Babylon denies "the power of God, the Holy One of Israel."[408] All the dominoes begin to fall when we ignore, discount, or deny the power of Christ. Not only do miracles cease, but we begin to doubt the reality of the Lord's perfections, upon which the scaffolding of faith is constructed—power, knowledge, love, consistency, justice, and truth.[409] Nephi explains that marginalizing the power of God leads to at least four false premises, which are calculated to retard our progress, empower men, enthrone self-reliance and personal wisdom, and discount modern-day miracles, God's consistency, and his treating his children with equal regard: (1) "there is no God today," (2) "the Lord and the Redeemer hath done his work," (3) "he hath given his power unto men,"

---

405   2 Nephi 28:4.
406   JS–H 1:19.
407   2 Nephi 28:26–30.
408   2 Nephi 28:5.
409   Smith, *Lectures on Faith*, 3.

and (4) "if they shall say there is a miracle wrought by the hand of the Lord, believe it not; for this day he is not a God of miracles; he hath done his work."[410]

Need we be reminded that Babylon's doctrine is exactly opposite that of Zion's? If we marginalize the power of God, we simultaneously deny the spirit of revelation and question whether God can or will intervene in our lives. Then we embrace scientific theories over faith; we look to man as the source of all knowledge and help; we disregard the justice of God; and we reduce to the level of myth the resurrection and the Atonement.

4. **Eat, drink, and be merry.** Babylon would like to portray life as a time to get, accumulate, indulge, and seek pleasure. Zion's goals of *giving* and *becoming* are foreign in Babylon, unless *giving* is done to get something better in return or *becoming* is done to become rich, popular, supposedly wise, or influential.[411] To eat, drink, and be merry is more than a decadent lifestyle; it is a wasted life, as life pertains to eternity; it is a life without accountability to God. Such a life is telestial and therefore Babylonian.

Nephi reveals that Babylon's philosophy of eat, drink, and be merry is one that telestial people worship. It is a perverse creed, and when it becomes life's goal it leads to all sorts of mischief. For example, the people of Babylon believe that they can either change the definition of sin or justify a little wrongdoing: "Yea, lie a little, take the advantage of one because of his words, dig a pit for thy neighbor; there is no harm in this." Living for today while taking no thought for eternity is Babylon's motto: "and do all these things, for tomorrow we die."

All of these follies lead to lack of accountability for one's actions, the prideful attitude of putting words in God's mouth, and inventing a private interpretation of justice and mercy: "and if it so be that we are guilty, God will beat us with a few stripes, and at last we shall be saved in the kingdom of God."[412] There is no evidence that God ever said such a thing. Satan invented this lie; it is his doctrine, and God has nothing to do with it. Nevertheless, in Babylon, "there shall be many which shall teach after this manner, false and vain and foolish doctrines."[413]

5. **Pride.** Nephi cannot say enough about this damning characteristic of Babylon. He says that Babylonians are "puffed up in their hearts." "Because of pride, and because of false teachers, and false doctrine, their churches have become corrupted, and their churches are lifted up; because of pride they are puffed up." Once again, we read the word *church* as a descriptor of Babylon. The people of Babylon worship their culture and practices as if they were holy. These people are elitists; they feel entitled; they indulge in every form of evil, with sex as the

---
410 2 Nephi 28:5–6.
411 Wickman, "Today," 103–5.
412 2 Nephi 28:7–8.
413 2 Nephi 28:9.

common denominator: "They wear stiff necks and high heads; yea, and because of pride, and wickedness, and abominations, and whoredoms, they have all gone astray save it be a few, who are the humble followers of Christ."[414]

Where does their pride lead them? As far from Zion as possible: "They rob the poor because of their fine sanctuaries [the monuments they build to themselves where they can worship the things of the world and practice the doctrines of Babylon]; they rob the poor because of their fine clothing; and they persecute the meek and the poor in heart, because in their pride they are puffed up."[415] Sadly, they could choose to help the poor with their money, but instead they selfishly accumulate riches, build elaborate houses that they adore, and wear elegant clothing—during all of which they persecute and rob the less fortunate. *Pride!*

Pride is death to Zion. We are not to build up ourselves. "God has commanded the Saints to 'seek to bring forth and establish the cause of Zion' (D&C 6:6). When Zion is established, its people will be 'of one heart and one mind' and will dwell together in righteousness (Moses 7:18). But 'pride is the great stumbling block to Zion' (Benson, 1989, p. 7). Pride leads people to diminish others in the attempt to elevate themselves, resulting in selfishness and contention."[416] President Ezra Taft Benson taught, "We must prepare to redeem Zion. It was essentially the sin of pride that kept us from establishing Zion in the days of the Prophet Joseph Smith. It was the same sin of pride that brought consecration to an end among the Nephites. (See 4 Ne. 1:24–25).”[417]

"President Benson brings the . . . message to our doorstep with the warning that 'pride is the great stumbling block to Zion. I repeat: Pride is the great stumbling block to Zion.' Our modern-day prophet said further: 'The central feature of pride is enmity—enmity toward God and enmity toward our fellowmen. Enmity means 'hatred toward, hostility to, or a state of opposition.' It is the power by which Satan wishes to reign over us. . . . Our enmity toward God takes on many labels, such as rebellion, hardheartedness, stiffneckedness, unrepentant, puffed up, easily offended, and sign seekers.'"[418]

Commenting on the proud of Babylon, Robert L. Millet writes: "They are proud, overly competitive, reactionary, and externally driven. Natural men and women—be they the irreverent and ungodly or the well-meaning but spiritually unregenerate—are preoccupied with self and obsessed with personal aggrandizement. Their lives are keyed to the rewards of this ephemeral sphere; their values derive solely from pragmatism and utility. They take their cues from the world and the worldly. The central feature of pride, as President Ezra Taft Benson warned the Latter-day Saints, is enmity—enmity toward God and enmity toward man. The look of natural men and women is neither up (to God)

---

414 2 Nephi 28:9, 12, 14.
415 2 Nephi 28:13.
416 *Encyclopedia of Mormonism*, 1132.
417 Benson, *The Teachings of Ezra Taft Benson*, 7.
418 Van Orden and Top, "Doctrines of the Book of Mormon," 16–17.

nor over (to their fellow humans), except as the horizontal glance allows them to maintain a distance from others. 'Pride is essentially competitive in nature,' President Benson explained. 'We pit our will against God's. When we direct our pride toward God, it is in the spirit of 'my will and not thine be done.' . . . The proud cannot accept the authority of God giving direction to their lives. . . . The proud wish God would agree with them. They aren't interested in changing their opinions to agree with God's.' With regard to other people, the proud 'are tempted daily to elevate [themselves] above others and diminish them.' There is no pleasure, as C. S. Lewis says, in 'having something,' only in 'having more of it than the next man.' In short, 'Pride is the universal sin, the great vice. . . . [It] is the great stumbling block to Zion.'"[419]

Explaining how pride brought down the Zion of the Nephites and caused the destruction of their society, Monte S. Nyman and Charles D. Tate Jr. write: "Mormon explicitly links apostasy and priestcraft with two other evils profoundly detrimental to the maintenance of a Zion society. These are pride and social stratification, which began to appear in A.D. 201—less than a decade after the initial cracks in the solidarity of the society were first noted by Mormon. The prosperity of the people of Nephi, owing to their faith in Christ, had produced great wealth among the populace. Unfortunately, this, in turn, led to pride and materialism as the people forgot the source of their strength. The result was that 'from that time forth they did have their goods and their substance no more in common among them' (4 Nephi 1:25).

"Here the insidious nature of pride is laid bare, and its destructive effects on Zion seen in an unmistakable way. Pride destroys unity and promotes selfishness. . . . Pride seeks to create divisions among people purely for the sake of self-interest, so that some may place themselves above others and exploit them. . . . Pride was the cause of social stratification among the people of 4 Nephi."[420] What is the destiny of the proud people of Babylon? "O the wise, and the learned, and the rich, that are puffed up in the pride of their hearts, and all those who preach false doctrines, and all those who commit whoredoms, and pervert the right way of the Lord, wo, wo, wo be unto them, saith the Lord God Almighty, for they shall be thrust down to hell!"[421] It is rare indeed for the Lord to pronounce three woes, but for the proud of Babylon he does not hesitate.

6. **Secrecy.** Babylon thrives in darkness. Babylonians "seek deep to hide their counsels from the Lord, and their works shall be in the dark."[422] Babylon is a brave sinner when she is not known, but shine a light on her and she shudders and runs for cover. The church of the devil promotes a secret double life: the first life is outwardly proper and pious, and the second is that of the secret

---

419 Millet, *The Power of the Word*, 77.
420 Nyman and Tate, *Fourth Nephi through Moroni*, 298.
421 2 Nephi 28:15.
422 2 Nephi 28:9.

sinner. Of necessity, the sinner in Babylon must learn the art of telling and living a lie. This is part of the "great secret" or Mahan doctrine that Satan taught Cain. "And Satan said unto Cain: Swear unto me by thy throat, and if thou tell it thou shalt die; and swear thy brethren by their heads, and by the living God, that they tell it not; for if they tell it, they shall surely die; and this that thy father may not know it; and this day I will deliver thy brother Abel into thine hands. And Satan sware unto Cain that he would do according to his commands. And all these things were done in secret. And Cain said: Truly I am Mahan, the master of this great secret, that I may murder and get gain. Wherefore Cain was called Master Mahan, and he gloried in his wickedness."[423]

Whether Babylon is a secret combination of willing participants who counsel and covenant to commit a crime, or an individual who rationalizes living a secret, sinful life, the result is the absence of remorse for the dark behavior. Why would Babylon be sorry for embracing its own doctrine? No, Babylon, like Cain, loves her wickedness and glories in it. She proclaims, "This is normal worldly behavior; everyone does it." Babylon acts in secrecy as a declaration of freedom: "And Cain gloried in that which he had done, saying: I am free; surely the flocks of my brother falleth into my hands."[424]

Babylon lurks in the shadows, deceiving herself into thinking that no one knows of her sinning, not even God. "All these things were done in secret." Over time, Babylon learns to secretly sin so well that she achieves a degree in wickedness—"Master Mahan, master of that great secret." Babylon becomes so arrogant in thinking that "none seeth me" that in her wickedness she begins to place her trust only in herself, saying, "I am, and none else beside me."[425] But what Zion people understand, which Babylonians will eventually discover, is that God knows; in fact, he knows in detail: "These things are not hid from the Lord."[426] Those people who sin in secret receive the Lord's curse: "And wo unto them that seek deep to hide their counsel from the Lord! And their works are in the dark; and they say: Who seeth us, and who knoweth us?. . . . But behold, I will show unto them, saith the Lord of Hosts, that I know all their works."[427]

7. **Reviling against anything good.** Babylon is not content simply with deceiving us. She might start out with that tactic, but her intent from the outset is our destruction by means of all-out war. Babylon will make a fierce, abusive, and insulting attack on each true doctrine, principle, sacred institution, and everything else that is just and holy. Babylon will cast the things of God as outdated, frivolous, unfair, limiting, foolish, vain, unscientific, ludicrous, cultish, unnatural, and even immoral.

---

423 Moses 5:29–31.
424 Moses 5:33.
425 Isaiah 47:10.
426 Moses 5:39.
427 2 Nephi 27:32.

Nephi pronounces a wo on those who "turn aside the just for a thing of naught and revile against that which is good, and say that it is of no worth!" Their opposition to Zion lands them on dangerous ground, and if they do not repent, their days are numbered: "For the day shall come that the Lord God will speedily visit the inhabitants of the earth; and in that day that they are fully ripe in iniquity they shall perish."[428]

8. **Carnal security.** With apostolic authority, Paul identified the love of money as the root of all evil.[429] This is an astounding revelation. Somewhere in the spectrum of wrongdoing, the accumulation, adoration, or envy of money seems to contribute to every sin. If Satan can convince us to covet, he can lead us into all sorts of mischief.

   The love of money is a powerful Babylonian lure, and if we step into the devil's trap, there is little hope of escape. Paul says, "But they that will be rich fall into temptation and a snare, and into many foolish and hurtful lusts, which drown men in destruction and perdition."[430]

   Nephi foresaw a latter-day epidemic of money loving, and he specifically identified the Saints who flirt with Babylon as Satan's target: "And others [of the Latter-day Saints] will he pacify, and lull them away into carnal security, that they will say: All is well in Zion; yea, Zion prospereth, all is well—and thus the devil cheateth their souls, and leadeth them away carefully down to hell."[431] Clearly, Nephi is talking about us, the only people who would be interested in Zion's welfare. Paul agrees. He condemns the Saints who persist in pursuing wealth as having "erred from the faith, and pierced themselves through with many sorrows."[432] Such a money-loving attitude is vintage Babylon and anti-Zion.

   The Book of Mormon prophet Jacob listed the love of money as one of the foremost offenses against God. Hugh Nibley wrote:

   > It is at the climax of his great discourse on the Atonement that Jacob cries out, "But wo unto the rich, who are rich as to the things of the world. For because they are rich they despise the poor." This is a very important statement, setting down as a general principle that the rich as a matter of course despise the poor, for "their hearts are upon their treasures; wherefore, their treasure is their God. And behold, their treasure shall perish with them also" (2 Nephi 9:30). Why does Jacob make this number one in his explicit list

---

428   2 Nephi 28:16.
429   1 Timothy 6:10.
430   1 Timothy 6:9.
431   2 Nephi 28:21.
432   1 Timothy 6:10.

of offenses against God? Because it is the number-one device among the enticings of "that cunning one" (2 Nephi 9:39), who knows that riches are his most effective weapon in leading men astray. You must choose between being at one with God or with Mammon, not both; the one promises everything in this world for money, the other a place in the kingdom after you have "endured the crosses of the world, and despised the shame of it," for only so can you "inherit the kingdom of God, which was prepared for them from the foundation of the world," and where your "joy shall be full forever" (2 Nephi 9:18). Need we point out that the main reason for having money is precisely to avoid 'the crosses of the world, and . . . the shame of it"?[433]

President Anthon H. Lund taught, "The riches of eternal life we ought to seek, not the riches of the world. There is a raging thirst for riches in this land. The love of money is growing, even in our midst. We do not look upon wealth in itself as a curse. We believe that those who can handle means rightly can do much to bless their fellows. But he who is ruled by the love of money is tempted to commit sin. The love of money is the root of all evil. *There is hardly a commandment but is violated through this seeking for riches.*"[434]

In the contest between mammon and God, mammon most often wins. But the stakes are high in making this choice. Jesus told his disciples, "How hard is it for them that trust in riches to enter into the kingdom of God!"[435] A scan of history shows us that there is no lasting security in mammon. Moreover, those who trust in riches receive the Lord's curse and risk losing everything: "And the day shall come that they shall hide up their treasures, because they have set their hearts upon riches; and because they have set their hearts upon their riches, and will hide up their treasures when they shall flee before their enemies, because they will not hide them up unto me, cursed be they and also their treasures; and in that day shall they be smitten, saith the Lord . . . ye are cursed because of your riches, and also are your riches cursed because ye have set your hearts upon them, and have not hearkened unto the words of him who gave them unto you."[436]

To the people of Babylon, however, such warnings are taken lightly. The love of money is a heady narcotic. In Babylon, making money is the fulfillment of one's existence, says Hugh Nibley; "he who has made money has already fulfilled his calling and has no further obligation—in fact, the whole virtue of money is that it frees one from any feeling of obligation to anyone . . . the worst

---

433 Nibley, *Approaching Zion*, 592–93.
434 Lund, Conference Report, April 1903, 24; emphasis added.
435 Mark 10:24.
436 Helaman 13:20–21.

thing is for a businessman to feel responsible for society."[437] We recall that Cain raised a jubilant shout of freedom after he had slain Abel to obtain his brother's flocks.[438] He supposed that his newly gotten wealth had liberated him and made him independent, even from accountability to God.

Trusting in riches is akin to another Babylonian doctrine: trusting in the arm of flesh—*man*. Nephi reveals that there is a curse on those who succumb to such a folly: "Cursed is he that putteth his trust in man, or maketh flesh his arm."[439] The *Encyclopedia of Mormonism* defines cursings as "the opposite of blessings."[440] To the degree that we look to man for strength, counsel, security, or safety, we cease depending on the Savior, "the Mighty One of Jacob,"[441] and we are left to the whims, devices, and frailties of weak, imperfect human beings. We are therefore "cursed." When we choose man over God, God willingly steps aside and allows us the consequences of our choice. As much as we cannot mix Zion and Babylon, we cannot choose or be supported by both God and man. We must decide, but as we do we should remember that the one choice will bring blessings while the other will bring a cursing.

9. **Flattery.** Joseph Smith said, "Flattery is a deadly poison."[442] Elder McConkie writes: "Flattery is the act of ingratiating oneself into another's confidence by excessive praise, or by insincere speech and acts. It includes the raising of false and unfounded hopes; there is always an element of dishonesty attending it."[443] We need only survey Babylon's long history to view lost fortunes, broken marriages, secret intrigues, lies, deceptions, and a host of other destructive conditions, all of which were perpetrated by flattering language.

The *Encarta Dictionary* defines flattery "an act or instance of complimenting somebody, often excessively or insincerely, especially in order to gain an advantage." This definition goes along with Nephi's depiction of Satan, whose tactic is to sweet-talk us down to hell: "And behold, others he flattereth away."[444] The devil's strategy is to ease into our lives by making us feel so good about ourselves that he can tell us almost anything and we will believe it. Over time, we become used to his silky voice, and because he butters us up whenever he speaks to us, we cannot wait for the next communication. Now we are in a position for Satan to easily feed us lies and false doctrines that ring of truth. Nephi says, he "telleth them there is no hell; and he saith unto them: I am no devil, for there is none—and thus he whispereth in their ears, until he grasps them with his awful chains, from whence there is no deliverance."

---

437 Nibley, *Approaching Zion*, 459–60.
438 Moses 5:33.
439 2 Nephi 28:31.
440 *Encyclopedia of Mormonism*, 352.
441 2 Nephi 6:18.
442 Smith, *Teachings of the Prophet Joseph Smith*, 137.
443 McConkie, *Mormon Doctrine*, 287.
444 2 Nephi 28:22.

If we listen to Satan long enough, we will contemplate then believe and finally act on his flattering message. Now Satan has us trapped, and we are doomed: "Yea, they are grasped with death, and hell; and death, and hell, and the devil, and all that have been seized therewith must stand before the throne of God, and be judged according to their works, from whence they must go into the place prepared for them, even a lake of fire and brimstone, which is endless torment."[445]

Babylon is awash in flattery. One can hardly get ahead in Babylon without employing this diabolical art of language. Satan tutors eager students as to how flattery can be used as an effective means to a sinister end: "Yea, he saith unto them: Deceive and lie in wait to catch, that ye may destroy; behold, this is no harm. And thus he flattereth them, and telleth them that it is no sin to lie that they may catch a man in a lie, that they may destroy him." He even teaches his pupils to flatter, lie, and deceive so that they might trump other flatterers, liars, and deceivers: "Verily, verily, I say unto you, wo be unto him that lieth to deceive because he supposeth that another lieth to deceive, for such are not exempt from the justice of God." Satan's goal is not to help his students, but rather to destroy them: 'And thus he flattereth them, and leadeth them along until he draggeth their souls down to hell; and thus he causeth them to catch themselves in their own snare. And thus he goeth up and down, to and fro in the earth, seeking to destroy the souls of men."[446]

10. **Taking and giving offense.** Babylon is a place or condition of discouragement and offense. Describing Babylon in the last days, Jesus said, "And then shall many be offended, and shall betray one another, and shall hate one another."[447] It is characteristic of Babylon to take offense at little things—to "make a man an offender for a word." Then the cycle of offense begins with the offended viciously turning on their offenders, laying snares for them, and discounting any good thing that their offenders might do "for a thing of naught."[448]

Both those who offend and take offense are cursed by the Lord: "Woe unto the world because of offences! for it must needs be that offences come; but woe to that man by whom the offence cometh!"[449] As much as Babylon is identified by people who take offense, she can also be detected by people who offend. Paul had no patience for offenders; to him they were divisive and selfish individuals who deserved to be avoided: "Now I beseech you, brethren, mark them which cause divisions and offences contrary to the doctrine which ye have learned; and avoid them. For they that are such serve not our Lord Jesus Christ, but their own belly."[450] Jesus was equally indignant when it came to

---

445 2 Nephi 28:22–23.
446 D&C 10:25–28.
447 Matthew 24:10.
448 2 Nephi 27:22.
449 Matthew 18:7.
450 Romans 16:17–18.

offenders: "But whoso shall offend one of these little ones which believe in me, it were better for him that a millstone were hanged about his neck, and that he were drowned in the depth of the sea."[451] Neither taking nor giving offense is a trait of Zion people; but such characteristics are readily evident in the people of Babylon.

Some people choose to take offense "because of the strictness of the word [of God]."[452] They would be more comfortable with extra latitude in the commandments and a more relaxed gospel. If Satan persuades us to collide with a troublesome doctrine, historical point, or someone else's actions or example, he can easily drag us down to his level. Worse, we become enemies with God—"angry because of the truth of God."[453] We recall that at the Lord's rebuke, Cain's countenance fell and that sealed his fate. Taking offense was the final stride in Cain's gallop to hell. "And Cain was wroth, and listened not any more to the voice of the Lord."[454]

Spiritual Babylon

Babylon exists both physically and spiritually; it is the physical environs of the world and the evil that exists therein. The Lord's continual cry to his people is: "Go ye out from Babylon. Be ye clean that bear the vessels of the Lord. . . . Go ye out from among the nations, even from Babylon, *from the midst of wickedness, which is spiritual Babylon.*"[455]

Occasionally, the Lord has removed his Saints from physical Babylon for their own safety. Enoch, Abraham, Moses, Lehi, the brother of Jared, and the Mormon pioneers are examples. But if we are to leave Babylon physically, it will be the Lord's prerogative. Unless he commands otherwise, our assignment is to live in the world without partaking of the things that characterize the world. For the present, the commandment is that we leave Babylon only spiritually. The Lord gives the reason for our remaining in physical Babylon. We are to minister among the people of the world and call them out of Babylon to the new and everlasting covenant associated with Zion, by which they might prepare for the coming of Christ:

> Send forth the elders of my church unto the nations which are afar off; unto the islands of the sea; send forth unto foreign lands; call upon all nations, first upon the Gentiles, and then upon the Jews. And behold, and lo, this shall be their cry, and the voice of the Lord unto all people: Go ye forth unto the land of Zion, that the borders of my people may be enlarged, and that

---

451 Matthew 18:6.
452 Alma 35:15.
453 2 Nephi 28:28.
454 Moses 5:21–26.
455 D&C 133:5, 14; emphasis added.

> her stakes may be strengthened, and that Zion may go forth unto the regions round about. Yea, let the cry go forth among all people: Awake and arise and go forth to meet the Bridegroom; behold and lo, the Bridegroom cometh; go ye out to meet him. Prepare yourselves for the great day of the Lord. . . . Let them, therefore, who are among the Gentiles flee unto Zion. And let them who be of Judah flee unto Jerusalem, unto the mountains of the Lord's house."[456]

Blaine Yorgason writes:

> Where or what, therefore, is this spiritual Babylon that we are commanded to leave? Two days before giving [D&C 133], the Lord had given another revelation (section 1) wherein He answered our question: "And the anger of the Lord is kindled, and his sword is bathed in heaven, and it shall fall upon the inhabitants of the earth. And the arm of the Lord shall be revealed; and the day cometh that they who will not hear the voice of the Lord, neither the voice of his servants, neither give heed to the words of the prophets and apostles, shall be cut off from among the people; for they have strayed from mine ordinances, and have broken mine everlasting covenant; they seek not the Lord to establish his righteousness, but every man walketh in his own way, and after the image of his own god, *whose image is in the likeness of the world, and whose substance is that of an idol,* which waxeth old and shall perish in Babylon, even Babylon the great, which shall fall (D&C 1:13–16; italics mine)."[457]

The spiritual Babylon that we are to leave, therefore, is the wickedness, idolatry, and man-made philosophies of the world.

Of interest, Elder McConkie reminds us that the name Babylon "is the Greek form of *Babel* and means *confusion.*" Babylon is awash in confusion, wickedness, and forbidden things that we term *worldliness.*[458] Money is at the root of Babylon's desires and indulgences. Commenting on John's revelation of the condition of spiritual Babylon, Hugh Nibley says that everything in the world is defined by business and the economy. Money, merchandising, and profiteering occupy our thoughts and confuse the more weighty is-

---

456 D&C 133:8–10, 12–13.
457 Yorgason, *I Need Thee Every Hour,* 14, quoting D&C 1:13–16.
458 McConkie, *Mormon Doctrine,* 58–69.

sues of God. Nibley reminds us that money can buy anything in Babylon: relationships, loyalties, recognition, influence, health, education, luxuriant clothing, leisure, mansions, military might, everything that men need to enrich themselves while impoverishing others—and love of money is always cast against the backdrop of the ever-prevalent preoccupation with sex:

> Babylon is a state of mind, as Zion is, with its appropriate environment. . . . The great world center of commerce and business, "the kings of the earth have committed fornication with her, and the merchants of the earth are waxed rich through the abundance of her delicacies" (Revelation 18:3). Indeed, "thy merchants were the great men of the earth; for by thy sorceries were all nations deceived" (Revelation 18:23). Babylon's economy is built on deceptions. Babylon is described fully in Revelation 18: She is rich, luxurious, immoral, full of fornications, merchants, riches, delicacies, sins, merchandise, gold, silver, precious stones, pearls, fine linens, purples, silks, scarlets, thyine wood, all manner of vessels, ivory, precious wood, brass, iron, marble, and so on. She is a giant delicatessen, full of wine, oil, fine flour, wheat; a perfume counter with cinnamon, odors, ointments, and frankincense; a market with beasts and sheep. It reads like a savings stamp catalog or a guide to a modern supermarket or department store. Horses and chariots and all manner of services are available; slaves in the souls of men. These are "the fruits thy soul lusted after . . . and all things which were dainty and goodly" (Revelation 18:14). And it is all for sale.[459]

Summing up spiritual Babylon, Blaine Yorgason writes:

> These worldly things, then,—habits, practices, policies, pleasures, possessions, entertainments, conversations, trappings, attitudes, and so forth—are described as unclean and having the substance of an idol, and they divert the children of God from hearing the apostles and prophets, seeking the Lord's ordinances, and keeping His everlasting covenant. It doesn't matter where we find these Babylonian "things" or even what they are; in subtle and not so subtle ways they distract or divert

---

[459] Nibley, *Approaching Zion*, 14.

us from diligently coming unto Christ and seeking His face, or of praying for charity, or His pure love. That is why, just four months after the Church was organized, the Lord declared, "Thou shalt lay aside the things of this world and seek for the things of a better" (D&C 25:10). Why? Because worldly things are not Godly things, and we are commanded to leave them behind![460]

Competition

Zion is distinguished by cooperation while Babylon is characterized by competition. Whereas cooperation ensures that no one loses, competition is structured so that everyone loses but one. While the winner rejoices, having defeated his opponent(s), the loser(s) are miserable. Neither equality nor unity nor charity can exist in such an atmosphere. Therefore, we might say with some certainty that competition does not exist in Zion—competition is wholly a phenomenon of Babylon.

Hugh Nibley states, "Competitiveness always rests on the assumption of a life-and-death struggle: 'There is no free lunch' is the clarion cry. The name of the game is survival. . . . It means to still be on the scene after everyone else has been wiped out. . . . If you're going to be successful, you can't let any person stand in the way. . . . In the end you are competing with everyone, or as everyone was saying when I was young, 'Self-preservation is the first law of nature,' a doctrine that justifies the commission of any possible crime in the name of survival. Nobody loves the rat race, but nobody can think of anything else—Satan has us just where he wants us."[461]

Nibley traces competition back to the Garden of Eden:

> Just as the order of Zion began with Adam in the garden, the rival system is just as old. It, too, was proposed to Adam, and he rejected it, while his son Cain accepted it. The plan Satan proposed to Adam was to put everything in this glorious and beautiful world up for sale. You could have anything in this world for money, but you had to have money. This launched a scramble that has gone on ever since Cain slew Abel, his brother, for gain; and he, says the Pearl of Great Price, "gloried in that which he had done, saying: I am free; surely the flocks of my brother falleth into my hands" (Moses 5:33). And this vigorous competition has imparted an air of dynamism and excitement to the scene that some find most attractive. What would the human drama

---
460 Yorgason, *I Need Thee Every Hour*, 199.
461 Nibley, *Approaching Zion*, 460.

> be to us without an element of conflict and competition? We would find it insufferably dull. Who would exchange this for the pale and bloodless activities of Eden? In the Book of Mormon, the Nephites, the Jaredites, and the Jews at Jerusalem all walked straight to their certain destruction because they were helpless to conceive of acting in any other way. They were so completely captivated by one way of life that they could not conceive of any other.[462]

What would life be like without pinewood derbies, increasing market share, or moving up the ladder of success at the expense of others? We are so entrenched in competition that we can hardly imagine a viable world without it. We equate progress with competition. Advancement, improvement, strength, ingenuity, success—all of these are supposedly products of competition and can be had in no other way. In society as we know it, we wink at competitive game playing as innocent fun, when in fact we know that it feeds the need of the natural man to conquer and ascend. Without debating the wisdom of engaging in lesser forms of competition, we simply note that the practice permeates our culture to such a degree that we believe it must be the natural order of things and therefore must exist in eternity. Surely heaven must be filled with stadiums, and gods must mount from one exaltation to another by proving themselves better than lesser gods. Have we forgotten that the war in heaven was caused by a competitor who pitted his will against the Father's?

Do we have the courage to admit that competition—every form of it—is an invention of Satan, and that he desensitizes us to it in playful forms? Then, when he has converted us as competitors, he sets out to teach us the finer points of competition. For example, we must never show that losing makes us miserable. That is bad sportsmanship. We have to pretend to feel good about being crushed by an opponent; we have to learn how to congratulate him for besting us. Moreover, we have to learn how to tell ourselves that being beaten does not matter; our damaged self-image will recover, we say; we will follow the rules of the defeated: lick our wounds, regroup, and hone our skills so we can come off conqueror next time. It is insanity! This attitude invades classrooms, businesses, marriages, and families, with devastating effects. Where are charity, cooperation, unity, equality, and service in competition? Where is Zion in this practice? President Lorenzo Snow said, "It is high time to establish Zion. . . . It is more pleasant and agreeable for the Latter-day Saints to enter into this work and build up Zion, than to build up ourselves and have this great competition which is destroying us. . . . There should be no unjust competition in matters that belong to the Latter-day Saints. That which creates division among us pertaining to our temporal interests should not be."[463]

---

462 Nibley, *Approaching Zion*, 17–18.
463 Snow, *The Teachings of Lorenzo Snow*, 181.

Section 4   Babylon the Great

In Babylon, commerce, invention, and economic expansion all depend on competition—and we are blind to see that there is another way. Hugh Nibley writes: "The doctrine as we hear it on every side is that if we do not grow, we must perish. It is not enough for the economy to hold its own, the Gross National Product must constantly increase, which means manufacturing must expand and consumption increase, demand must increase, nothing must relax lest everything contract and collapse."[464] When we finally arrive in Zion, will we be shocked at its stability, uniformity, and ability to rapidly progress *without* competition? Or will we be bored to death and retreat to Babylon where self-image is measured by wins and losses; husbands and wives pit their wills against each other and fracture love; siblings vie for attention, position, and privilege; educational prizes go to the few; quarterbacks get the cheerleaders; co-workers stab each other in the back to obtain the better job; nations dispute borders and treasures; and the economy spikes and plummets; and fortunes are made and lost by the world's most skilled competitors?

Perhaps this sounds like heresy. Some might cry, "Treason! Socialism! Our beloved competition is as American as apple pie and therefore holy." Not true. Search the scriptures. Competition is Babylonian, and cooperation is Zion. Nevertheless, we are wont to lump competition alongside constitutional freedom. We say, "We are a free people, and thus we are free to compete." This perverse definition of freedom, which promotes the idea that *winners are made free by defeating all others,* is completely Babylonian and hearkens back, as we have learned, to Cain, who competed with Abel and slew his brother "for the sake of getting gain." Need we be reminded that Cain gloried in his newly found freedom?[465] Thus competition became the anchor of the "great secret" that Satan taught Cain: "The Mahan principle . . . the exchange of life for property." This is *competition!*

Cain was not bothered by his action. Competitors cannot allow themselves to lapse into empathy or compassion. Hugh Nibley explains, "Thus when the Lord asked him, 'Where is your brother Abel?' Cain said, 'That is none of my business; he can take care of himself. If not, that is just too bad for him—he deserves what he gets' (cf. Moses 5:34). It's a dog-eat-dog world, says the entrepreneur who comforts his ruined investors with the magnanimous submission that life is unfair after all." Thus competition thrives on ruined losers and the winner's "descending scale of accountability."[466]

The doctrine of competitive enterprise reads like a chapter from the book of Korihor, the anti-Christ: "Every man prospered according to his genius, and . . . every man conquered according to his strength; and whatsoever a man did was no crime."[467] In a competitive world there are myriad losers and a handful of winners. Moreover, competition classifies and stratifies people. It guarantees that there will always be poor among us, and it ensures that the poor will likely remain at their level. Competition wants to conquer, not to help. It makes opponents of otherwise friendly people and engenders hatred, depression, feelings of inferiority, contention, selfishness, and entitlement for the winners. By competitive action, we elevate our wants over others' needs and judge ours as more important. Competition makes for

---
464   Nibley, *Approaching Zion,* 448.
465   Moses 5:33, 50.
466   Nibley, *Approaching Zion,* 436.
467   Alma 30:17.

vertical rather than horizontal relationships—we are on the top and others are beneath us. Competition is propelled by the false assumption of scarcity, when the Lord has plainly stated that there is enough and to spare,[468] that is, unless we hoard. Competition leads to a variety of sins, including lying, stealing, coveting, committing fornication and adultery; and, taken to extremes, competition causes murder and war.

If we are competitive by nature, we are not Zion. Of course, competition in this telestial world can offer healthy advantages, allowing us to enjoy affordable products and services that enhance our well-being. Nevertheless, if we espouse competition as a way of life, we had better get our fill of it now. Competition simply does not exist in Zion. To become Zion-like, we must abandon this destructive tendency and learn to become cooperative.

Hypocrites

A prevalent practice in Babylon is that of hypocrisy. A hypocrite is "a person who pretends to be what he is not; one who pretends to be better than he really is, or to be pious, virtuous, etc., without really being so."[469] Explaining, Elder McConkie writes: "Thus if a person knows what is right and makes open profession of conforming thereto and yet does not in reality live the gospel law, he is a hypocrite. Hypocrisy is to profess religion and not practice it. If a teacher advocates the payment of tithing, but does not himself pay an honest tithing, he is a hypocrite. If a person prays and seeks temporal and spiritual blessings from the Lord, and then turns away the naked and needy and fails to visit the sick and afflicted, he is a hypocrite. He has professed religion, but not practiced it."[470]

Amulek taught that prayer without the action of charity is hypocritical: "And now behold, my beloved brethren, I say unto you, do not suppose that this is all; for after ye have done all these things, if ye turn away the needy, and the naked, and visit not the sick and afflicted, and impart of your substance, if ye have, to those who stand in need—I say unto you, if ye do not any of these things, behold, your prayer is vain, and availeth you nothing, and ye are as hypocrites who do deny the faith."[471] It makes sense. How is it that on the one hand we feel justified to pray for our needs while on the other hand we ignore the needs of others?

Hugh Nibley wrote: "The worst sinners, according to Jesus, are not the harlots and publicans, but the religious leaders with their insistence on proper dress and grooming, their careful observance of all the rules, their precious concern for status symbols, their strict legality, their pious patriotism. . . . Babylon is . . . rich, respectable, immovable, with its granite walls and steel vaults, its bronze gates, its onyx trimmings and marble floors . . . and its bullet-proof glass—the awesome symbols of total security. Keeping her orgies decently private, she presents a front of unalterable propriety to all."[472] Wherever hypocrisy rears its ugly head, there is Babylon.

---

468 D&C 104:17.
469 *Webster's New World Dictionary*, s.v. "hypocrite."
470 McConkie, *Mormon Doctrine*, 371.
471 Alma 34:28.
472 Nibley, *Approaching Zion*, 53–54.

False Philosophies

Babylon is always promoting a new philosophy to replace God or ascribe his power to phenomena of nature or the mind of man. These pseudo religions come and go like flavors of the month, but they are damning to those who believe and practice them. One popular philosophy states that the universe itself is capable of delivering benefits to those who cast their thoughts "out there," and then, by simply maintaining a positive attitude, those thoughts will return with a caravan of blessings. God is never mentioned in the equation.

The ancient practice of astrology pretends to be a science to predict the future. This abominable craft has ensnared countless people over time, according to Elder McConkie.[473] He wrote: "A form of divination and fortune telling akin to sorcery, astrology is a pseudo science that pretends to divulge the influence of the stars upon human affairs; it is a false science that claims to foretell earthly events by means of the positions and aspects of these heavenly luminaries. It is, of course, one of Satan's substitutes for the true science of astronomy and for the true principle of receiving revelation of future events from divine sources."[474] Modern-day computers have added an element of scientific legitimacy to astrology, and therefore have made the practice appear credible. But the underlying philosophy and motive can be traced back to Satan, who continues to decoy gullible people by shifting their focus away from the true source of revelation and prophecy.

Another equally damaging Babylonian philosophy is humanism, a "rationalist movement that holds that man is capable of self-fulfillment, ethical conduct, etc., without recourse to [God]."[475] Rationalism is the doctrine that human reason alone is the supreme authority and source of knowledge, and that "reason, unaided by divine revelation, is an adequate or the sole guide to all attainable religious truth."[476] President Joseph Fielding Smith quoted prominent rationalists as declaring, "'The religious forms and ideas of our fathers are no longer adequate.'" Then President Smith commented,

> As a substitute they offer 'humanism,' and give an explanation of their "faith" in 15 points. . . . Let it suffice to say that they maintain that Christianity has failed, and that "religion must formulate its hopes and plans in the light of the scientific spirit and method." They say the distinction between the sacred and the secular cannot be maintained, that worship of the supreme ruler and religious prayer to him are futile. Men must find expression to their emotions in "a higher sense of personal life and in a cooperative effort to promote social

---

473 Isaiah 47; Daniel 1:20; 2:27; 4:7; 5:7.
474 McConkie, *Mormon Doctrine*, 56.
475 *Webster's New World Dictionary*, s.v. "humanism."
476 *Webster's New World Dictionary*, s.v. "rationalism."

> well being." To these "worshipers" the universe is self-existing—it had no creator; Dr. Charles E. Schofield, in his book, *The Adventurous God*, says, "The major trend of unbelief today seems to be more and more towards the position that we very much need a religion, but it must be a religion without a God."[477]

Humanism itself or humanistic trends account for all sorts of philosophies that approach but reside just outside the boundaries of atheism. Each of these philosophies discounts or limits God while enthroning the human mind. Intellectualism is an example. Like humanism, intellectualism is devotion to intellectual pursuits. It places excessive emphasis on the mind of man as the summit of genius, and therefore that to which we should pay homage. Both intellectualism and humanism are agnostic and an affront to God.

President Harold B. Lee wrote: "Humanism is a threat to the work of the Lord. One of the greatest threats to the work of the Lord today comes from false educational ideas. There is a growing tendency of teachers within and without the Church to make academic interpretations of gospel teachings—to read, as a prophet-leader has said, 'by the lamp of their own conceit.' Unfortunately, much in the sciences, the arts, politics, and the entertainment field, as has been well said by an eminent scholar, is 'all dominated by this humanistic approach which ignores God and His word as revealed through the prophets.' This kind of worldly system apparently hopes to draw men away from God by making man the 'measure of all things,' as some worldly philosophers have said."[478]

Relativism promotes tolerance as the ultimate human virtue. This philosophy is a plague of the latter days. Relativism preaches open-mindedness to other people's lifestyles and values regardless of traditional ethics. At the foundation of relativism is the falsehood that there is no universal standard to measure the truth of an ethical proposition, so lifestyle becomes a matter of individual choice, which is made relative to one's conscience. Moreover, to relativists, conscience itself is the product of a person's environment or preferences; therefore, one person's morals are no better or worse than another's. To relativists, good and bad are relative and not absolute but rather subjective; therefore, we ought to be tolerant.

The number of "-isms" Babylon promotes is dizzying. For example, universalism holds that all persons will be reconciled to God, regardless of church affiliation. A universalistic organization would teach the common tenets held by most religions while accepting other religions inclusively. In the end, they say, it does not matter, because there looms universal reconciliation between God and mankind.

Monism holds that in a given field, everything comes down to one thing and only one correct opinion. Monistic theologians support the view that there is one God who can manifest himself in any number of religions.

---

477 Smith, *Doctrines of Salvation*, 3:275.
478 Lee, *The Teachings of Harold B. Lee*, 342.

Section 4   Babylon the Great 83

Subjectivism is the view that people can know only what they experience directly; everything else is subjective. Like relativism, subjectivism states that the only moral standard is the one that emerges from one's own conscience; therefore, moral codes that are held by society are invalid.

Fundamentalism is another Babylonian philosophy that retards man's progress and diminishes God. Fundamentalism mixes man's philosophies with the scriptures to give them an air of legitimacy. This clever philosophy "stresses the infallibility of the Bible, not only in matters of faith and morals, but also as a literal historical record." Of course, this means that there can be no revelation outside the Bible. The fundamentalist movement arose in American Protestantism in the early part of the twentieth century in reaction to Modernism,[479] which was comprised of various attempts to "redefine Biblical and Christian dogma and traditional teachings in light of modern science, historical and critical research."[480]

Considering this maze of "-isms," we could go crazy trying to find the truth. Clearly, Satan does not care which doctrine we believe as long as it is not the true one. Taking advantage of our natural tendency to search for truth, he keeps us off-balance by bouncing us from one philosophical room to another in a house that can be escaped only by burning it down. In the 1950 October general conference, Elder Albert E. Bowen of the Quorum of the Twelve taught: "Under the impact of agnosticism, atheism, and the extreme humanism which denies God and makes man the source of all meaning, the Christian church as a body has compromised its basic doctrines to make its teachings more harmonious with the current of popular opinion. And where has it got itself? It has lost its saving faith, weakened its influence, and almost forfeited its moral leadership. In consequence, men are floundering about in confusion, not knowing what they ought to do, but well-assured that the fair promises of irreligion and unbelief and human sufficiency have failed them, and they are casting about for anchorage. That is the sorry plight of man in this age."[481] Since the time that Elder Bowen issued his denunciation of "-isms," they have only increased in number and followers.

False, man-made philosophies permeate Babylon and run counter to the gospel truth that everything—*absolutely everything*—that is good comes from God.[482] President James E. Faust taught that while advances in science and technology are wonderful and provide amazing opportunities, they can also be fraught with hazard. Satan can use them to titillate the human ego and point gullible people to man's genius as the source of good things. The future holds great challenges, President Faust said, and we will be able to survive those challenges only by our compensating the expansion of secular knowledge with proportionate virtues of faith, judgment, honesty, decency, self-control, and character.[483]

The people of Babylon who embrace the philosophies of men will share the doom of that fallen system. Nephi wrote: "O that cunning plan of the evil one! O the vainness,

---

479   Dr. Frederick J. Pack, "Was the Earth Created in Six Days of Twenty-Four Hours Each?"
480   *Webster's New World Dictionary,* s.v. "modernism."
481   Bowen, *Conference Report,* Oct. 1950, 71.
482   Omni 1:25.
483   Faust, "The Shield of Faith," 17.

and the frailties, and the foolishness of men! When they are learned they think they are wise, and they hearken not unto the counsel of God, for they set it aside, supposing they know of themselves, wherefore, their wisdom is foolishness and it profiteth them not. And they shall perish.... And the wise, and the learned, and they that are rich, who are puffed up because of their learning, and their wisdom, and their riches—yea, they are they whom he despiseth; and save they shall cast these things away, and consider themselves fools before God, and come down in the depths of humility, he will not open unto them."[484]

Popularity

Nehor, the anti-Christ, taught "the people that every priest and teacher ought to become popular; and they ought not to labor with their hands, but that they ought to be supported by the people."[485] Because Nehor was promoting a *priestcraft*—a false religion—his inference was that recognition or influence should be worshipped and that it could be bought or sold for money. This attitude is a mainstay of Babylon.

To be popular is to be liked and accepted by most people. But Babylon places a demonic twist on popularity. In Babylon the goal of popularity is to seek recognition to obtain money, power, rank, and influence. According to Nehor, popular people are in a position to cease laboring with their hands and to be supported by the people. Is this not a primary goal of wealth and popularity today?

Flattering words are an avenue to popularity. Likewise, to pleasingly, and often falsely, present one's self in public promotes popularity. Other tools to become popular are the deft use of fashion, exploiting one's beauty or intelligence, offering vacant promises, and applying the skill of rhetoric. Nephi lumps the popular in with the wealth seekers, power brokers, the lustful, and the sinful—and he predicts a swift collapse of those people and institutions: "For the time speedily shall come that all churches [or individuals and institutions] which are built up to get gain, and all those who are built up to get power over the flesh, and those who are built up to become popular in the eyes of the world, and those who seek the lusts of the flesh and the things of the world, and to do all manner of iniquity; yea, in fine, all those who belong to the kingdom of the devil are they who need fear, and tremble, and quake; they are those who must be brought low in the dust; they are those who must be consumed as stubble; and this is according to the words of the prophet."[486]

In Zion, prominent people deflect popularity. They do not seek it, but if recognition comes, they are quick to use it to bless others.

Latter-day Babylon—Prophetic Description of Our Time

Through the eyes of a prophet and seer, President Kimball looked upon the condition of Babylon and said that he was appalled and frightened. Three things in particular distressed him: (1) *The abuse of the environment:* allowing filth and contaminants to pollute

---
484   2 Nephi 9:28, 42.
485   Alma 1:3.
486   1 Nephi 22:23.

our minds, bodies, and surroundings; (2) *The pursuit of personal affluence:* transferring our trust in God to a trust in material things in an effort to assure security and happiness for the remainder of our life; and (3) *Trust in military security:* expending enormous resources to purchase and develop armaments with the intention of depending upon them for protection rather than depending upon God. "When threatened, we become anti-enemy instead of pro-kingdom of God; we train a man in the art of war and call him a patriot, thus, in the manner of Satan's counterfeit of true patriotism, perverting the Savior's teaching: 'Love your enemies, bless them that curse you, do good to them that hate you, and pray for them which despitefully use you, and persecute you.'"

President Kimball was unabashedly pro-Zion. Certainly Babylon would have considered him idealistic and detached from reality. Babylon would teach us to flex our military muscle and destroy our enemy, but President Kimball taught: "We forget that if we are righteous the Lord will either not suffer our enemies to come upon us—and this is the special promise to the inhabitants of the land of the Americas—or he will fight our battles for us. . . . What are we to fear when the Lord is with us?"[487]

As we have mentioned, Jesus, looking forward to our day, foretold that many of the "very elect" would be deceived.[488] Our leaders have referred to the parable of the ten virgins, warning us about the arithmetic of this parable. Of the ten, who were meant to depict Latter-day Saints, only five actually prepared themselves to attend the marriage of the Bridegroom.[489] To decoy the unprepared five virgins in the last days, Babylon will dish up a menu of evils and deceptions that exceed the wickedness of former generations. Some of these deceptions will come from a preponderance of anti-Christs and false prophets (seducers, imposters, alarmists, promoters of new doctrines and philosophies), whom we deify and follow because of their titillating ideas and predictions. These things, however, are nothing more or less than a manifestation of priestcraft, which is motivated by money, influence, and popularity. The latter-day anti-Christs and false prophets build their professions and practices upon the anti-Christ doctrine and manage to mislead many. Some of these anti-Christs and false prophets come from the ranks of the Saints. They are people who zero in on a gospel topic and promote it as an essential issue. They *prophesy* of future events and call people to action without priesthood keys or the mantle of a prophet. They are extremists, dooms-dayers, catastrophists, and conspiracy promoters, those whom the Savior predicted would spread "rumors of wars." These anti-Christs and false prophets can frighten and deceive even the very elect. They can be detected by their enthusiastic embracing of a gospel subject while neglecting the more weighty parts of the true gospel or by stepping in front of the Lord's prophet and leaders.

Jesus prophesied that latter-day Babylon would become an environment of continual unrest, disobedience, contention, and war, which conditions would escalate and increasingly torment and devastate the earth until he came. Moreover, latter-day Babylon would be a place of widespread hunger caused by natural and man-made pestilences.

---
487 Kimball, *The Teachings of Spencer W. Kimball*, 417.
488 Matthew 24:24.
489 Oaks, "Preparation for the Second Coming," 7; see Matthew 25:1–13.

Babylon would be characterized by persecution, anger, hatred, and betrayal. Her people would become easily offended, and "because iniquity shall abound, the love of many shall wax cold."[490]

Babylon in the latter days is a time when "darkness covereth the earth, and gross darkness the minds of the people, and all flesh has become corrupt before my face."[491] Well did Jeremiah say that "Babylon hath . . . made all the earth drunken: the nations have drunken of her wine; therefore the nations are mad."[492] As it was in the days of the wicked Nephites before the resurrected Lord appeared, so it will be in latter-day Babylon: "disputings among the people," many being "lifted up unto pride and boastings because of their exceedingly great riches," "great persecutions," "many merchants, lawyers, and officers," people being "distinguished by ranks, according to their riches and their chances for learning," widespread ignorance and poverty, preferential educational opportunities proffered to the rich. Moreover, people will return "railing for railing," and there will be "great inequality in all the land," which condition, in the days of the Nephites, infiltrated the Church and gave Satan "great power unto the stirring up of the people to do all manner of iniquity, and to the puffing them up with pride, tempting them to seek for power, and authority, and riches, and the vain things of the world."

We have been warned! The people of Babylon, whether inside or outside the Church, were carried about by the temptations of the devil whithersoever he listed to carry them. Without much resistance, he managed to convince them to do whatsoever iniquity he desired—and thus "they were in a state of awful wickedness." Babylon leads people to destruction by initially deceiving them into sinning; but eventually the people sin because they like it: "Now they did not sin ignorantly, for they knew the will of God concerning them, for it had been taught unto them; therefore they did willfully rebel against God."[493]

Babylon Today Compared to the Days of Noah

We remain in Babylon as though we had no other option. Often we feel paralyzed, and therefore make no attempt to flee or cease partaking of her lifestyle and philosophies. We assume that this is just the way life is and that we are powerless to change things. The people in Noah's and Lot's days held similar views and were caught up in the destructions. The Lord's words hang over us heavily: "And as it was in the days of [Noah], so shall it be also in the days of the Son of man. They did eat, they drank, they married wives, they were given in marriage, until the day that [Noah] entered into the ark, and the flood came, and destroyed them all. Likewise also as it was in the days of Lot; they did eat, they drank, they bought, they sold, they planted, they builded; but the same day that Lot went out of Sodom it rained fire and brimstone from heaven, and destroyed them all. Even thus shall it be in the day when the Son of man is revealed."[494]

---

490 Matthew 24:5–24.
491 D&C 112:24.
492 Jeremiah 51:7.
493 3 Nephi 6:10–18.
494 Luke 17:26–30.

What was it like in former days when Babylon was destroyed? The Pearl of Great Price describes the world of Enoch and Noah as wicked beyond anything that had been created by God, which, in this context, suggests wickedness beyond anything that God had created in the *universe*. Of those wicked people, the Lord said, "Satan shall be their father, and misery shall be their doom; and the *whole* heaven shall weep over them, even *all* the workmanship of mine hands."[495] We would do well to consider the descriptions of the evil in that day. We are told that our generation's wickedness is equal to or exceeds that of Noah's generation, and because of that level of wickedness, Noah's generation was completely obliterated.

Noah's generation was an extension of Enoch's generation. Moses, who wrote the account, explained that Enoch's people were pursued by their enemies from place to place, but they were always protected by God and his prophet.[496] We could say the same today. In the days of Enoch, the enemies of the people of God turned against each other, "and from that time forth there were wars and bloodshed among them."[497] This statement gives a key to how we might be protected in the last days—by aligning ourselves with the true God and his anointed prophets. War and violence continued to define ancient Babylon: "The earth was corrupt before God, and it was filled with violence."[498] Moreover, the world of Enoch and Noah was filled with men of "great renown,"[499] popular people of influence, who swayed the populace to commit evil. Consequently, the majority of the people rejected the gospel and the prophets.[500]

Of all the words that Moses could have used to describe that ancient world, he chose *corrupt*: "And God looked upon the earth, and, behold, it was corrupt, for all flesh had corrupted its way upon the earth."[501] The word *corrupt* has a variety of meanings: "changed from a sound condition to an unsound one; spoiled; contaminated; rotten; deteriorated from the normal or standard; morally unsound or debased; perverted; evil; depraved."[502] This widespread corruption retarded the people's ability to show love and attacked their marriages and families: "Behold, they are without affection, and they hate their own blood."[503] Their corruption made them wicked and immoral beings; evil pervaded their minds constantly: "And God saw that the wickedness of men had become great in the earth; and every man was lifted up in the imagination of the thoughts of his heart, being only evil continually."[504] Even the most righteous parents could not hold back wickedness and immorality from infiltrating their homes: "And the Lord said unto Noah: The daughters of thy sons have sold themselves; for behold mine anger is kindled against the sons of men, for they will not hearken to my voice."[505]

---

495 Moses 7:36–37; emphasis added.
496 Moses 7:14–15; see Moses 8:18.
497 Moses 7:16.
498 Moses 8:28.
499 Moses 8:21.
500 Moses 8:19–20, 24.
501 Moses 8:29.
502 *Webster's New World Dictionary*, s.v. "corrupt."
503 Moses 7:33.
504 Moses 8:22.
505 Moses 8:15.

Moses' description reads like the evening news. These people were suddenly swept off the planet and sent to a hellish place: "Behold, I will shut them up; a prison have I prepared for them. . . . And until that day [Christ's Resurrection] they shall be in torment; . . . wherefore Enoch knew, and looked upon their wickedness, and misery, and wept."[506]

Why do we remain in Babylon? Does the example of these ancient people mean nothing to us?

Paul's Prophecy

Paul's description of Babylon in the last days confirms Moses' portrayal. With apostolic boldness, he declared: "In the last days perilous times shall come." Paul's statement runs counter to Babylon's assertion that her institutions are sound and secure. What is the source of the peril? Paul answers with a terrifying depiction of pervasive personal wickedness:

"Lovers of their own selves"—those who are self-centered, conceited.

"Covetous"—those who are easily distracted from spiritual things; those who set their hearts on something other than God; those who are idolatrous and adulterous; those who are completely unfaithful.

"Boasters"—those braggers who strut and gloat in their accomplishments, who think they are great in their own eyes and who glory in their wickedness.

"Proud"—those who have an exaggerated opinion of themselves and who selfishly pit their will against God's.

"Blasphemers"—those who insult God or treat him and sacred things with contempt.

"Disobedient to parents"—those who compete with their parents so as to cause contention; those who exhibit willful rebellion against righteous parental authority.

"Unthankful"—those who are spoiled and feel entitled; those who offend God by not confessing his hand in all things (see D&C 59:21).

"Unholy"—those who are deliberately defiant, intentionally evil, profane, and ungodly; those who reject or neglect the sacred gospel ordinances that assure holiness.

"Without natural affection"—those who are hard-hearted, whose actions break apart marriages, families, and friendships; those whose affections divert to alternative lifestyles.

"Trucebreakers"—these are the opposite of peacemakers: those who would make a pact of peace with no intention of keeping it; those who have not the discipline to keep the peace; or those would make a pact of peace to gain an advantage and then break it.

"False accusers"—those who are slanderers; they who would criticize to destroy another person while elevating themselves, or those who would accuse while knowing that their accusation is a lie.

"Incontinent"—those people who are without self-restraint, especially with regard to sexual activity, or those who are incapable of keeping a trust or promise or holding to a virtue.

"Fierce"—those who are violently cruel or aggressively, intensely, or uncontrollably angry.

"Despisers of those that are good"—those who scorn, mock, and show contempt for the children and things of God.

---

506   Moses 7:38–41.

"Traitors"—those who are disloyal to vows; these people can be treacherous and for selfish reasons will betray causes, friends, and family.

"Heady"—those who are impetuous, rash, and willful, especially when following impulses to gratify their senses.

"Highminded"—those who are proud and conceited and show an excessively high opinion of themselves.

"Lovers of pleasures more than lovers of God"—those who are carnal, sensual, and devilish; like the heady, these people seek to gratify their senses without thought to spiritual consequences, accountability, and realities

"Having a form of godliness, but denying the power thereof"—these people appear godly and go through the motions of religiosity, but they reject the idea of saving covenants and ordinances that must be performed by proper authority; their pseudo religions and teachings are man-made and based on selected scriptures, which they interpret to suit their philosophies and desires.

"They which creep into houses, and lead captive silly women laden with sins, led away with divers lusts"—those who are overly enthusiastic about pleasing and satisfying their multiple carnal and sensual desires, especially gratifying their desire to have sexual relations without feelings of love and affection for their partner; these people practice their works of evil in the darkness of secrecy.

"Ever learning but never able to come to a knowledge of the truth"—those who immerse themselves in the knowledge of man without giving credit to God as the source of true knowledge; these people "resist the truth;" they have "corrupt minds," and are "reprobate concerning the faith"; they congratulate, worship, and deify man's genius. Of such people, Paul prophesies. "For the time will come when they will not endure sound doctrine; but after their own lusts shall they heap to themselves teachers, having itching ears; and they shall turn away their ears from the truth, and shall be turned unto fables."[507]

Inverting the Truth

One neat trick of Babylon is to confuse and reverse the order of good and bad. Those in Babylon all too frequently "call evil good, and good evil, . . . put darkness for light, and light for darkness, [and] put bitter for sweet, and sweet for bitter!"[508] Hugh Nibley explains how Satan manages this deception:

> In order to reconcile the ways of Babylon with the ways of Zion it has been necessary to circumvent the inconvenient barriers of scripture and conscience by the use of the tried and true device of *rhetoric*, defined by Plato as the art of making true things seem false and false things seem true by the use of words. This invalu-

---
507 2 Timothy 3:1–8; 4:3–4.
508 2 Nephi 15:20; see also Isaiah 5:20.

able art has, since the time of Cain, invested the ways of Babylon with an air of high purpose, solid virtue, and impeccable respectability. "The servants of sin should appear polished and pious, . . . able to call to their assistance . . . the subtle, persuasive power of rhetoric." "The devil is an orator; he is powerful; . . . he can tempt all classes."[509] . . . [We have, for example, the philosophy stating that] "Rome was great because Rome was good, giving expression to the old Roman belief in the close association between piety and success." This was the rhetoric of wealth, and it was inevitable—it always follows in such a situation, because people simply can't live virtuously and viciously at the same time. Yet they want to be good and rich at the same time, and so they reach a compromise called respectability, which is nothing less than Babylon masquerading as Zion. . . . It is not enough for the wicked to make excuses or explanations; in order to live with themselves and succeed in their undertakings, they must stand forth and be counted as pillars of righteousness, raising a hue and cry with practiced skill against those who would jeopardize their position, demonstrating, usually with the aid of paid rhetoricians, ministers, and lawyers, that it is not they but their opponents who are wicked.[510]

Hence, by the clever use of language and appealing to a sense of morality, Babylon manages to murder unborn children under the rhetoric of *pro-choice, individual liberty, reproductive freedom,* and *reproductive rights,* and Babylon redefines marriage by waving the flag of *tolerance.* A comparison of gospel beliefs—such as the purposes of money, relationships, education, health, personal management, religious beliefs, and so forth—against the issues and doctrines of Babylon—reveals a host of inversions of the truth. With certainty, in Babylon we can expect to find a falsehood wherever we find a truth, and that falsehood will be upheld by rhetoric.

Moroni's Prophecy

Through eyes of a seer, Moroni gazed into the future and saw our day in detail. He wrote, "Behold, I speak unto you as if ye were present, and yet ye are not. But behold, Jesus Christ hath shown you unto me, and I know your doing." Then Moroni described latter-day Babylon as if he were a modern-day journalist: "And I know that ye do walk in the

---

509 Nibley, *Approaching Zion,* 45, quoting Brigham Young, *Journal of Discourses,* 11:234–35; quoting Smith, *Teachings of the Prophet Joseph Smith,* 162.
510 Nibley, *Approaching Zion,* 45–46.

pride of your hearts; and there are none save a few only who do not lift themselves up in the pride of their hearts, unto the wearing of very fine apparel, unto envying, and strifes, and malice, and persecutions, and all manner of iniquities; and your churches, yea, even every one, have become polluted because of the pride of your hearts. For behold, ye do love money, and your substance, and your fine apparel, and the adorning of your churches, more than ye love the poor and the needy, the sick and the afflicted."[511]

Moroni's vision was essentially the same vision as that seen by Jesus, Paul, and John the Revelator. He foresaw pervasive pride, attention to fashion, envy, strife, malice, persecution, iniquity, and polluted churches, which are both actual religious institutions and the philosophies of men, all of which are worshipped and followed devoutly. Sadly, Moroni reported, these conditions would exist among the Saints, whose affiliation with Babylon would defile the holy Church of God: "O ye pollutions, ye hypocrites, ye teachers, who sell yourselves for that which will canker, *why have ye polluted the holy church of God?* Why are ye ashamed to take upon you the name of Christ? Why do ye not think that greater is the value of an endless happiness than that misery which never dies—because of the praise of the world?" Moreover, Moroni said that our embracing Babylon while professing Zion would serve to persecute, rank, alienate, and maltreat the less fortunate among us: "Why do ye adorn yourselves with that which hath no life, and yet suffer the hungry, and the needy, and the naked, and the sick and the afflicted to pass by you, and notice them not?"

Frighteningly, he noted that some Saints would adopt Babylon's strategy of sinful secret dealings to get rich. Once again, our selfish attitude toward money holds the vulnerable and poor in captivity: "Yea, why do ye build up your secret abominations to get gain, and cause that widows should mourn before the Lord, and also orphans to mourn before the Lord, and also the blood of their fathers and their husbands to cry unto the Lord from the ground, for vengeance upon your heads?" Unless we Saints repent and flee Babylon, we will suffer her fate: "Behold, the sword of vengeance hangeth over you; and the time soon cometh that he avengeth the blood of the saints upon you, for he will not suffer their cries any longer."[512]

Moroni describes latter-day Babylon as "a day when the blood of saints shall cry unto the Lord, because of secret combinations and the works of darkness. Yea, it shall come in a day when the power of God shall be denied, and churches become defiled and be lifted up in the pride of their hearts, yea, even in a day when leaders of churches and teachers shall rise in the pride of their hearts, even to the envying of them who belong to their churches."

Beyond the preponderance of latter-day secret combinations, denials of the power of God, and myriad competing churches and man-made philosophies that are built up to get gain, Babylon boasts one continual scene of natural disasters and war: "Yea, it shall come in a day when there shall be heard of fires, and tempests, and vapors of smoke in foreign lands; and there shall also be heard of wars, rumors of wars, and earthquakes in divers places." Moreover, Babylon is a place and condition of "great pollutions,' both physical and spiritual: "Yea, it shall come in a day when there shall be great pollutions

---

511   Mormon 8:35–37.
512   Mormon 8:38–41; emphasis added.

upon the face of the earth." Every conceivable sin abounds: "There shall be murders, and robbing, and lying, and deceivings, and whoredoms [every form of sexual sin], and all manner of abominations." Babylon is a place and condition of apathy and lack of accountability to God: "Many . . . will say, Do this, or do that, and it mattereth not, for the Lord will uphold such at the last day. But wo unto such, for they are in the gall of bitterness and in the bonds of iniquity."[513]

As we recall, the word *church,* in Babylonian terms, means both a religious institution and a worshipped philosophy of man—anything that we worship other than God, whose leaders and teachers are those to whom we give our allegiance in place of God. Therefore, for example, Moroni prophesies: "Yea, it shall come in a day when there shall be churches built up that shall say: Come unto me, and for your money you shall be forgiven of your sins."[514]

Beyond spawning many corrupt religious institutions and man-made philosophies, Babylon promotes the attitude of entitlement, the doctrines that having money equals personal goodness, and that money exalts its owner above those of lesser fortunes. In the process, Zion's equality, unity, and oneness become nonexistent. To achieve her goals, Babylon first focuses her people on seeking riches for self-serving purposes; then she soothes their consciences with the lie that God will favor or at least wink at the rich (they must be good because they are rich), and eventually usher them into heaven where more riches await. This is false doctrine. Hugh Nibley notes, "God recognizes only one justification for seeking wealth, and that is with the express intent of helping the poor (Jacob 2:19)."[515] Moroni holds out no comfort to those who espouse such Babylonian attitudes: "O ye wicked and perverse and stiffnecked people, why have ye built up churches [worshipped philosophies] unto yourselves to get gain? Why have ye transfigured [reinvented] the holy word of God, that ye might bring damnation upon your souls?"[516] Clearly, Babylon wants money so badly that she will ignore or wrest the scriptures to justify her actions.

The Fall of Babylon

Babylon is like a cancer: her presence is destructive to the system. She is an unwelcomed intruder that must be excised completely, or she will overwhelm and kill her host. Babylon can be neither converted nor saved. Total annihilation is the only answer. "We would have healed Babylon, but she is not healed: forsake her, and let us go every one into his own country: for her judgment reacheth unto heaven, and is lifted up even to the skies."[517] The future of Babylon is absolute destruction: "Behold, that great and abominable church, the whore of all the earth, must tumble to the earth, and great must be the fall thereof. For the kingdom of the devil must shake, and they which belong to it must needs be stirred up unto repentance, or the devil will grasp them with his everlasting

---

513 Mormon 8:27–31.
514 Mormon 8:32.
515 Nibley, *Approaching Zion,* 53.
516 Mormon 8:33.
517 Jeremiah 51:9.

chains, and they be stirred up to anger, and perish."[518] Unfortunately, many people who are aware of these scriptures will still choose to wait it out, then try to jump ship to Zion at the very last minute.

We should take to heart these prophecies. Babylon and Zion do not mix. Zion merged with even a little bit of Babylon is no longer Zion. For Zion to be Zion—a Zion person, a Zion family, or a Zion priesthood community—there can be no hint of Babylon. Hugh Nibley writes: "Zion is pure, which means 'not mixed with any impurities, unalloyed'; it is all Zion and nothing else. . . . It is all pure—it is a society, a community, and an environment into which no unclean thing can enter. 'Henceforth there shall no more come into thee the uncircumcised and the unclean' (3 Nephi 20:36). It is not even pure people in a dirty environment, or pure people with a few impure ones among them; it is the perfectly pure in a perfectly pure environment."[519] If we partake of Babylon or embrace her teachings in any degree, we are not Zion, and we will suffer Babylon's fate.

In the revelation of John, the Apostle saw a powerful angel descend from heaven, "and the earth was lightened with his glory. And he cried mightily with a strong voice, saying, Babylon the great is fallen, is fallen, and is become the habitation of devils."[520] John lists five reasons for Babylon's fall: (1) illicit relationships, interactions, and transactions that bring power and wealth. Described as "fornication," these universally accepted things stand contrary to the Covenant; (2) the intolerable sin of wealth-seeking: "and the merchants of the earth are waxed rich through the abundance of her delicacies"; (3) pride: "How much she hath glorified herself"; (4) excess and selfishness: "[Babylon] lived deliciously"; (5) ignoring the underprivileged: "I sit a queen, and am no widow, and shall see no sorrow." But enough is too much: "her sins have reached unto heaven, and God hath remembered her iniquities."

The first angel's voice is now joined by a voice from heaven, which is directed at the Saints: "And I heard another voice from heaven, saying, Come out of her, my people, that ye be not partakers of her sins, and that ye receive not of her plagues." This merciful warning is dire; the Lord has undertaken to judge Babylon, and neither she nor the people who remain in her will be able to withstand his judgment: "Therefore shall her plagues come in one day, death, and mourning, and famine; and she shall be utterly burned with fire: for strong is the Lord God who judgeth her."

The reference to a sudden and astonishing fall is repeated throughout the prophecy: "in one day"; "Alas, alas, that great city Babylon, that mighty city! for in one hour is thy judgment come"; "For in one hour so great riches is come to nought"; "in one hour is she made desolate." Babylon's fall will be violent and permanent: "Thus with violence shall that great city Babylon be thrown down, and shall be found no more at all."

The wicked who have loved Babylon will greatly miss her; their reaction will be widespread mourning: "And the kings of the earth, who have committed fornication and lived deliciously with her, shall bewail her, and lament for her, when they shall see the smoke of her burning, standing afar off for the fear of her torment."

---

518   2 Nephi 28:18–19.
519   Nibley, *Approaching Zion*, 26–27.
520   Revelation 18:1–2.

The world's economy will collapse, and those who have bought and sold will never recover: "And the merchants of the earth shall weep and mourn over her; for no man buyeth their merchandise any more." John then records the words of a voice from heaven, as if it were speaking directly to Babylon, saying, "All things which were dainty and goodly are departed from thee, and thou shalt find them no more at all." Then, viewing the merchants, the voice adds, "The merchants of these things, which were made rich by her, shall stand afar off for the fear of her torment, weeping and wailing, and saying, Alas, alas." But the merchants are not the only ones to mourn. The fall of Babylon is lamented by everyone who has remained within her precincts: "And every shipmaster, and all the company in ships, and sailors, and as many as trade by sea, stood afar off, and cried when they saw the smoke of her burning, saying, What [city is] like unto this great city! And they cast dust on their heads, and cried, weeping and wailing, saying, Alas, alas, that great city, wherein were made rich all that had ships in the sea by reason of her costliness! for in one hour is she made desolate."

Then a mighty angel assesses the extent of the destruction: "And the voice of harpers, and musicians, and of pipers, and trumpeters, shall be heard no more at all in thee; and no craftsman, of whatsoever craft he be, shall be found any more in thee; and the sound of a millstone shall be heard no more at all in thee; and the light of a candle shall shine no more at all in thee." No more of the world's carnal music and art; no more worldly crafts; no more worldly manufacturing. Babylon's light has been snuffed out forever, and the world mourns, "For thy merchants were the great men of the earth; for by thy sorceries were all nations deceived. And in her was found the blood of prophets, and of saints, and of all that were slain upon the earth."

But Zion's hour has come at last. While the people of Babylon mourn, the people of Zion rejoice. "Rejoice over her, thou heaven, and ye holy apostles and prophets; for God hath avenged you on her." We have a choice: we can remain in Babylon, suffer her plagues and mourn, or we can come to Zion, obtain safety in the Covenant, and rejoice.

According to Nephi, the fall of Babylon will be "exceedingly great."[521] Babylon will be destroyed "speedily; . . . it shall be at an instant, suddenly."[522] Lehi's foundationless "great and spacious building" that "stood as it were in the air, high above the earth" will collapse, to the astonishment and fear of the world. Then a voice from heaven will be heard: "Babylon the great is fallen, is fallen, and is become the habitation of devils, and the hold of every foul spirit."[523] Moreover, when Babylon, "the glory of kingdoms," falls, it "shall be as when God overthrew Sodom and Gomorrah." That is, Babylon will be so fully eradicated that "it shall never be inhabited, neither shall it be dwelt in from generation to generation; . . . her time is near to come, and her day shall not be prolonged. For I will destroy her speedily; yea, for I will be merciful unto my people, but the wicked shall perish."[524]

Speaking to the Prophet Joseph Smith, the Lord said, "Behold, vengeance cometh speedily upon the inhabitants of the earth, a day of wrath, a day of burning, a day of des-

---

521 1 Nephi 11:35–36; 12:18.
522 2 Nephi 26:18.
523 Revelation 18:2.
524 2 Nephi 23:19–22.

olation, of weeping, of mourning, and of lamentation; and as a whirlwind it shall come upon all the face of the earth, saith the Lord. *And upon my house shall it begin,* and from my house shall it go forth, saith the Lord; first among those among you, saith the Lord, who have professed to know my name and have not known me, and have blasphemed against me in the midst of my house, saith the Lord."[525] The Saints are not exempt. Those Saints who hold to Babylon and its philosophies will suffer the consequences of Babylon's fall. Either we must decide to be safe in Zion or defenseless in Babylon. To the extent that we dabble with Babylon, we are vulnerable.

Samuel the Lamanite's Parallel Denunciation of Babylon

A few years before the birth of Christ, Samuel, a Lamanite prophet, entered the land of the Nephites to warn the people, cry repentance, and prophesy of simultaneously glorious and catastrophic events. That Mormon would record Samuel's words in such detail should signal to us their latter-day import. Furthermore, that Samuel delivered his message only years before the advent of the Savior, with the advent's attendant destructions, should add more weight to our latter-day consideration. The fact that the resurrected Jesus drew attention to Samuel's prophecies and insisted that they be added to the Nephite record in detail should further signal their importance to us in the latter days.[526]

Let us consider Samuel's denunciation of the Nephites' Babylon as that denunciation parallels Babylon today.

To set the stage, Mormon describes the Nephite world as one of "great wickedness." Only a few "did observe strictly to keep the commandments of God." The Nephites' reaction to the prophet's preaching ranged from disregard to violence.[527] Immediately, we see our latter-day condition mirroring that of the Nephites.

Samuel warned that "the sword of justice hangeth over this people. . . . Yea, heavy destruction awaiteth this people, and it surely cometh unto this people, and nothing can save this people save it be repentance and faith on the Lord Jesus Christ." The Nephites' condition had resulted from "the hardness of the hearts of the people." That hardness of heart was being manifested in a variety of ways:
- Misusing the money the Lord had given them.
- Setting their hearts on acquiring riches.
- Not hearkening unto the Lord or his words.
- Neither remembering the Lord or his blessings nor thanking him for them.
- Always thinking about their riches and how to acquire more of them
- Not allowing their hearts to be "drawn out unto the Lord."
- Giving themselves over to "great pride, unto boasting, and unto great swelling, envyings, strifes, malice, persecutions, and murders, and all manner of iniquities."
- Mocking and rejecting the prophets.[528]

---
525   D&C 112:24–26; emphasis added.
526   3 Nephi 23:7–14.
527   Helaman 13:1–2.
528   Helaman 13:19–24.

Another sinful condition of the Nephites was their willingness to follow, idolize, and uphold people who flattered their egos— Samuel called these deceivers "blind guides."[529] The Nephites were more interested in the philosophies of these smooth-tongued "guides" than the prophets. They would enrich these people and canonize their words as if they were scripture. "But behold, if a man shall come among you and shall say: Do this, and there is no iniquity; do that and ye shall not suffer; yea, he will say: Walk after the pride of your own hearts; yea, walk after the pride of your eyes, and do whatsoever your heart desireth—and if a man shall come among you and say this, ye will receive him, and say that he is a prophet. Yea, ye will lift him up, and ye will give unto him of your substance; ye will give unto him of your gold, and of your silver, and ye will clothe him with costly apparel; and because he speaketh flattering words unto you, and he saith that all is well, then ye will not find fault with him."[530]

"Blind guides" are those people who receive our support and adoration for flattering us with their mouth, but more often with their lifestyle. We give them riches not for what they produce or contribute; we give them riches for being famous. They are famous for being famous. They flatter us by parading before us the rewards that come with a lifestyle that glamorizes Babylon, and we applaud them for their having legitimized a life of wealth, self-indulgence, power, recognition, and excess.

The Lord's Spirit cannot abide in such wickedness. In Samuel's day, only the presence of a few righteous individuals was holding back the judgments. But the clock was ticking. The gathering of the righteous was taking place. Soon the faithful few would be called out (or cast out), and only the repentant would be spared. Then the wicked would be ripe for destruction.[531] A fruit that is ripe will fall from the tree, an interesting analogy of separating one's self from the tree of life. In its insistence for a sinful, independent life from the tree, the ripe and fallen fruit can ultimately do nothing on its own except lie on the ground and rot.

Speaking for the Lord, Samuel pronounced a series of curses: (1) "I will take away my word from them"; (2) "I will withdraw my spirit"; (3) "I will suffer them no longer," that is, *I will not allow them to continue living this way;* (4) "I will turn the hearts of their [enemies] against them"; (5) "I will cause that they shall be smitten . . . with the sword and with famine and with pestilence. . . . I will visit them in my fierce anger"; and (6) "Whoso shall hide up treasures in the earth shall find them no more . . . save he be a righteous man."[532]

If the people cared little about the first five curses, the last one was sure to get their attention. This curse was aimed at what they loved most: their treasures. The curse stipulated that a righteous person was exempt; he could "hide up" his treasure unto the Lord—that is, he could consecrate it—and it would remain safe. But a wicked person would not be so fortunate. Because he was in the selfish habit of hiding his treasure unto

---

529 Helaman 13:29.
530 Helaman 13:27–28.
531 Helaman 13:12–14.
532 Helaman 13:8–10, 18.

himself and not the Lord, he would discover that his treasure had become "slippery."[533] Consequently, the fortunes of those who were wicked would slip away from them; the economy would collapse, and financial ruin would result. "And behold, the time cometh that he curseth your riches, that they become slippery, that ye cannot hold them; and in the days of your poverty ye cannot retain them."[534]

Then things would go from bad to worse. In the people's impoverished situation, they would be vulnerable to attack from their enemies, particularly those enemies who constitute secret combinations. We note that Samuel's prophecies were followed by the near destruction of the nation by the Gadianton robbers.[535] Samuel foretold that the people would "flee before their enemies" following the economic collapse.[536] Their lamentations should strike fear in every person who trusts in his riches and adores Babylon:

> And in the days of your poverty ye shall cry unto the Lord; and in vain shall ye cry, for your desolation is already come upon you, and your destruction is made sure; and then shall ye weep and howl in that day, saith the Lord of Hosts. And then shall ye lament, and say: O that I had repented, and had not killed the prophets, and stoned them, and cast them out. Yea, in that day ye shall say: O that we had remembered the Lord our God in the day that he gave us our riches, and then they would not have become slippery that we should lose them; for behold, our riches are gone from us.
>
> Behold, we lay a tool here and on the morrow it is gone; and behold, our swords are taken from us in the day we have sought them for battle.
>
> Yea, we have hid up our treasures and they have slipped away from us, because of the curse of the land.
>
> O that we had repented in the day that the word of the Lord came unto us; for behold the land is cursed, and all things are become slippery, and we cannot hold them.
>
> Behold, we are surrounded by demons, yea, we are encircled about by the angels of him who hath sought to destroy our souls. Behold, our iniquities are great. O Lord, canst thou not turn away thine anger from us? And this shall be your language in those days.
>
> But behold, your days of probation are past; ye have procrastinated the day of your salvation until it is everlastingly too late, and your destruction is made

---

533   Helaman 13:18–19, 31, 33, 36.
534   Helaman 13:31.
535   3 Nephi 1–4.
536   Helaman 13:20.

> sure; yea, for ye have sought all the days of your lives for that which ye could not obtain; and ye have sought for happiness in doing iniquity, which thing is contrary to the nature of that righteousness which is in our great and Eternal Head.
>
> O ye people of the land, that ye would hear my words! And I pray that the anger of the Lord be turned away from you, and that ye would repent and be saved.[537]

Samuel's prophecies began to be fulfilled, but the Nephites did not repent. Mormon reported that "there was but little alteration in the affairs of the people, save it were the people began to be more hardened in iniquity." Even when "great signs [were] given unto the people, and wonders; and the words of the prophets began to be fulfilled," the Nephites hardened their hearts.[538] They simply would not believe the signs or respond to the Lord's invitation to repent, which invitation he offered by means of cataclysmic events. Mormon identified four reasons why the people did not repent:

1. Prophecies are nothing more than good guesses: "Some things they [the prophets] may have guessed right, among so many; but behold, we know that all these great and marvelous works cannot come to pass, of which has been spoken."
2. Prophecies do not make sense: "And they began to reason and to contend among themselves, saying: That it is not reasonable that such a being as a Christ shall come.
3. Prophecies are false traditions: "But behold, we know that this is a wicked tradition, which has been handed down unto us by our fathers, to cause us that we should believe in some great and marvelous thing which should come to pass . . . ; therefore they can keep us in ignorance."
4. Prophets deceive us to keep us bound to them: "And they [the prophets] will, by the cunning and the mysterious arts of the evil one, work some great mystery which we cannot understand, which will keep us down to be servants to their words, and also servants unto them, for we depend upon them to teach us the word; and thus will they keep us in ignorance if we will yield ourselves unto them, all the days of our lives."

Mormon informed us that the Nephites "began to depend upon their own strength and upon their own wisdom." They "imagine[d] up in their hearts" "many more things" "which were foolish and vain." Mormon said that the people "were much disturbed, for Satan did stir them up to do iniquity continually; yea, he did go about spreading rumors and contentions upon all the face of the land, that he might harden the hearts of the people against that which was good and against that which should come. And notwithstanding the signs and the wonders which were wrought among the people of the Lord, and the many miracles which they did, Satan did get great hold upon the hearts of the people upon all the face of the land."[539]

---

537 Helaman 13:32–39.
538 Helaman 16:12–15.
539 Helaman 16:15, 22–24.

It is difficult to read this account and not see the condition of Babylon today. Clearly, we are mere years away from the Savior's advent. The prophets are widely mocked, ignored, and often soundly rejected. Only a few Zion people practice righteousness, and for the sake of those few the Lord is holding back the destructions. The condition of Babylon's people is defined by hardness of heart. They love their money and selfishly misuse it; they always think about their riches and how to acquire more. They will not hearken unto the Lord or his words; they will not remember or thank him for their blessings. Their hearts are not "drawn out unto the Lord." Their lives are marked with "great pride," boastings, envyings, strifes, malice, persecutions, and murders, and all manner of iniquities." They follow "blind guides," who use flattering words to stroke their egos and legitimize a lifestyle that glamorizes wealth, self-indulgence, popularity, power, and excess.

Now the curses of the Lord are becoming apparent. Personal treasures are becoming slippery; economies are lying in ruins. In this condition, the people of Babylon are vulnerable to their enemies, especially those of secret combinations. Despite cataclysmic events, they will not repent and return to the Lord. Rather, they find all sorts of reasons not to repent, and they grow in wickedness. Samuel might as well have been warning and prophesying to us.

Go Ye Out from Babylon

Knowing the condition and future of Babylon, why do we try so hard to stay there? The Lord has instructed us implicitly: "Go ye out from Babylon. Be ye clean that bear the vessels of the Lord. . . . Yea, verily I say unto you again, the time has come when the voice of the Lord is unto you: Go ye out of Babylon; gather ye out from among the nations, from the four winds, from one end of heaven to the other. . . . Go ye out from among the nations, even from Babylon, from the midst of wickedness, which is spiritual Babylon."[540]

As we have learned, Babylon is simultaneously a location, the sum of false philosophies and doctrines, and a condition of the heart. While our present circumstances might not involve moving away from physical Babylon, we nevertheless must flee from spiritual Babylon. In unmistakable language, the Lord has commanded us to "forsake the world,"[541] and "lay aside the things of this world, and seek for the things of a better."[542] He charges us to escape for our own safety: "For after today cometh the burning—this is speaking after the manner of the Lord—for verily I say, tomorrow all the proud and they that do wickedly shall be as stubble; and I will burn them up, for I am the Lord of Hosts; and I will not spare any that remain in Babylon."[543] If we choose to remain in spiritual Babylon, we do so at our own risk. Most certainly, we will be caught up in the destructions: "That great whore, who hath perverted the right ways of the Lord, yea, that great and abominable church, shall tumble to the dust and great shall be the fall of it."[544]

---

540 D&C 133:5, 7, 14.
541 D&C 53:2.
542 D&C 25:10.
543 D&C 64:24.
544 1 Nephi 22:14.

The Lord's command to leave Babylon is also an invitation to come to Zion, with the Lord's offer to help us. Still, there is nothing easy about leaving Babylon and converting to a Zion-like way of life founded on celestial doctrines. Occasionally, we must be "stirred up" so that we might see the truth about Babylon and decide once and for all to leave. Blaine Yorgason writes:

> Whether we think we need to give up [the things of Babylon] or not, it seems that the Lord is frequently willing to help us in the giving up of worldly things. He might do this by allowing financial reversals to occur, bringing loss of homes, cars, boats, and incomes; personal or corporate bankruptcy; and so forth. We might also experience a severe loss of health or death of a loved one, which can do the same thing by making worldly things unattractive or meaningless. . . . This is called being stirred up unto repentance. In this case, however, I will substitute the word *humility*, which always strikes at the heart of pride, vanity, and worldliness! "Behold, the world is ripening in iniquity; and it must needs be that the children of men are stirred up unto *humility*, both the Gentiles and also the house of Israel" (D&C 18:6); and, "The kingdom of the devil must shake, and they which belong to it must needs be stirred up unto repentance, or the devil will grasp them with his everlasting chains, and they . . . perish" (2 Nephi 28:19).
>
> When we experience this divine assistance in leaving behind the things of the world—and to some degree we will all experience it—then above all else we ought to be filled with joy and rejoicing in the Lord's goodness and mercy (D&C 52:43).[545]

Summary and Conclusion

Babylon is the inverse of Zion. Wherever we detect any of the loathsome things that we have discussed in this section (and this section is not exhaustive), we find Babylon. If we desire to become Zion-like, we must not partake of or participate in anything that Babylon does, believes, or promotes; otherwise, we will suffer her fate. To the degree that we embrace Babylon, we reject Zion. Only when we make a clean break from Babylon and never turn back will we finally qualify as Zion people. There are only two choices.

The process of leaving Babylon and coming to Zion begins with the discovery that we are not home; we have fallen into a lone and dreary world that is as foreign to heaven

---

545 Yorgason, *I Need Thee Every Hour*, 206–7.

as is hell. From that moment of discovery for the rest of our lives, our direction must be away and up.

This earth began as Zion but was soon infiltrated by a being who determined to wrest ownership from its Creator and reign as the god of this world. That being was Satan, who systematically reversed every Zion doctrine and replaced it with his anti-Christ philosophy, which he designed to appear so reasonable and close to the truth that it could deceive even the very elect. Attempting to imitate God the Father, Satan searched for a *son* to champion his anti-Christ *gospel*. He found a willing candidate in Cain, who advanced a doctrine so damning that the entire antediluvian world became irretrievably corrupt, and in the days of Noah, it eventually warranted annihilation.

After the Flood, Cain's descendant Nimrod became heir to Cain's diabolical throne, and a new anti-Christ *dispensation* began. Nimrod advanced what Cain had started by conquering much of the world and building a capital with a tower, or *temple,* to attempt to ascend illegitimately into heaven. Nimrod's temple city was called Babel, or Babylon. Forevermore, *Babylon* would be the code name by which the prophets of God would identify and describe the Satanic kingdom, culture, and doctrines that always led people to individual damnation and collective destruction. Sodom and Gomorrah are examples.

Today, the anti-Christ philosophy dominates the earth. Both figuratively and literally, it "slayeth the saints of God, yea, and tortureth them and bindeth them down, and yoketh them with a yoke of iron, and bringeth them down into captivity."[546]

In one way or another we have all partaken of Babylon, and when we become sufficiently sick, we seek heavenly help to get out and go home. To make a clean break from Babylon requires making the new and everlasting covenant, receiving priesthood authority by ordination with the Father's oath and our covenant, receiving priesthood power by means of temple ordinances and righteous living, being endowed with knowledge from on high, and, of course, enduring in the Covenant to the end and its perfect conclusion. For a season, we might react like Laman and Lemuel, constantly looking back and longing for life in Babylon; but at some point we will realize that Zion and Babylon cannot coexist, and therefore we have to make a choice. We can only straddle the gulf between Zion and Babylon for so long; because the two go in opposite directions, we will eventually be forced to jump to one side or another. Nephi gives us the key to escape Babylon and come to Zion: "We heeded [Babylon] not."[547]

Babylon is so diverse, pervasive, and disgusting that the prophets seem to struggle to find adequate language to describe her. Babylon is often called "the world," but that term usually gives way to more graphic descriptors that focus us on Babylon's central elements: "whore" to portray her many sexual perversions; "The Mother of Harlots and Abominations of the Earth" to illustrate her continually spawning myriad seductive evils; "carnal, sensual, and devilish" to depict her ability to exploit human nature and to tempt us to gratify our senses, which will cause us to become like the devil; "Great and Abominable Church" to illustrate that she is full of idolatry, envy, and covetousness, and that her vile

---

546 1 Nephi 13:5.
547 1 Nephi 8:33.

desires and philosophies are worshipped by her adherents; and "great and spacious building" to express her excessive pride and the scope of her influence. By whatever name, Babylon's aim is to trap and destroy us.

Babylon's fourfold strategy to torture and "murder" us centers on the pursuits of money, power, recognition, and selfishness and self-indulgence. According to Nephi, these pursuits are facilitated by:
1. The desire for wealth.
2. Fashion and materialism.
3. Sexual sins.
4. The desire for peer acceptance, recognition, and popularity.[548]

This strategy is so successful that even Satan is taken aback by Babylon's "dark and blackening deeds [which] are enough to make hell itself shudder, and to stand aghast and pale, and the hands of the very devil to tremble and palsy."[549] Babylon has made us to "bow down with grief, sorrow, and care, under the most damning hand of murder, tyranny, and oppression."[550]

Nephi describes Babylon in terms of the extent of her detestable deeds and the depth her corruption. His list includes contention; man's wisdom replacing God's wisdom; denying the power of God; "eat, drink and be merry" as a way of life; pride; secret sinning; reviling against that which is good; placing trust in carnal security; flattery; and taking and giving offense.[551] These items and more define Babylon as a physical location and a spiritual condition, which condition includes false philosophies and doctrines and a corruption of the heart.

As mentioned earlier, in Babylon, competition rather than cooperation is the name of the game. In Babylon, competitive enterprise is the primary engine that drives progress. Competition, however, spawns more losers than winners and therefore is the cause of widespread misery. Competition accounts for social classes, educational disparity, poverty, oppression, dishonesty, murder, and war.

Babylon is filled with hypocrites, whom Jesus labeled the worst sinners—those people who pretend to be what they are not, to seem better than they really are, or to appear pious and virtuous when they are not.

Babylon bounces her adherents from one false philosophy to another, always keeping them off balance so that they will never find the truth. These man-made philosophies are embraced by the people of Babylon as pseudo religions; humanism, intellectualism, atheism, fundamentalism, relativism, universalism, monism, subjectivism, and modernism are a few. All of these are designed to limit or remove God from our consciousness and to enthrone man and his genius.

Prophets have compared modern Babylon to the days of Noah and Lot, whose worlds, along with the societies of Sodom and Gomorrah, were completely obliterated as

---

548   1 Nephi 13:5–9.
549   D&C 123:10.
550   D&C 123:7.
551   2 Nephi 28:4–16, 26–30.

punishment for their sins. To help us negotiate through Babylon's filthiness in the last days, the Lord has given us the Book of Mormon. This book of scripture contains two accounts of once-mighty nations that imploded as a result of their embracing Babylonian ideals. Do we really believe we are immune? President Kimball stated that latter-day Babylon would deceive even the very elect—as many as half the Saints, according to the parable of the ten virgins.

Jesus, John, Paul, and Moroni join Nephi and other prophets who foresaw Babylon's latter-day dominance. Their descriptions are chilling, and yet many of us still make no attempt to flee. Jesus portrayed our day as a time when "darkness covereth the earth, and gross darkness the minds of the people, and all flesh has become corrupt before my face."[552] We live in physical Babylon and partake of spiritual Babylon as though we have no option. At times, we seem powerless to cease partaking of her lifestyle and philosophies. We assume that this is just the way life is and that we are helpless to change things. The people in Noah's and Lot's day held similar views and were caught up in the destructions: "And as it was in the days of [Noah], so shall it be also in the days of the Son of man. They did eat, they drank, they married wives, they were given in marriage, until the day that [Noah] entered into the ark, and the flood came, and destroyed them all. Likewise also as it was in the days of Lot; they did eat, they drank, they bought, they sold, they planted, they builded; but the same day that Lot went out of Sodom it rained fire and brimstone from heaven, and destroyed them all. Even thus shall it be in the day when the Son of man is revealed."[553]

Babylon will fall again. Can there be any doubt? From the days of Enoch to the present, Babylon's fall has been prophesied repeatedly. Moreover, there are countless prophetic descriptions of Babylon and authoritative declarations concerning why she must be destroyed once and for all. When we consider Babylon's characteristics, we are astonished that anyone would want to stay. The one and only solution for safety and security in a world gone mad is to flee to Zion.

Postlude

Zion was our origin, our birthright, and Zion will be our destiny. She is our ideal. Her establishment should be our greatest desire. Remember, Joseph Smith said that the building of Zion should be our main focus.[554] Brigham Young laid the responsibility of Zion upon each of us individually: "[Zion] commences in the heart of each person."[555] We cannot read the scriptures, especially latter-day scriptures, and avoid personal responsibility for becoming Zion people. Without reservation, our obligation is to accept every revealed Zion principle and put it into practice.

As mentioned previously, Zion is the standard among celestial and celestial-seeking beings.[556] The celestial condition of Zion is the exact opposite of the telestial condition of

---

552 D&C 112:24.
553 Luke 17:26–30.
554 Smith, *Teachings of the Prophet Joseph Smith*, 60.
555 Young, *Discourses of Brigham Young*, 118.
556 D&C 105:5.

Babylon;[557] therefore, we are constantly faced with choosing between the two. We cannot have it both ways. Nothing good has ever come from attempting to mix Zion with Babylon.

As members of the dispensation of the fulness of times, we are under covenant to build up the kingdom of God for the purpose of establishing Zion. A key to establishing Zion in our lives is found in Doctrine and Covenants 42, the revelation called the law of the Church,[558] which comprises the law of Zion. In one sentence, the Lord prophesies of three significant events that will make us Zion individuals: "And ye shall hereafter receive church covenants, such as shall be sufficient to establish you, both here and in the New Jerusalem."[559] The references in this scripture lead to what we are calling in this series, The Three Pillars of Zion:

The New and Everlasting Covenant (D&C 132:4–7)
The Oath and Covenant of the Priesthood (D&C 84:33–44)
The Law of Consecration (D&C 82:11–15)

These three covenants (pillars) are sufficient to establish Zion-like qualities in our individual lives, as well as in our marriages, families, or other groups of people under the direction of the priesthood.

Therefore, to become Zion-like and thus ensure our salvation and exaltation, we enter into the new and everlasting covenant. By this act, we specify that we have made a choice between Zion and Babylon and that forevermore we will not attempt to mix the two. We agree to follow the Covenant to its perfect conclusion: to snatch us from Babylon, to single us out, to purify and sanctify our hearts, to prepare us in every way to regain the presence of God, and to obtain our inheritance and our crown. "This is Zion: THE PURE IN HEART."[560]

---

557 Nibley, *Approaching Zion*, 30.
558 D&C 42 section heading.
559 D&C 42:67.
560 D&C 97:21.

Bibliography

American Heritage Dictionary. Boston, MA: Houghton Mifflin, 2000.

Anderson, Dawn Hall, Susette Fletcher Green, and Dlora Hall Dalton, eds. *Clothed with Charity: Talks from the 1996 Women's Conference*. Salt Lake City, UT: Deseret Book, 1997.

Asay, Carlos E. "The Oath and Covenant of the Priesthood," *Ensign*, November 1985.

—*Family Pecan Trees: Planting a Legacy of Faith at Home*. Salt Lake City, UT: Deseret Book, 1992.

—*The Seven M's of Missionary Service: Proclaiming the Gospel as a Member or Full-time Missionary*. Salt Lake City, UT: Bookcraft, 1996.

Ashton, Marvin J. "Be a Quality Person," *Ensign*, February 1993.

—"Love Takes Time," *Ensign*, November 1975.

Bednar, David A. "Pray Always," *Ensign*, November 2008.

Benson, Ezra Taft. "A Vision and a Hope for the Youth of Zion," *Devotional Speeches of the Year*. Provo, UT: Brigham Young University Press, 1978.

—*A Witness and a Warning: A Modern-Day Prophet Testifies of the Book of Mormon*. Salt Lake City, UT: Deseret Book, 1988.

—"Beware of Pride," *Ensign*, May 1989.

—*Devotional Speeches of the Year*. Provo, UT: Brigham Young University Press, 1978.

—*God, Family, Country: Our Three Great Loyalties*. Salt Lake City, UT: Deseret Book, 1975.

—"In His Steps," *Ensign*, September 1988.

—"Jesus Christ—Gifts and Expectations," *New Era*, May 1975.

—*The Teachings of Ezra Taft Benson*. Salt Lake City, UT: Deseret Book, 1988.

—"What I Hope You Will Teach Your Children about the Temple," *Ensign*, August 1985;

Bible Dictionary. Salt Lake City, UT: The Church of Jesus Christ of Latter-day Saints, 1989;

Black, Susan Easton, et al. *Doctrines for Exaltation: The 1989 Sperry Symposium on the Doctrine and Covenants*. Salt Lake City, UT: Deseret Book, 1989.

—*The Iowa Mormon Trail: Legacy of Faith and Courage*. Orem, UT: Helix Publishing, 1997.

Bowen, Albert E. *The Church Welfare Plan*. Salt Lake City, UT: The Church of Jesus Christ of Latter-day Saints, 1946.

Brewster, Hoyt W. Jr. *Doctrine and Covenants Encyclopedia*. Salt Lake City, UT: Bookcraft, 1988.

Brown, Hugh B. *Continuing the Quest*. Salt Lake City, UT: Bookcraft, 1961.

Brown, Matthew B. *Prophecies: The Gate of Heaven*. American Fork, UT: Covenant Communications, 1999.

—*Signs of the Times, Second Coming, Millennium*. American Fork, UT: Covenant Communications, 2006.

Budge, Ernest A. Wallis. *Coptic Martyrdoms Discourse on Abbaton*. London: British Museum, 1914.

Burton, Alma P., ed. *Discourses of the Prophet Joseph Smith*. Salt Lake City, UT: Deseret Book, 1956.

Cannon, Donald Q. *Teachings of the Latter-day Prophets*. Salt Lake City, UT: Bookcraft, 1998.

Cannon, Elaine. "Agency and Accountability." Salt Lake City, *Ensign*, November 1983.

Bibliography

Cannon, George Q. "Beware Lest Ye Fall." Discourse delivered at the Morgan Utah Stake Conference, Sunday, February 16, 1896.

—*Gospel Truth: Discourses and Writings of President George Q. Cannon.* Salt Lake City, UT: Deseret Book, 1974.

Cannon, Joseph A. "Sanctification," *Mormon Times,* June 12, 2008, http://www.mormontimes.com.

Clark, E. Douglas. *The Blessings of Abraham—Becoming a Zion People.* American Fork, UT: Covenant Communications, 2005.

Clark, J. Reuben. *Church Welfare Plan: A Discussion.* Salt Lake, City, UT General Church Welfare Committee, 1939.

Clark, James R., comp., *Messages of the First Presidency of The Church of Jesus Christ of Latter-day Saints.* Salt Lake City: Bookcraft, 1965–75.

Clarke, Adam. *Clarke's Commentary on the Bible.* Grand Rapids, MI: Baker Book House, 1967.

Clarke, J. Richard. "Successful Welfare Stewardship," *Ensign,* November 1978.

Conference Report, 1897–2009, Salt Lake City, UT: The Church of Jesus Christ of Latter-day Saints.

Cook, Gene R. "Home and Family: A Divine Eternal Pattern," *Ensign,* May 1984.

—"The Seat Next to You," *New Era,* October 1983.

Cook, Lyndon. *Joseph Smith and the Law of Consecration.* Provo, UT: Keepsake Books, 1991.

Cowley, Matthew. *Matthew Cowley Speaks: Discourses of Elder Matthew Cowley of the Quorum of the Twelve of the Church of Jesus Christ of Latter-day Saints.* Salt Lake City, UT: Deseret Book Company, 1954.

Dalrymple, G. Brent. *The Age of the Earth.* Stanford, CA: Stanford University Press, 1991.

Dellenbach, Robert K. "Hour of Conversion," *New Era,* June 2002.

DeMille, Cecil B. *BYU Speeches of the Year.* Provo, UT: Brigham Young University Press, May 1957.

Durham, G. Homer, ed. *The Gospel Kingdom: Selections from the Writings and Discourses of John Taylor, Third President of The Church of Jesus Christ of Latter-day Saints.* Salt Lake City, UT: Bookcraft, 1943.

—*Gospel Ideals: Selections from the Discourses of David O. McKay.* Salt Lake City, UT: Improvement Era, 1953.

Dibble, Philo. "Recollections of the Prophet Joseph Smith," *Juvenile Instructor,* June 1892.

Duffin, James G. "A Character Test," *Improvement Era,* February 1911.

Easton, M. G. *Illustrated Bible Dictionary.* Nashville: TN: Thomas Nelson, 1897.

"The Bondage of Sin," *Improvement Era,* February 1923.

Ehat, Andrew F. and Lyndon W. Cook. *The Words of Joseph Smith: The Contemporary Accounts of the Nauvoo Discourses of the Prophet Joseph.* Provo, UT: Religious Studies Center Brigham Young University, 1980.

Encarta World English Dictionary. New York, NY: St. Martins Press, 1999.

Eyring, Henry B. "Faith and the Oath and Covenant of the Priesthood," *Ensign,* May 2008.

Farley, S. Brent. "The Oath and Covenant of the Priesthood." *Sperry Symposium on the Doctrine and Covenants.* Salt Lake City: Deseret Book, 1989.

First Presidency, "What is the Doctrine of the Priesthood?" Salt Lake City, UT: *Improvement Era*, February 1961.

Faust, James E. "A Royal Priesthood," *Ensign*, May 2006.

—*In the Strength of the Lord: The Life and Teachings of James E. Faust.* Salt Lake City, UT: Deseret Book, 1999.

—"He Healeth the Broken Heart," *Ensign* July 2005.

—"Our Search for Happiness, *Ensign*, Oct. 2000.

—"Standing in Holy Places," *Ensign*, May 2005.

—"The Devil's Throat," *Ensign*, May 2003.

—"The Gift of the Holy Ghost—A Sure Compass," *Ensign*, April 1996.

—"The Shield of Faith," *Ensign*, May 2000.

"Galaxy Map." Washington D.C.: The National Geographic Society, June 1983.

Galbraith, David B., D. Kelly Ogden, and Andrew C. Skinner. *Jerusalem—The Eternal City.* Salt Lake City, UT: Deseret Book, 1996.

Gardner, R. Quinn. "Becoming a Zion Society," *Ensign*, February 1979.

—. "I Have a Question," *Ensign*, March 1978.

Gibbons, Ted L. *Be Not Afraid,* Springville, UT: Cedar Fort, Inc., 2009.

Goddard, Wallace H. "Blessed by Angels." *MeridianMagazine.com,* July 27, 2009.

—. *Drawing Heaven into Your Marriage.* Fairfax, VA: Meridian Publishing, 2007.

Grant, Heber J. *Teachings of Presidents of the Church.* Salt Lake City, UT: The Church of Jesus Christ of Latter-day Saints, 2002.

Guralnik, David B., ed. *Webster's New World Dictionary, 2nd College Edition.* New York City, NY: The New World Publishing Company, 1970.

Hafen, Bruce C. *The Broken Heart: Applying the Atonement to Life's Experiences.* Salt Lake City, UT: Deseret Book, 1989.

Haight, David B. "The Sacrament and the Sacrifice," *Ensign*, November 1989.

Hamilton, Edith. *Spokesman for God.* New York, NY: Norton and Company, 1977.

Hinckley, Gordon B. "Blessed Are the Merciful," *Ensign*, May 1990.

—*Faith: The Essence of True Religion.* Salt Lake City, UT: Deseret Book, 1989.

—"Our Mission of Saving," *Ensign*, November 1991.

—"Priesthood: The Power of Godliness," *Improvement Era*, December 1970.

—*Stand a Little Taller.* Salt Lake City, UT: Eagle Gate, 2000.

—*Standing for Something.* New York, NY: Three Rivers Press, 2000.

—*Teachings of Gordon B. Hinckley.* Salt Lake City, UT: Deseret Book, 2002.

—"The Dawning of a Brighter Day," *Ensign*, May 2004.

—"The Stone Cut Out of the Mountain," *Ensign*, 2007.

—"Till We Meet Again," *Ensign*, November 2001.

—"We Thank Thee for This Sacred Structure," *Church News*, 8 November 1997.

— "Your Greatest Challenge, Mother," *Ensign*, November 2000.

Holland, Jeffrey R. "Broken Things to Mend," *Ensign*, May 2006.

—"However Long and Hard the Road," *Ensign*, September 2002.

—*On Earth As It Is in Heaven.* Salt Lake City, UT: Deseret Book, 1989.

Holzapfel, Richard Neitzel and Thomas A. Wayment, eds., *The Life and Teachings of Jesus Christ: From the Transfiguration through the Triumphant Entry.* Salt Lake City, UT: Deseret Book, 2006.

Horton, George A. "Abraham's Act of Faith Reflects 'a Soul Like Unto Our Savior.'" *LDS Church News,* April 2, 1994.

"'Hymn of the Pearl': an Ancient Counterpart To 'O My Father.'" *BYU Studies,* vol. 36, 1996–97.

Hymns of the Church of Jesus Christ of Latter-day Saints. Salt Lake City, UT: The Church of Jesus Christ of Latter-day Saints, 1985.

Jackson, Kent P. and Robert L. Millet. eds. *Studies in Scripture.* Salt Lake City, UT: Deseret Book 1989.

Jensen, Marlin K. "Living after the Manner of Happiness," *Ensign,* December 2002.

—"An Eye Single to the Glory of God," Ensign, Nov. 1989.

Jenson, Andrew, *Historical Record: A Monthly Periodical.* Salt Lake City, UT: Deseret News, 1886—1890.

Jessee, Dean. "Joseph Knight's Recollection of Early Mormon History." Provo, UT: BYU *Studies,* vol. 17, no. 1, 1976.

Johnson, Clark V. *Doctrines for Exaltation: The 1989 Sperry Symposium on the Doctrine and Covenants.* Salt Lake City, UT: Deseret Book, 1989.

Josephus. *Complete Works.* William Whiston, trans., Grand Rapids, MI: Kregal Publications, 1960.

Kimball, Spencer W. "A Gift of Gratitude," *Tambuli,* December 1977.

—"Becoming the Pure in Heart," *Ensign,* May 1978.

—*Faith Precedes the Miracle: Based on Discourses of Spencer W. Kimball.* Salt Lake City, UT: Deseret Book, 1972.

—"The Fruit of Our Welfare Services Labors," *Ensign,* November 1978.

—"The Role of Righteous Women," *Ensign,* November 1979.

—*The Teachings of Spencer W. Kimball.* Salt Lake City, UT: Bookcraft, 1982.

—"Welfare Services: The Gospel in Action," *Ensign,* November 1977.

—"Young Women Fireside 1981—In Love and Power and without Fear," *New Era,* July 1981.

Kirchhoff, Frederick. "Reconstruction of Self in Wordsworth's 'Ode on Intimations of Immortality from Recollections of Early Childhood.'" *Narcissism and the Text.* New York, NY: New York University Press, 1986.

Kirtland Council Minute Book, eds. Fred Collier and William S. Hartwell, Salt Lake City, UT: Collier's Publishing, 1996.

Largey, Dennis L. *Book of Mormon Reference Companion.* Salt Lake City, UT: Deseret Book, 2003.

Larsen, Dean L. "A Royal Generation," *Ensign,* May 1983.

Larson, Stan "The King Follett Discourse: a Newly Amalgamated Text." Provo, UT: *BYU Studies,* Vol. 18, 1977–1978.

Layton, Lynne and Schapiro, Barbara A. *Narcissism and the Text: Studies in Literature and the Psychology of Self.* New York, NY: New York University Press, 1986.

Lee, Harold B. *Decisions for Successful Living.* Salt Lake City, UT: Deseret Book, 1973.
—"Stand Ye in Holy Places," *Ensign,* July 1973.
—*The Teachings of Harold B. Lee.* Salt Lake City, UT: Deseret Book, 1974.
Lightner, Mary. Address to Brigham Young University. *BYU Archives and Manuscripts, Writings of Early Latter-day Saints,* 1905.
Ludlow, Daniel H. *A Companion to Your Study of the Book of Mormon.* Salt Lake City, UT: Deseret Book, 1976.
—*Encyclopedia of Mormonism.* New York City, NY: Macmillan Publishing, 1992.
Lund, Gerald N. *Jesus Christ, Key to the Plan of Salvation.* Salt Lake City, UT: Deseret Book, 1991.
—"Old Testament Types and Symbols," *A Witness of Jesus Christ: The 1989 Sperry Symposium on the Old Testament.* ed. Richard D. Draper, Salt Lake City, UT: Deseret Book, 1990.
Lundquist, John M. and Stephen D. Ricks, eds. *By Study and Also by Faith: Essays in Honor of Hugh W. Nibley on the Occasion of His Eightieth Birthday.* Provo, UT: Maxwell Institute, 1992.
Lundwall, N. B. *Temples of the Most High.* Salt Lake City, UT: Bookcraft, 1965.
"Map: Old Testament Stories: Part Two," *Deseret News.* Jan. 8, 1994.
Maxwell, Cory H., ed. *The Neal A. Maxwell Quote Book.* Salt Lake City, UT: Bookcraft, 1997.
Maxwell, Neal A. *A Wonderful Flood of Light.* Salt Lake City, UT: Deseret Book, 1991.
—*But for a Small Moment.* Salt Lake City, UT: Bookcraft, 1987.
—"Consecrate Thy Performance." *Ensign,* May 2002.
—*Disposition of a Disciple.* Salt Lake City, UT: Deseret Book, 1976.
—"Enduring Well," *Ensign,* April 1997.
—*Even As I Am.* Salt Lake City, UT: Deseret Book, 1991.
—*If Thou Endure It Well.* Salt Lake City, UT: Bookcraft, 2002.
—*Lord, Increase Our Faith.* Salt Lake City, UT: Bookcraft, 1994.
—*Men and Women of Christ.* Salt Lake City, UT: Deseret Book, 1991.
—*Notwithstanding My Weakness.* Salt Lake City, UT: Deseret Book, 1981.
—*One More Strain of Praise.* Salt Lake City, UT: Deseret Book, 2003.
—"Patience," *Ensign,* October 1980.
—*That Ye May Believe.* Salt Lake City, UT: Bookcraft, 1994.
—*The Promise of Discipleship.* Salt Lake City, UT: Deseret Book, 2001.
—"These Are Your Days," *New Era,* January 1985.
McConkie, Bruce R. *A New Witness for the Articles of Faith.* Salt Lake City, UT: Deseret Book, 1985.
—*Doctrinal New Testament Commentary.* Salt Lake City, UT: Deseret Book, 1972.
—*Doctrines of Salvation: Sermons and Writings of Joseph Fielding Smith,* Salt Lake City, UT: Bookcraft, 1954–1956.
—*Mormon Doctrine.* Salt Lake City, UT: Bookcraft: 1966.
—"Obedience, Consecration, and Sacrifice," *Ensign,* May 1975.

—"The Doctrine of the Priesthood," *Ensign*, May 1982.
—*The Mortal Messiah: From Bethlehem to Calvary*. Salt Lake City, UT: Deseret Book, 1981.
—"The Probationary Test of Mortality." Address delivered at the University of Utah Institute, January 10, 1982.
—*The Promised Messiah: The First Coming of Christ*. Salt Lake City, UT: Deseret Book, 1981.
—"The Ten Blessings of the Priesthood," *Ensign*, November 1977.
McConkie, Joseph Fielding and Robert L. Millet. *Doctrinal Commentary on the Book of Mormon*. Salt Lake City, UT: Deseret Book, 1987–1993.
—*Joseph Smith: The Choice Seer*. Salt Lake City, UT: Bookcraft, 1996.
—*Revelations of the Restoration*. Salt Lake City, UT: Deseret Book, 2000.
McKay, David O. *Gospel Ideals: Selections from the Discourses of David O. McKay*. Salt Lake City, UT: Deseret Book, 1993.
———*Pathways to Happiness*. Salt Lake City, UT: Bookcraft, 1957.
McMullin, Keith B. "Come to Zion! Come to Zion!" Salt Lake City, UT: *Ensign*, November 2002.
Merriam Webster's New World Dictionary, Third Edition. New York, NY: Simon and Schuster, 1998
Middlemiss, Clare. *Man May Know for Himself: Teachings of President David O. McKay*. Salt Lake City, UT: Deseret Book, 1967.
Millet, Robert L. "Quest for the City of God: The Doctrine Of Zion In Modern Revelation," *1989 Sperry Symposium on the Doctrine and Covenants*. Salt Lake City, UT: Deseret Book, 1989.
—*The Capstone of Our Religion: Insights into the Doctrine and Covenants*. Salt Lake City, UT: Deseret Book, 1989.
—*The Life Beyond*. Salt Lake City, UT: Deseret Book, 1986.
—*The Power of the Word: Saving Doctrines from the Book of Mormon*. Salt Lake City, UT: Deseret Book, 2000.
Monson, Thomas S. "In Quest of the Abundant Life." *Ensign*, March 1988.
Nelson, Russell M. "Personal Priesthood Responsibility," *Ensign*, October 2005.
—*The Power within Us*. Salt Lake City, UT: Deseret Book, 1989.
Nelson, William O. "Enoch and His Message for Latter Days," *Deseret News*, Feb. 5, 1994.
Neuenschwander, Dennis. "Ordinances and Covenants," *Ensign*, August 2001.
Nibley, Hugh. *Abraham in Egypt*. Salt Lake City, UT and Provo, UT: Deseret Book and FARMS, 2000.
—*An Approach to the Book of Mormon*. Salt Lake City, UT: Deseret Book, 1988.
—*Approaching Zion*. Salt Lake City, UT: Deseret Book, 1989.
—"Educating the Saints—A Brigham Young Mosaic." Provo, UT: *BYU Studies*, Vol. 11, Autumn 1970.
—*Nibley on the Timely and the Timeless*. Provo, UT: Religious Studies Center, Brigham Young University, 2004.
—*Teachings of the Book of Mormon*. Provo, UT: Covenant Communications, 2004.
—*Temple and Cosmos: Beyond This Ignorant Present*. Salt Lake City, UT: Deseret Book, 1992.

Nibley, Preston. *Brigham Young: The Man and His Work*, 4th ed. Salt Lake City, UT: Deseret Book, 1960.

Nielsen, Donna B. *Beloved Bridegroom*. Salt Lake City, UT: Onyx Press, 1999.

Nyman, Monte S. and Charles D. Tate, Jr., eds. *Fourth Nephi through Moroni: From Zion to Destruction*. Salt Lake City, UT: Bookcraft, 1992.

—*The Capstone of Our Religion: Insights into the Doctrine and Covenants*. Salt Lake City, UT: Bookcraft, 1989.

Oaks, Dallin H. "Good, Better, Best," *Ensign*, November 2007.

—"He Heals the Heavy Laden," *Ensign*, November 2006

—"Preparation for the Second Coming," *Ensign*, November 2004.

—"Taking Upon Us the Name of Jesus Christ," *E nsign*, May 1985.

—"The Challenge to Become," *Ensign*, November 2000.

—"Timing," *Ensign*, October 2003.

Oaks, Robert C. "The Power of Patience," *Ensign*, November 2006.

Otten, L. G. and C. M. Caldwell. *Sacred Truths of the Doctrine and Covenants*. Salt Lake City, UT: Deseret Book, 1982–1983.

Pack, Frederick J. "Was the Earth Created in Six Days of Twenty-Four Hours Each?" *Improvement Era*, October 1930.

Packer, Boyd K. "Personal Revelation: The Gift, the Test, and the Promise," *Ensign*, November 1994.

—"Restoration," *First Worldwide Leadership Training Meeting*. Salt Lake City, UT: The Church of Jesus Christ of Latter-day Saints, January 2003.

—*That All May Be Edified*. Salt Lake City, UT: Bookcraft, 1982.

—"The Candle of the Lord," *Ensign*, January 1983.

—"The One Pure Defense (An Evening with President Boyd K. Packer)," Intellectual Reserve, 2004. Address to CES Religious Educators, 6 February 2004, Salt Lake Tabernacle.

Parry, Donald W., ed. *Temples of the Ancient World: Ritual and Symbolism*. Salt Lake City, UT and Provo, UT: Deseret and FARMS, 1994.

—*Understanding the Book of Revelation*. Salt Lake City, UT: Deseret Book, 1998.

Peterson, H. Burke. "Your Special Purpose," *New Era*, October 2001.

Pratt, Orson. *Times and Seasons*, vol. 6. no. 10, 1 June 1845.

Riddle, Chauncey C. "The New and Everlasting Covenant," 1989 *Sperry Symposium on the Doctrine and Covenants*. Salt Lake City: Desert Book, 1989.

Roberts, B.H. *Comprehensive History of the Church of Jesus Christ of Latter-day Saints*. Salt Lake City, UT: Church of Jesus Christ of Latter-day Saints, 1930.

—*Seventy's Course of Theology*. Salt Lake City, UT: Deseret Book, 1931.

Romney, Marion G. "Church Welfare Services' Basic Principles," *Ensign*, May 1976.

—"Church Welfare—Temporal Service in a Spiritual Setting," *Ensign*, May 1980

—"Priesthood," *Ensign*, May 1982.

—"'In Mine Own Way,'" *Ensign*, November 1976.

—"The Celestial Nature of Self-reliance," *Ensign*, November 1982.

—"The Oath and Covenant Which Belongeth to the Priesthood," *Ensign*, November 1980.

—"The Purpose of Church Welfare Services," *Ensign*, May 1977.
—"The Royal Law of Love," *Ensign*, May 1978.
—"Unity," *Ensign*, May 1983.
—"Welfare Services: The Savior's Program," *Ensign*, October 1980.
Salt Lake School of the Prophets Minutes. Salt Lake City, UT: The Church of Jesus Christ of Latter-day Saints, 1899.
"Sermon Given to Different People," *LDS Church News*, Feb. 18, 1995.
Skidmore, Rex A. "What Part Should a Teenager Play in a Family?" *Improvement Era*, 1952.
Skinner, Andrew C. *Temple Worship: 20 Truths That Will Bless Your Life*. Salt Lake City, UT: Deseret Book, 2008.
—*The Old Testament and the Latter-Day Saints*. Salt Lake City, UT: Deseret Book, 2005.
Smith, Hyrum M. and Janne M. Sjodahl. *Doctrine and Covenants Commentary*. Salt Lake City, UT: Deseret Book, 1960.
Smith, Joseph. *Evening and Morning Star*, July, 1833.
—*History of The Church of Jesus Christ of Latter-day Saints*. Salt Lake City, UT: Deseret Book, 1980.
—*Lectures on Faith*. Salt Lake City, UT: Deseret Book, 1993.
Smith, Joseph F. *Gospel Doctrine: Selections from the Sermons and Writings of Joseph F. Smith*. Deseret News Press, 1919.
—*Teachings of Presidents of the Church*. Salt Lake City, UT: The Church of Jesus Christ of Latter-day Saints, 1998.
Smith, Joseph Fielding. *Church History and Modern Revelation*. Salt Lake City, UT: The Church of Jesus Christ of Latter-day Saints, 1946.
—"Our responsibility as Priesthood Holders," *Ensign*, June 1971.
—*Teachings of the Prophet Joseph Smith*. Salt Lake City, UT: Deseret Book, 1938.
—"The Duties of the Priesthood in Temple Work," *The Utah Genealogical and Historical Magazine*, vol. 30, no. 1, January 1939.
—*The Restoration of All Things*. Salt Lake City, UT: Deseret News Press, 1945.
Snow, Lorenzo. *The Teachings of Lorenzo Snow*, Salt Lake City, UT: Bookcraft, 1984.
Sorensen, A. D. "No Respecter of Persons: Equality in the Kingdom." ed. Mary E. Stoval, .*As Women of Faith: Talks Selected from the BYU Women's Conferences*. Salt Lake City, UT: Deseret Book, 1989, 55.
Stevenson, Edward. "Life and History of Elder Edward Stevenson." Provo, UT: Special Collections, Harold B. Lee Library, Brigham Young University, n.d.
Stuy, Brian H., comp., *Collected Discourses*. Burbank, CA: B.H.S. Publishing, 1988.
Summerhays, James T. "The Stripling Elect." *MeridianMagazine.com*, February 20, 2009.
Talmage, James E. *Articles of Faith*. Salt Lake City, UT: Deseret Book, 1984.
—*Jesus the Christ*. Salt Lake City: Deseret News Press, 1915.
—"The Eternity of Sex," *Young Woman's Journal*, October 1914.
—*The House of the Lord*. Salt Lake City, UT: Bookcraft, 1962.
Tanakh: A New Translation of the Holy Scriptures According to the Traditional Hebrew Text. Philadelphia, PA: Jewish Publication Society of America, November 1985.

Tanner, N. Eldon. "Constancy Amid Change," Ensign, November 1979.
Tanner, Susan W. "All Things Shall Work Together for Your Good," *Ensign*, May 2004.
—"My Soul Delighteth in the Things of the Lord," *Ensign*, 2008.
Taylor, John. *Teachings of the Latter-day Prophets*. Salt Lake City, UT: Bookcraft, 1998.
Times and Seasons, vol. 6. no. 10, 1 June 1845.
Thomas, M. Catherine. "Alma the Younger, Part 1," Provo, UT: Neal A. Maxwell Institute for Religious Scholarship, 1996.
—"Alma the Younger, Part 2," Provo, UT: Neal A. Maxwell Institute for Religious Scholarship, 1996.
—"Benjamin and the Mysteries of God," *King Benjamin's Speech*. Provo, UT: Foundation for Ancient Research and Mormon Studies, 1998.
Turner, Rodney. *Woman and the Priesthood*. Salt Lake City, UT: Deseret Book, 1972.
Tvedtnes, John A. *The Church of the Old Testament*. Salt Lake City, UT: Deseret Book, 1967.
—"They Have Their Reward." *MeridianMagazine.com*, February 21, 2007.
Van Orden, Bruce A. and Brent L. Top. *Doctrines of the Book of Mormon: The 1991 Sperry Symposium*, Provo, UT: Maxwell Institute, 1993.
Watt, George D., ed. *Journal of Discourses*. Liverpool, England: F.D. Richards, et al., 1854–1886.
Whitney, Newell K. in *Messenger and Advocate*, 3 September 1837.
Whitney, Orson F. *Gospel Themes*. Salt Lake City, UT: n.p., 1914.
—*Life of Heber C. Kimball*. Salt Lake City, UT: Bookcraft, 1975.
—*Saturday Night Thoughts*. Salt Lake City, UT: Deseret News, 1927.
Wickman, Lance B. "Today," *Ensign*, May 2008.
Widtsoe, John A. *An Understandable Religion*. Salt Lake City, UT: The Church of Jesus Christ of Latter-day Saints, 1944.
—*Priesthood and Church Government*. Salt Lake City, UT: Deseret Book, 1939.
—*Utah Genealogical and Historical Magazine*. Salt Lake City, UT: October 1934.
Williams, Clyde J. *The Teachings of Lorenzo Snow, Fifth President of the Church of Jesus Christ of Latter-day Saints*. Salt Lake City, UT: Bookcraft, 1984.
Wilson, Marvin. *Our Father Abraham*, Grand Rapids, MI: Eerdmans Publishing Co., 1989.
Winder, Barbara W. "Finding Joy in Life," *Ensign*, November 1987.
Wirthlin, Joseph B. "The Great Commandment," *Ensign*, November 2007.
—"The Law of the Fast," *Ensign*, May 2001.
Woodruff, Wilford. *The Discourses of Wilford Woodruff*. Salt Lake City, UT: Bookcraft, 1946.
Yarn, David H. *The Gospel: God, Man, and Truth*. Salt Lake City, UT: Deseret Book, 1965.
Yorgason, Blaine M. *I Need Thee Every Hour*. Salt Lake City, UT: Deseret Book, 2003.
—*Spiritual Progression in the Last Days*. Salt Lake City, UT: Deseret Book, 1994.
Young, Brigham in *Deseret News*, 10 October 1866.
—*Discourses of Brigham Young*. Salt Lake City, UT: Deseret Book, 1926.
—*Journal History*. 28 September 1846.
—*Millennial Star, Vol. 16*. Salt Lake City, UT: The Church of Jesus Christ of Latter-day Saints, 1840–1970.

Index and Concordance

This is a master index of the book series. The page number is specific to the book in which it is located. For example: 101:3 means page 101 in book 3. Marker "P" refers to Portrait of a Zion Person.

Aaronic Priesthood. *See* **Oath and Covenant of the Priesthood;** *See* **Patriarchal Order of the Priesthood;** *See* **Priesthood**
>40:2, 41:2, 12:3, 22:3, 23:3, 36:3, 39:3, 42:3, 59:3, 60:3, 76:3, 92:3, 93:3, 103:3, 104:3, 202:3, 204:3, 50:4, 131:5

abundance
>5:6, 8:6, 10:6, 13:6, 17:6, 18:6, 31:6, 41:6, 44:6, 46:6, 52:6, 70:6, 82:6, 87:6, 96:6, 101:6, 103:6, 106:6, 107:6, 110:6, 111:6, 112:6, 114:6, 115:6

Adam
>empowered to become a savior to his family
>>11:1

adultery. *See also* **immoral**
>Babylon distinguished by
>>50:2

adversary. *See also* **devil;** *See also* **hell;** *See also* **Lucifer;** *See also* **Satan**
>attacks Saints more viciously than others
>>44:1

adversity. *See also* **opposition;** *See also* **trial(s)**
>33:2, 51:2, 54:2, 56:2, 58:2, 61:2, 34:3, 66:3, 117:3, 132:3, 186:3, 178:4, 10:5, 27:5, 30:5, 76:5, 50:6, 101:6

affluence. *See also* **mammon;** *See also* **riches;** *See also* **wealth**
>85:1, 139:4, 103:5, 64:6, 71:6

agency
>a discussion of
>>62–68:4

Amulek
>52:1, 80:1, 51:2, 52:2, 55:3, 42:4, 59:4, 133:4, 180:4, 36:5, 71:5, 56:6, 104:6

angels
>involved in crucible experiences
>>26:5

anger. *See also* **contention**
>19:1, 57:1, 64:1, 75:1, 86:1, 87:1, 93:1, 96:1, 97:1, 98:1, 55:2, 23:3, 152:3, 169:3, 176:3, 5:4, 29:4, 34:4, 101:4, 111:4, 116:4, 121:4, 136:4, 165:4, 179:4, 180:4, 4:5, 15:5, 22:5, 41:5, 46:5, 79:5, 104:5, 107:5, 124:5, 17:6, 28:6, 34:6, 39:6, 60:6, 94:6, 116:6

anti-Christ
>17:P, 21:1, 49:1, 50:1, 51:1, 61:1, 79:1, 84:1, 85:1, 101:1, 54:2, 67:3, 87:4, 127:4, 175:4, 176:4, 33:5, 48:5, 7:6, 47:6, 88:6

apostasy
>27:1, 33:1, 34:1, 60:1, 68:1, 84:4, 108:5

apostle
>59:1, 17:2

Index & Concordance

Atonement
> 6:P, 14:P, 15:P, 24:P, 42:P, 11:1, 12:1, 22:1, 23:1, 42:1, 45:1, 47:1, 66:1, 70:1, 1:2, 3:2, 6:2, 7:2, 9:2, 10:2, 16:2, 17:2, 18:2, 19:2, 20:2, 23:2, 24:2, 25:2, 26:2, 27:2, 28:2, 29:2, 30:2, 31:2, 32:2, 34:2, 35:2, 36:2, 37:2, 38:2, 39:2, 45:2, 55:2, 57:2, 66:2, 67:2, 72:2, 93:2, 98:2, 1:3, 10:3, 17:3, 20:3, 21:3, 35:3, 63:3, 70:3, 73:3, 76:3, 158:3, 180:3, 196:3, 211:3, 214:3, 1:4, 16:4, 18:4, 19:4, 20:4, 31:4, 41:4, 42:4, 56:4, 57:4, 59:4, 64:4, 99:4, 122:4, 162:4, 185:4, 1:5, 4:5, 29:5, 64:5, 84:5, 87:5, 91:5, 106:5, 107:5, 111:5, 113:5, 117:5, 129:5, 133:5, 137:5, 15:6, 42:6, 67:6, 75:6

Babel
> a counterfeit gate of God
>> 54:1
> Nimrod established kingdom in
>> 53:1

Babylon. *See also* world
> a discussion of
>> 49–105:1
> state of mind defined by excess, self-indulgence
>> 54:1

baptism
> 2:P, 18:P, 21:P, 25:P, 11:1, 19:1, 23:1, 9:2, 18:2, 19:2, 21:2, 28:2, 31:2, 33:2, 34:2, 35:2, 36:2, 37:2, 38:2, 40:2, 41:2, 44:2, 45:2, 49:2, 53:2, 60:2, 63:2, 64:2, 67:2, 68:2, 70:2, 73:2, 75:2, 81:2, 82:2, 91:2, 93:2, 98:2, 1:3, 2:3, 4:3, 5:3, 9:3, 10:3, 11:3, 17:3, 21:3, 23:3, 27:3, 39:3, 42:3, 66:3, 70:3, 71:3, 76:3, 80:3, 93:3, 99:3, 117:3, 143:3, 144:3, 153:3, 179:3, 187:3, 193:3, 200:3, 210:3, 214:3, 1:4, 14:4, 26:4, 39:4, 51:4, 52:4, 88:4, 142:4, 144:4, 145:4, 1:5, 17:5, 18:5, 60:5, 61:5, 62:5, 63:5, 82:5, 83:5, 106:5, 117:5, 133:5, 134:5, 135:5, 68:6, 75:6, 76:6, 106:6

Beatitudes. *See also* Sermon on the Mount
believe. *See* faith
> 16:P, 18:P, 28:P, 28:1, 49:3, 41:5, 82:5
> in order to see
>> 68:5

Beloved Son. *See also* Christ; *See also* Exemplar; *See also* Jehovah; *See also* Lamb; *See also* Savior
> 47:1, 65:3, 111:3, 55:5, 56:5, 110:5, 115:5

Bible
> 39:1, 63:1, 83:1, 54:2, 7:3, 138:3, 153:3, 203:3, 8:5

blasphemy
> 59:1, 82:3

bloodline
> men ordained to priesthood regardless of
>> 17:1

Book of Mormon
12:P, 19:P, 21:P, 30:P, 39:P, 42:P, 1:1, 2:1, 5:1, 12:1, 17:1, 31:1, 34:1, 37:1, 61:1, 64:1, 67:1, 70:1, 78:1, 103:1, 18:2, 51:2, 7:3, 17:3, 19:3, 45:3, 46:3, 69:3, 70:3, 92:3, 120:3, 123:3, 132:3, 141:3, 146:3, 153:3, 163:3, 171:3, 180:3, 5:4, 26:4, 40:4, 69:4, 85:4, 97:4, 99:4, 104:4, 108:4, 124:4, 135:4, 138:4, 139:4, 157:4, 161:4, 4:5, 8:5, 11:5, 23:5, 34:5, 59:5, 78:5, 96:5, 103:5, 109:5, 118:5, 127:5, 129:5, 11:6, 15:6, 20:6, 25:6, 44:6, 59:6, 61:6, 63:6, 113:6

Bridegroom. *See also* **Christ, Jesus**
75:1, 85:1, 58:2, 71:2, 72:2, 73:2, 74:2, 75:2, 76:2, 77:2, 78:2, 79:2, 80:2, 81:2, 82:2, 83:2, 84:2, 85:2, 86:2, 87:2, 88:2, 89:2, 90:2, 91:2, 92:2, 93:2, 94:2, 95:2, 96:2, 97:2, 98:2, 111:3, 161:3, 173:3, 183:3, 98:4, 11:6

Brigham Young
14:P, 26:P, 39:P, 41:P, 3:1, 5:1, 6:1, 12:1, 39:1, 40:1, 44:1, 46:1, 90:1, 103:1, 1:2, 61:2, 1:3, 3:3, 19:3, 56:3, 96:3, 101:3, 102:3, 127:3, 128:3, 142:3, 164:3, 192:3, 193:3, 201:3, 214:3, 1:4, 10:4, 30:4, 47:4, 62:4, 75:4, 85:4, 87:4, 89:4, 97:4, 105:4, 106:4, 109:4, 113:4, 125:4, 131:4, 132:4, 133:4, 135:4, 137:4, 140:4, 141:4, 149:4, 150:4, 152:4, 1:5, 4:5, 11:5, 28:5, 41:5, 56:5, 73:5, 81:5, 84:5, 90:5, 91:5, 96:5, 97:5, 99:5, 101:5, 109:5, 127:5, 134:5, 136:5, 137:5, 11:6, 20:6, 21:6, 27:6, 30:6, 31:6, 45:6, 55:6, 56:6, 57:6, 58:6, 59:6, 61:6, 64:6, 65:6, 71:6, 105:6

brother of Jared
13:1, 74:1, 58:2, 184:3, 196:3, 209:3, 210:3, 8:5, 21:5, 29:5, 32:5, 34:5, 41:5, 43:5, 53:5, 58:5, 66:5, 68:5, 69:5, 70:5, 73:5, 86:5, 112:5, 119:5

Bruce R. McConkie
34:P, 36:P, 37:P, 11:1, 45:1, 85:2, 93:2, 2:3, 9:3, 11:3, 14:3, 21:3, 25:3, 33:3, 79:3, 214:3, 2:4, 8:4, 62:4, 68:4, 82:4, 135:4, 2:5, 7:5, 60:5, 64:5, 129:5, 58:6

business. *See* **mammon**

Cain
13:1, 51:1, 52:1, 53:1, 54:1, 61:1, 69:1, 72:1, 74:1, 77:1, 79:1, 90:1, 101:1, 109:3, 82:4, 127:4, 150:4, 175:4, 176:4, 47:6, 88:6

calling and election made sure
    chronology of
        83:3

carnal
20:P, 25:P, 41:P, 19:1, 23:1, 59:1, 62:1, 70:1, 89:1, 94:1, 101:1, 102:1, 8:2, 23:2, 25:2, 29:2, 33:2, 62:2, 23:3, 109:3, 172:3, 178:3, 64:4, 65:4, 100:4, 109:4, 149:4, 14:5, 44:5, 67:5, 93:5, 16:6, 26:6, 76:6

celestial kingdom
14:P, 16:P, 18:P, 22:P, 28:P, 34:P, 48:1, 14:2, 15:2, 16:2, 18:2, 21:2, 27:2, 37:2, 74:2, 2:3, 22:3, 23:3, 28:3, 34:3, 69:3, 71:3, 79:3, 103:3, 115:3, 121:3, 124:3, 125:3, 153:3, 168:3, 182:3, 186:3, 199:3, 2:4, 3:4, 4:4, 6:4, 8:4, 10:4, 15:4, 26:4, 29:4, 30:4, 38:4, 51:4, 52:4, 54:4, 63:4, 68:4, 73:4, 77:4, 79:4, 89:4, 90:4, 91:4, 95:4, 126:4, 132:4, 141:4, 144:4, 148:4, 150:4, 152:4, 185:4, 2:5, 11:5, 31:5, 50:5, 78:5, 120:5, 132:5, 134:5, 135:5, 3:6, 6:6, 9:6, 13:6, 31:6, 46:6, 56:6, 66:6, 68:6, 72:6, 94:6, 105:6, 110:6

Index & Concordance

charity
> a discussion of
>> 165–184:4
> characteristics of
>> 147–173:3

chaste
> 5:2, 22:2, 66:2, 24:5 57:5

Christ, Jesus. *See also* **Beloved Son;** *See also* **Exemplar;** *See also* **Jehovah;** *See also* **Lamb;** *See also* **Savior**
> a discussion of
>> as Bridegroom
>>> 72–98:2
>> coming into his presence
>>> 77:2
>> taking name of, upon us
>>> 59:2
> frees us from the powers of Babylon
>> 26:1

city of Enoch
> 14:1, 16:1, 36:1, 5:3, 19:3, 23:5, 34:5, 72:5, 2:6

comforter. *See also* **Holy Ghost**
> 37:2, 86:2, 71:3

commerce. *See also* **mammon**
> 76:1, 79:1

compete, competition
> 79:1, 88:1, 119:3, 132:3

consecrate, consecration
> a discussion of
>> blessings of living
>>> 33–50:4
>> characteristics of the law of
>>> 3–31:4
>> guiding principles of
>>> 62–91:4
> living law of, brings blessings of abundance
>> 18:1
> to set apart
>> 160:4

contention. *See also* **anger**
> 6:P, 12:P, 43:P, 19:1, 21:1, 24:1, 29:1, 64:1, 67:1, 79:1, 85:1, 88:1, 102:1, 8:3, 119:3, 128:3, 42:4, 48:4, 179:4, 180:4, 4:5, 43:5, 102:5, 103:5, 104:5, 107:5 108:5, 2:6, 117:6

cooperate
>25:P, 6:2, 9:2, 100:5

corn
>kernel of, represents potential of grace freely given
>>55:3

coronation
>1:2, 9:2, 98:2, 29:3, 30:3, 36:3, 184:3, 194:3, 195:3, 65:5, 73:5, 135:5

counterfeit
>Satan always has, to God's works
>>61:1

covet
>36:P, 24:1, 70:1, 69:4, 86:4, 100:4, 102:4, 148:4, 16:6, 17:6, 18:6, 115:6

Creator. See **Christ, Jesus**

crown. See coronation

crucibles
>angels involved in
>>26:5
>
>many, last fourteen years
>>25:5

deceive. See deception

deception
>victims of, will not be condemned
>>22:1

Deity. See **God**

deliverance
>20:P, 18:1, 25:1, 72:1, 8:2, 22:2, 35:2, 51:2, 52:2, 26:3, 121:3, 128:3, 140:3, 148:3, 44:4, 84:4, 125:4, 131:4, 161:4, 162:4, 163:4, 174:4, 178:4, 180:4, 185:4, 3:5, 16:5, 17:5, 19:5, 23:5, 26:5, 27:5, 29:5, 36:5, 38:5, 39:5, 40:5, 45:5, 48:5, 49:5, 50:5, 51:5, 52:5, 55:5, 57:5, 68:5, 69:5, 70:5, 71:5, 72:5, 73:5, 75:5, 76:5, 78:5, 45:6, 52:6, 101:6

descend
>we must, below all things to ascend above all
>>39:1

devil. See also **adversary**; See also **hell**; See also **Lucifer**; See also **Satan**
>6:P, 35:P, 41:P, 21:1, 24:1, 44:1, 51:1, 52:1, 60:1, 61:1, 62:1, 63:1, 64:1, 68:1, 70:1, 72:1, 73:1, 84:1, 86:1, 90:1, 92:1, 100:1, 101:1, 102:1, 28:2, 32:2, 49:2, 89:2, 98:2, 97:3, 109:3, 131:3, 160:3, 163:3, 172:3, 188:3, 189:3, 19:4, 45:4, 63:4, 64:4, 65:4, 67:4, 70:4, 109:4, 113:4, 120:4, 138:4, 141:4, 149:4, 151:4, 152:4, 14:5, 18:5, 47:5, 55:5, 101:5, 104:5, 107:5, 120:5, 26:6, 27:6, 30:6, 38:6, 63:6, 65:6, 71:6, 117:6

disputations
>6:P, 17:P, 26:P, 30:1, 49:1, 57:1, 19:3, 42:4, 119:4, 107:5, 108:5, 109:5, 122:5, 2:6, 37:6, 117:6

Index & Concordance   121

elect
> 57:1, 63:1, 85:1, 101:1, 103:1, 43:2, 48:2, 92:2, 40:3, 63:3, 79:3, 80:3, 81:3, 82:3, 84:3, 85:3, 87:3, 105:3, 114:3, 140:3, 154:3, 203:3, 73:5, 74:5, 90:5, 96:5, 7:6

Elijah
> 23:P, 35:P, 31:1, 81:2, 12:3, 13:3, 14:3, 15:3, 16:3, 17:3, 65:3, 116:3, 121:3, 66:4, 130:4, 8:5, 51:5, 70:5, 92:5, 52:6

Eliza R. Snow
> 34:1

endow, endowment
> Abraham administered, regardless of bloodline
>> 17:1

Enoch
> 3:P, 12:P, 15:P, 33:P, 37:P, 39:P, 3:1, 4:1, 6:1, 7:1, 13:1, 14:1, 15:1, 16:1, 18:1, 32:1, 33:1, 36:1, 37:1, 55:1, 58:1, 74:1, 87:1, 88:1, 103:1, 11:2, 12:2, 5:3, 7:3, 9:3, 18:3, 19:3, 20:3, 24:3, 25:3, 27:3, 30:3, 46:3, 57:3, 72:3, 73:3, 89:3, 93:3, 116:3, 184:3, 198:3, 204:3, 207:3, 208:3, 209:3, 10:4, 11:4, 82:4, 86:4, 157:4, 23:5, 34:5, 37:5, 69:5, 72:5, 86:5, 89:5, 90:5, 94:5, 96:5, 100:5, 101:5, 112:5, 124:5, 125:5, 127:5, 132:5, 1:6, 2:6

equal
> 6:P, 7:P, 12:P, 33:P, 27:1, 41:1, 57:1, 65:1, 87:1, 13:2, 64:2, 4:3, 18:3, 40:3, 41:3, 50:3, 60:3, 90:3, 105:3, 106:3, 119:3, 132:3, 200:3, 9:4, 24:4, 26:4, 27:4, 30:4, 36:4, 37:4, 38:4, 39:4, 49:4, 58:4, 59:4, 61:4, 73:4, 74:4, 77:4, 90:4, 96:4, 125:4, 156:4, 183:4, 185:4, 4:5, 122:5, 123:5, 3:6, 10:6, 45:6, 53:6, 77:6, 107:6, 116:6

exalt
> 25:P, 1:2, 9:2, 32:2, 33:2, 45:2, 54:2, 57:2, 61:2, 28:3, 59:3, 132:3, 134:3, 142:3, 146:3, 4:4, 37:4, 52:4, 56:4, 109:4, 184:4, 93:5, 26:6, 76:6, 78:6, 108:6, 116:6

Exemplar. *See also* **Christ, Jesus;** *See also* **Jehovah;** *See also* **Lamb;** *See also* **Savior**
> 39:1, 65:3

Ezra Taft Benson
> 34:P, 8:1, 24:1, 41:1, 61:1, 67:1, 26:3, 109:3, 116:3, 205:3, 6:4, 15:4, 25:4, 26:4, 27:4, 28:4, 48:4, 59:4, 1:6, 80:6, 105:6

face-to-face
> coming, with God is ultimate blessing and right of Zion people
>> 97:3

family, families
> 3:P, 4:P, 23:P, 27:P, 29:P, 31:P, 32:P, 33:P, 34:P, 36:P, 37:P, 38:P, 42:P, 43:P, 6:1, 11:1, 12:1, 13:1, 14:1, 17:1, 18:1, 24:1, 26:1, 40:1, 42:1, 43:1, 45:1, 47:1, 54:1, 89:1, 93:1, 5:2, 23:2, 29:2, 32:2, 36:2, 37:2, 41:2, 50:2, 51:2, 52:2, 53:2, 62:2, 64:2, 68:2, 80:2, 83:2, 92:2, 5:3, 8:3, 12:3, 13:3, 14:3, 15:3, 16:3, 17:3, 20:3, 25:3, 26:3, 27:3, 28:3, 31:3, 32:3, 34:3, 65:3, 69:3, 70:3, 76:3, 78:3, 92:3, 100:3, 111:3, 113:3, 120:3, 136:3, 139:3, 146:3, 170:3, 178:3, 185:3, 186:3, 199:3, 200:3, 201:3, 204:3, 206:3, 207:3, 212:3, 4:4, 6:4, 8:4, 9:4, 23:4, 26:4, 27:4, 29:4, 30:4, 39:4, 41:4, 69:4, 72:4, 73:4,

74:4, 79:4, 82:4, 84:4, 86:4, 87:4, 133:4, 134:4, 141:4, 151:4, 157:4, 170:4, 171:4, 179:4, 180:4, 4:5, 21:5, 24:5, 42:5, 50:5, 51:5, 52:5, 62:5, 66:5, 71:5, 94:5, 95:5, 104:5, 107:5, 127:5, 133:5, 134:5, 5:6, 57:6, 65:6, 78:6, 87:6, 98:6, 102:6, 103:6, 104:6, 111:6, 112:6, 113:6, 114:6, 115:6

fathers

6:P, 18:1, 28:1, 35:1, 45:1, 63:1, 81:1, 91:1, 98:1, 32:2, 75:2, 13:3, 15:3, 17:3, 23:3, 27:3, 65:3, 77:3, 91:3, 104:3, 160:3, 161:3, 207:3, 118:4, 124:4, 128:4, 137:4, 141:4, 152:4, 67:5, 109:5, 124:5, 128:5, 136:5, 4:6, 37:6, 43:6, 48:6, 60:6, 66:6

fear

11:P, 26:P, 29:P, 42:P, 43:P, 23:1, 35:1, 37:1, 40:1, 53:1, 56:1, 64:1, 84:1, 85:1, 93:1, 94:1, 97:1, 59:2, 86:2, 39:3, 128:3, 130:3, 142:3, 149:3, 158:3, 169:3, 186:3, 196:3, 4:4, 22:4, 116:4, 141:4, 171:4, 172:4, 177:4, 27:5, 37:5, 57:5, 101:5, 133:5, 1:6, 35:6, 66:6, 90:6, 97:6, 98:6, 112:6

flatter

73:1, 96:1

forgive

10:P, 39:2, 40:2, 116:4, 178:4, 183:4, 35:6, 101:6

fornication

56:1, 57:1, 58:1, 59:1, 76:1, 80:1, 93:1, 50:2, 22:5

fourteen years

many crucibles last
25:5

fruit

ripe, falls from tree of life to rot on ground
96:1

fundamentalism

definition of
83:1

Gadianton robbers. *See also* **secret combinations**

97:1

Garden of Eden

13:1, 77:1, 108:4, 8:5, 28:5, 36:5, 72:5, 25:6

gathering

always associated with Zion
20:1

generosity. *See* **selflessness**

give yourself rich. *See* **abundance**

8:P, 176:4, 89:6

God-like, godliness

become, by learning how to lift others
5:1

Index & Concordance

gold
    28:P, 38:P, 42:P, 27:1, 50:1, 52:1, 58:1, 59:1, 62:1, 76:1, 96:1, 22:2, 80:2, 94:2, 129:3, 151:3, 9:4, 40:4, 44:4, 82:4, 101:4, 103:4, 106:4, 109:4, 116:4, 118:4, 124:4, 132:4, 139:4, 140:4, 145:4, 146:4, 3:5, 21:5, 23:5, 24:5, 25:5, 26:5, 17:6, 19:6, 22:6, 27:6, 35:6, 36:6, 44:6, 55:6, 64:6, 65:6, 68:6, 69:6, 70:6

good
    definition of
        9:1

goods. *See* **mammon**

Gordon B. Hinckley
    6:P, 7:1, 28:2, 55:3, 172:3, 211:3, 37:4, 40:4, 41:4, 56:4, 59:4, 60:4, 164:4, 170:4, 87:5, 78:6, 83:6, 93:6

grace. *See also* **mercy**
    15:P, 19:P, 22:P, 4:1, 6:1, 10:1, 11:1, 28:1, 42:1, 4:2, 17:2, 18:2, 19:2, 20:2, 22:2, 23:2, 26:2, 29:2, 36:2, 38:2, 43:2, 45:2, 78:2, 16:3, 21:3, 24:3, 52:3, 53:3, 54:3, 55:3, 60:3, 64:3, 86:3, 104:3, 153:3, 198:3, 200:3, 57:4, 66:4, 79:4, 89:4, 92:4, 139:4, 146:4, 174:4, 175:4, 177:4, 181:4, 184:4, 7:5, 20:5, 31:5, 32:5, 45:5, 90:5, 124:5, 64:6, 70:6, 75:6, 80:6, 81:6, 82:6, 83:6, 89:6, 90:6, 100:6, 101:6

Harold B. Lee
    16:P, 28:P, 28:1, 82:1, 49:3, 130:3, 131:3, 204:3, 82:5, 147:5

heal
    21:P, 1:1, 2:1, 46:1, 135:3, 142:3, 152:3, 165:3, 171:3, 73:4, 77:4, 142:4, 144:4, 159:4, 160:4, 161:4, 184:4, 15:5, 113:5, 68:6, 86:6

healing
    we prepare for Zion by experiencing
        160:4

health
    23:P, 9:1, 76:1, 90:1, 100:1, 24:2, 29:2, 123:3, 18:4, 161:4, 180:4, 185:4, 15:5, 24:5, 25:5, 37:5, 57:5, 71:5, 72:5, 1:6, 86:6, 103:6, 109:6

heart
    a discussion of
        pure in
            77–108:5
    is altar of soul
        49:5
    must be changed to attain Zion
        12:1

Heber C. Kimball
    , 83:3, 100:3, 101:3, 148:5

heir
    11:1, 53:1, 101:1, 29:3, 76:3, 195:3, 45:5

hell. *See also* **adversary**; *See also* **devil**; *See also* **Lucifer**; *See also* **Satan**
>   18:P, 41:P, 47:1, 63:1, 68:1, 70:1, 72:1, 73:1, 74:1, 101:1, 102:1, 26:2, 97:3, 109:3, 128:3, 131:3, 154:3, 160:3, 163:3, 188:3, 75:4, 109:4, 112:4, 113:4, 120:4, 126:4, 141:4, 149:4, 13:5, 14:5, 47:5, 56:5, 97:5, 5:6, 26:6, 29:6, 30:6, 39:6, 46:6, 65:6

Holy Ghost. *See also* **comforter**
>   presence of, signifies we are retaining remission of sins
>>   38:2

homosexuality
>   56:1

Hugh Nibley
>   5:P, 26:P, 33:P, 5:1, 7:1, 8:1, 33:1, 34:1, 50:1, 51:1, 56:1, 57:1, 70:1, 71:1, 75:1, 77:1, 79:1, 80:1, 89:1, 92:1, 93:1, 47:3, 109:3, 110:3, 137:3, 6:4, 7:4, 16:4, 28:4, 50:4, 56:4, 85:4, 87:4, 93:4, 94:4, 98:4, 99:4, 105:4, 108:4, 110:4, 113:4, 127:4, 132:4, 136:4, 138:4, 150:4, 21:5, 22:5, 96:5, 7:6, 8:6, 12:6, 15:6, 21:6, 25:6, 27:6, 30:6, 47:6, 56:6, 59:6, 61:6, 105:6, 116:6

hundredfold
>   8:P, 25:2, 27:2, 29:2, 123:3, 126:3, 127:3, 141:3, 151:3, 36:4, 58:4, 67:4, 92:4, 145:4, 153:4, 170:4, 177:4, 184:4, 70:5, 118:5, 3:6, 6:6, 69:6, 70:6, 72:6, 87:6, 89:6, 106:6, 107:6, 108:6, 109:6, 110:6

husband. *See also* **marriage**
>   24:2, 66:2, 75:2, 76:2, 77:2, 78:2, 79:2, 80:2, 81:2, 83:2, 84:2, 85:2, 89:2, 90:2, 94:2, 97:2, 13:3, 15:3, 17:3, 23:3, 59:3, 64:3, 85:3, 110:3, 136:3, 179:3, 183:3, 198:3, 211:3, 41:4, 43:4, 98:4, 155:4, 156:4, 157:4, 42:5, 117:5, 11:6

hypocrisy
>   80:1, 41:2, 44:3, 47:3, 108:3, 110:3, 119:3, 159:3, 160:3, 165:3, 167:3, 140:4, 64:6

idleness
>   38:P, 27:1, 56:1, 119:3, 129:3, 20:4, 39:4, 83:4, 84:4, 85:4, 86:4, 101:4, 121:4, 157:4, 18:6, 41:6, 50:6

idolatrous
>   54:1, 88:1, 54:2, 171:3, 109:4, 117:4, 27:6, 35:6

immoral. *See also* **adultery**
>   58:1, 69:1, 76:1, 87:1, 171:3, 172:3, 176:4, 88:6

inequality
>   7:P, 86:1, 114:3, 124:3, 132:3, 139:3, 19:4, 29:4, 36:4, 39:4, 73:4, 85:4, 119:4, 124:4, 125:4, 150:4, 103:5, 38:6, 44:6, 45:6, 78:6

inherit, inheritance
>   a discussion of the chosen few
>>   63–105:3

Israel
>   26:P, 18:1, 29:1, 32:1, 36:1, 42:1, 43:1, 45:1, 46:1, 65:1, 100:1, 14:2, 72:2, 81:2, 90:2, 91:2, 94:2, 14:3, 23:3, 31:3, 70:3, 76:3, 77:3, 111:3, 176:3, 180:3, 196:3, 18:4, 73:4, 100:4, 101:4, 104:4, 106:4, 126:4, 130:4, 131:4, 135:4, 150:4, 160:4, 35:5, 36:5, 41:5, 79:5, 110:5, 111:5, 112:5, 113:5, 114:5, 132:5, 4:6, 16:6, 17:6, 20:6, 21:6, 22:6, 46:6, 52:6, 58:6

Index & Concordance

James E. Faust
    8:P, 83:1, 93:3, 117:3, 43:4, 156:4, 162:4, 45:5, 91:5, 142:5

Jehovah. *See also* **Christ, Jesus;** *See also* **Exemplar;** *See also* **Lamb;** *See also* **Savior**
    18:1, 30:3, 66:4, 98:4, 100:4, 88:5, 98:5, 12:6, 16:6

Jerusalem. *See also* **Salem**
    14:P, 2:1, 9:1, 15:1, 16:1, 33:1, 36:1, 37:1, 47:1, 53:1, 55:1, 61:1, 75:1, 78:1, 104:1, 1:2, 3:2, 51:2, 97:2, 1:3, 9:3, 18:3, 49:3, 100:3, 202:3, 1:4, 41:4, 1:5, 8:5, 20:5, 23:5, 63:5, 73:5, 87:5, 96:5, 97:5, 98:5, 113:5, 117:5, 118:5, 127:5, 128:5, 131:5, 134:5, 1:6

John A. Widtsoe
    8:1, 45:1, 61:1, 72:2, 164:4, 67:5, 93:6

Joseph Fielding Smith
    14:1, 81:1, 15:3, 21:3, 41:3, 56:3, 78:3, 102:3, 103:3, 190:3, 194:3, 208:3, 3:6

Joseph Smith
    4:P, 12:P, 18:P, 33:P, 39:P, 40:P, 41:P, 3:1, 5:1, 15:1, 26:1, 31:1, 32:1, 41:1, 44:1, 46:1, 48:1, 65:1, 67:1, 72:1, 90:1, 94:1, 103:1, 1:2, 3:2, 4:2, 6:2, 10:2, 15:2, 22:2, 23:2, 25:2, 26:2, 27:2, 28:2, 31:2, 42:2, 44:2, 45:2, 50:2, 58:2, 61:2, 62:2, 63:2, 87:2, 88:2, 90:2, 1:3, 5:3, 6:3, 7:3, 12:3, 13:3, 14:3, 15:3, 16:3, 17:3, 18:3, 20:3, 22:3, 25:3, 30:3, 31:3, 36:3, 43:3, 44:3, 57:3, 68:3, 69:3, 77:3, 81:3, 82:3, 83:3, 85:3, 86:3, 87:3, 88:3, 91:3, 93:3, 97:3, 98:3, 99:3, 100:3, 101:3, 104:3, 116:3, 120:3, 122:3, 125:3, 126:3, 140:3, 141:3, 160:3, 166:3, 177:3, 181:3, 182:3, 184:3, 188:3, 190:3, 191:3, 192:3, 193:3, 195:3, 196:3, 198:3, 200:3, 202:3, 203:3, 207:3, 208:3, 1:4, 4:4, 7:4, 10:4, 11:4, 12:4, 13:4, 28:4, 29:4, 30:4, 38:4, 39:4, 44:4, 45:4, 46:4, 48:4, 57:4, 61:4, 65:4, 76:4, 77:4, 78:4, 100:4, 104:4, 107:4, 114:4, 133:4, 137:4, 142:4, 148:4, 157:4, 169:4, 171:4, 1:5, 4:5, 5:5, 8:5, 9:5, 14:5, 20:5, 24:5, 25:5, 27:5, 30:5, 31:5, 33:5, 34:5, 42:5, 45:5, 47:5, 54:5, 55:5, 56:5, 58:5, 64:5, 66:5, 68:5, 77:5, 81:5, 86:5, 88:5, 89:5, 93:5, 94:5, 95:5, 96:5, 97:5, 98:5, 99:5, 100:5, 108:5, 112:5, 118:5, 119:5, 123:5, 124:5, 126:5, 127:5, 129:5, 136:5, 1:6, 3:6, 5:6, 6:6, 16:6, 20:6, 22:6, 25:6, 31:6, 51:6, 56:6, 57:6, 60:6, 87:6, 98:6, 105:6, 106:6, 113:6, 116:6

journey
    a discussion of
        life's journey
            7–57:5

J. Reuben Clark
    44:1, 79:3, 21:4, 28:4

justice, justification
    discussion of
        6–17:2
    rewards those who are obedient to God's laws
        17:2

justified. *See* **justice, justification**

key(s)
    8:P, 23:P, 26:P, 2:1, 13:1, 18:1, 87:1, 101:1, 104:1, 28:2, 61:2, 22:3, 23:3, 24:3, 43:3, 44:3, 57:3, 60:3, 76:3, 83:3, 94:3, 95:3, 97:3, 98:3, 121:3, 122:3, 136:3, 141:3, 156:3,

157:3, 164:3, 176:3, 179:3, 181:3, 184:3, 190:3, 191:3, 192:3, 198:3, 9:4, 62:4, 66:4, 89:4, 106:4, 146:4, 153:4, 159:4, 164:4, 182:4, 26:5, 46:5, 47:5, 54:5, 64:5, 66:5, 87:5, 88:5, 108:5, 134:5, 22:6, 70:6, 94:6, 106:6, 108:6

King Benjamin
20:P, 19:1, 20:1, 21:1, 22:1, 23:1, 24:1, 25:1, 26:1, 8:2, 66:2, 7:3, 8:3, 9:3, 10:3, 11:3, 20:3, 51:3, 67:3, 152:3, 9:4, 35:4, 39:4, 78:4, 120:4, 121:4, 126:4, 127:4, 170:4, 36:5, 42:5, 59:5, 62:5, 63:5, 64:5, 66:5, 106:5, 108:5, 39:6, 46:6, 48:6, 76:6, 79:6, 106:6

king(s)
15:1, 16:1, 20:1, 21:1, 23:1, 25:1, 49:1, 85:2, 90:2, 92:2, 94:2, 95:2, 5:3, 7:3, 9:3, 10:3, 11:3, 29:3, 45:3, 111:3, 112:3, 113:3, 119:3, 139:3, 152:3, 198:3, 199:3, 20:4, 39:4, 76:4, 100:4, 108:4, 134:4, 8:5, 9:5, 39:5, 51:5, 54:5, 58:5, 60:5, 62:5, 63:5, 89:5, 1:6, 2:6, 16:6, 26:6, 46:6, 58:6

Korihor
50:1, 79:1, 127:4, 175:4, 47:6, 88:6

labor. *See also* **work**
35:P, 37:P, 38:P, 42:P, 20:1, 24:1, 27:1, 30:1, 42:1, 84:1, 39:2, 7:3, 19:3, 55:3, 146:3, 171:3, 17:4, 19:4, 39:4, 58:4, 62:4, 70:4, 71:4, 80:4, 82:4, 83:4, 84:4, 85:4, 86:4, 87:4, 88:4, 89:4, 90:4, 91:4, 92:4, 127:4, 135:4, 136:4, 140:4, 141:4, 151:4, 152:4, 156:4, 174:4, 176:4, 183:4, 185:4, 4:5, 26:5, 32:5, 33:5, 50:5, 92:5, 93:5, 95:5, 122:5, 137:5, 48:6, 59:6, 60:6, 65:6, 66:6, 71:6, 72:6, 100:6

lack. *See* **poor**

Laman
101:1, 20:5, 27:5

Lamb. *See also* **Christ, Jesus;** *See also* **Exemplar;** *See also* **Jehovah;** *See also* **Savior**
18:1, 172:4, 98:6

lawyers
86:1, 90:1, 119:4, 103:5, 37:6

Lehi
17:P, 27:P, 63:1, 64:1, 74:1, 94:1, 52:2, 58:2, 78:2, 195:3, 21:4, 42:4, 59:4, 3:5, 8:5, 9:5, 10:5, 17:5, 19:5, 21:5, 23:5, 26:5, 28:5, 31:5, 34:5, 41:5, 42:5, 51:5, 52:5, 58:5, 67:5, 73:5

lies
30:P, 9:1, 18:1, 22:1, 51:1, 63:1, 72:1, 19:2, 97:2, 9:3, 55:3, 60:3, 95:3, 97:3, 117:3, 139:3, 160:3, 181:3, 13:4, 41:4, 47:4, 65:4, 74:4, 137:4, 142:4, 156:4, 166:4, 7:5, 9:5, 19:5, 26:5, 87:5, 2:6, 60:6, 67:6, 101:6, 112:6

Lorenzo Snow
78:1, 6:4, 15:4, 17:4, 31:4, 47:4, 4:5, 94:5, 95:5, 100:5, 131:5, 136:5, 148:5

love. *See also* **charity;** *See also* **heart**
2:P, 7:P, 9:P, 10:P, 11:P, 12:P, 17:P, 20:P, 21:P, 22:P, 24:P, 27:P, 28:P, 34:P, 39:P, 43:P, 19:1, 22:1, 23:1, 24:1, 26:1, 29:1, 30:1, 33:1, 34:1, 42:1, 49:1, 64:1, 65:1, 70:1, 71:1, 76:1, 77:1, 79:1, 86:1, 87:1, 89:1, 91:1, 99:1, 3:2, 4:2, 5:2, 18:2, 19:2, 27:2, 38:2, 41:2, 44:2, 50:2, 54:2, 56:2, 57:2, 60:2, 61:2, 62:2, 66:2, 67:2, 69:2, 70:2,

Index & Concordance

72:2, 73:2, 74:2, 75:2, 76:2, 77:2, 78:2, 79:2, 80:2, 81:2, 82:2, 84:2, 86:2, 93:2, 95:2, 96:2, 97:2, 98:2, 99:2, 17:3, 30:3, 33:3, 44:3, 47:3, 48:3, 49:3, 50:3, 51:3, 52:3, 56:3, 57:3, 61:3, 68:3, 74:3, 75:3, 85:3, 86:3, 87:3, 90:3, 91:3, 92:3, 93:3, 95:3, 104:3, 108:3, 109:3, 111:3, 113:3, 114:3, 117:3, 118:3, 119:3, 122:3, 124:3, 125:3, 131:3, 132:3, 134:3, 138:3, 139:3, 140:3, 141:3, 142:3, 146:3, 147:3, 148:3, 153:3, 154:3, 155:3, 156:3, 157:3, 158:3, 159:3, 168:3, 169:3, 170:3, 171:3, 173:3, 178:3, 182:3, 185:3, 189:3, 203:3, 2:4, 19:4, 21:4, 23:4, 25:4, 26:4, 27:4, 33:4, 34:4, 35:4, 37:4, 38:4, 41:4, 42:4, 47:4, 50:4, 51:4, 52:4, 54:4, 55:4, 56:4, 57:4, 58:4, 60:4, 64:4, 70:4, 72:4, 73:4, 90:4, 91:4, 93:4, 95:4, 97:4, 98:4, 99:4, 100:4, 102:4, 107:4, 114:4, 116:4, 120:4, 121:4, 123:4, 138:4, 141:4, 142:4, 143:4, 146:4, 147:4, 148:4, 149:4, 152:4, 153:4, 155:4, 156:4, 157:4, 158:4, 163:4, 164:4, 165:4, 166:4, 167:4, 168:4, 169:4, 170:4, 171:4, 172:4, 173:4, 174:4, 175:4, 178:4, 179:4, 181:4, 182:4, 183:4, 184:4, 185:4, 186:4, 2:5, 16:5, 24:5, 30:5, 33:5, 42:5, 43:5, 52:5, 64:5, 66:5, 67:5, 69:5, 70:5, 71:5, 74:5, 77:5, 78:5, 79:5, 81:5, 85:5, 89:5, 92:5, 100:5, 106:5, 107:5, 108:5, 122:5, 124:5, 127:5, 133:5, 135:5, 137:5, 2:6, 5:6, 7:6, 8:6, 9:6, 11:6, 13:6, 15:6, 16:6, 18:6, 23:6, 31:6, 35:6, 38:6, 39:6, 43:6, 61:6, 66:6, 67:6, 70:6, 78:6, 79:6, 80:6, 85:6, 86:6, 87:6, 88:6, 91:6, 93:6, 94:6, 95:6, 96:6, 97:6, 98:6, 99:6, 100:6, 101:6, 102:6, 106:6, 107:6, 108:6, 113:6, 116:6, 117:6

low

    to make, is not demeaning

        34:4

Lucifer. *See also* **adversary**; *See also* **devil**; *See also* **hell**; *See also* **Satan**

    10:1

lukewarm

    being, is a one-way ticket to hell

        47:1

Mahan

    51:1, 52:1, 69:1, 79:1, 127:4, 151:4, 47:6

mammon. *See also* **materialism**; *See also* **money**; *See also* **riches**

    a discussion of

        choosing, over God

            99–137:4

    making friends with

        109:4

mansions

    37:P, 76:1, 73:2, 82:2, 86:2, 89:2, 93:2, 168:3, 203:3, 81:4, 175:4, 50:5, 100:6

marriage. *See also* **new and everlasting covenant**

    a discussion of

        how it's likened to new and everlasting covenant

            72–99:2

martyrdom

    34:1, 58:2

materialism. *See also* **mammon**
    25:P, 41:P, 62:1, 64:1, 68:1, 102:1, 109:4, 93:5, 26:6, 76:6

Matthew Cowley
    3:P, 4:P, 6:1, 46:1, 105:6

Melchizedek
    administered priesthood to Abraham/built temple in Salem
        16:1

Melchizedek Priesthood. *See also* **Aaronic Priesthood**; *See also* **oath and covenant of the priesthood**; *See also* **patriarchal order of the priesthood**; *See also* **priesthood**
    a discussion of
        4–209:3

merchandise. *See* **mammon**; *See* **money**

mercy. *See also* **grace**
    10:P, 17:P, 20:P, 21:P, 22:P, 23:P, 24:P, 23:1, 26:1, 30:1, 66:1, 100:1, 4:2, 6:2, 7:2, 8:2, 9:2, 10:2, 15:2, 16:2, 17:2, 18:2, 20:2, 23:2, 24:2, 26:2, 27:2, 28:2, 29:2, 30:2, 32:2, 34:2, 35:2, 36:2, 45:2, 57:2, 97:2, 54:3, 71:3, 156:3, 159:3, 165:3, 167:3, 98:4, 112:4, 122:4, 129:4, 130:4, 143:4, 148:4, 151:4, 179:4, 15:5, 16:5, 19:5, 44:5, 64:5, 77:5, 106:5, 113:5, 114:5, 124:5, 12:6, 29:6, 41:6, 49:6, 51:6, 82:6, 102:6

miracle
    17:P, 25:1, 30:1, 66:1, 64:2, 155:3, 9:4, 36:4, 51:4, 57:4, 60:4, 67:4, 70:4, 159:4, 160:4, 162:4, 163:4, 173:4, 25:5, 32:5, 39:5, 66:5, 101:5, 109:5, 99:6

miserable
    49:1, 50:1, 51:1, 60:1, 77:1, 78:1, 8:2, 16:2, 89:2, 132:3, 63:4, 13:5, 14:5, 16:5, 56:5, 30:6

money. *See also* **mammon**; *See also* **materialism**; *See also* **riches**
    love of, is root of all evil
        70:1

Moroni
    1:1, 31:1, 61:1, 90:1, 91:1, 92:1, 103:1, 12:3, 65:3, 68:3, 92:3, 166:3, 195:3, 209:3, 210:3, 5:4, 6:4, 107:4, 123:4, 124:4, 149:4, 165:4, 166:4, 174:4, 175:4, 178:4, 181:4, 182:4, 183:4, 31:5, 44:5, 53:5, 55:5, 70:5, 77:5, 109:5, 112:5, 118:5, 119:5, 22:6, 23:6, 43:6, 86:6, 100:6

mortality
    is testing ground for our genuine desires
        47:1

Moses
    4:P, 26:P, 18:1, 19:1, 28:1, 32:1, 34:1, 51:1, 74:1, 87:1, 88:1, 8:2, 22:2, 40:2, 81:2, 84:2, 14:3, 15:3, 16:3, 17:3, 18:3, 20:3, 23:3, 24:3, 40:3, 55:3, 63:3, 65:3, 66:3, 76:3, 77:3, 88:3, 89:3, 99:3, 104:3, 110:3, 175:3, 176:3, 177:3, 184:3, 195:3, 207:3, 208:3, 47:4, 50:4, 100:4, 101:4, 112:4, 118:4, 120:4, 126:4, 129:4, 151:4, 165:4, 166:4, 8:5, 9:5, 18:5, 23:5, 31:5, 32:5, 35:5, 41:5, 42:5, 54:5, 55:5, 67:5, 72:5, 74:5, 79:5, 86:5, 89:5, 112:5, 131:5, 16:6, 17:6, 29:6, 36:6, 38:6, 46:6, 49:6, 50:6, 94:6, 95:6

Index & Concordance

mother
    46:1, 61:1, 62:1, 25:2, 51:2, 85:2, 59:3, 126:3, 158:3, 28:4, 110:4, 172:4, 21:5, 129:5, 27:6, 52:6, 98:6, 106:6, 109:6

murder
    50:1, 53:1, 60:1, 62:1, 63:1, 69:1, 80:1, 90:1, 102:1, 96:2, 119:3, 146:3, 160:3, 53:4, 118:4, 137:4, 14:5, 108:5, 36:6, 60:6

murmur
    22:2, 26:5

mysteries
    26:P, 32:P, 39:P, 40:P, 18:1, 61:1, 44:2, 8:3, 10:3, 24:3, 30:3, 31:3, 43:3, 47:3, 49:3, 57:3, 72:3, 81:3, 87:3, 93:3, 95:3, 96:3, 97:3, 98:3, 176:3, 177:3, 181:3, 183:3, 187:3, 188:3, 189:3, 190:3, 191:3, 192:3, 46:4, 100:4, 108:4, 149:4, 59:5, 60:5, 65:5, 79:5, 85:5, 86:5, 87:5, 88:5, 116:5, 119:5, 16:6, 25:6, 115:6

natural man
    25:P, 22:1, 78:1, 20:2, 21:2, 50:2, 178:3, 64:4, 95:4, 169:4, 182:4, 23:5, 25:5, 42:5, 43:5, 44:5, 45:5, 68:5, 76:5, 84:5, 91:5, 9:6, 86:6

Neal A. Maxwell
    12:1, 40:1, 110:3, 118:3, 148:3, 15:4, 27:4, 57:4, 79:4, 148:5

needy. *See also* poor
    3:1, 20:1, 24:1, 27:1, 56:1, 80:1, 91:1, 48:3, 114:3, 129:3, 7:4, 11:4, 14:4, 23:4, 24:4, 29:4, 33:4, 40:4, 54:4, 72:4, 75:4, 82:4, 90:4, 107:4, 117:4, 121:4, 122:4, 123:4, 124:4, 125:4, 126:4, 129:4, 130:4, 133:4, 139:4, 144:4, 149:4, 153:4, 158:4, 170:4, 179:4, 180:4, 71:5, 5:6, 8:6, 23:6, 36:6, 41:6, 43:6, 44:6, 45:6, 46:6, 50:6, 52:6, 56:6, 63:6, 67:6, 72:6, 76:6, 87:6, 95:6, 104:6, 105:6, 106:6, 107:6, 109:6, 113:6

Nehor
    26:1, 84:1, 145:3

neighbor
    7:P, 8:P, 9:P, 28:P, 30:P, 19:1, 29:1, 66:1, 18:3, 49:3, 96:3, 182:3, 21:4, 26:4, 33:4, 38:4, 56:4, 58:4, 77:4, 91:4, 100:4, 104:4, 118:4, 122:4, 158:4, 164:4, 165:4, 169:4, 184:4, 93:5, 94:5, 127:5, 16:6, 20:6, 36:6, 41:6, 77:6, 93:6, 94:6, 113:6

new and everlasting covenant. *See also* marriage
    a discussion of
        how it's likened to marriage
            72–99:2

Nimrod
    51:1, 52:1, 53:1, 54:1, 55:1, 58:1, 61:1, 101:1

Noah
    15:P, 14:1, 15:1, 16:1, 18:1, 36:1, 53:1, 55:1, 86:1, 87:1, 101:1, 102:1, 103:1, 7:3, 27:3, 207:3, 107:4, 32:5, 88:5, 101:5, 124:5, 125:5, 127:5, 22:6

oath and covenant of the priesthood. *See also* priesthood
    1:P, 6:1, 32:1, 9:2, 34:2, 36:2, 47:2, 61:2, 98:2, 1:3, 2:3, 3:3, 4:3, 6:3, 21:3, 25:3, 30:3, 33:3, 35:3, 36:3, 39:3, 40:3, 41:3, 43:3, 47:3, 49:3, 53:3, 54:3, 55:3, 58:3, 59:3, 60:3, 61:3, 63:3,

64:3, 66:3, 68:3, 71:3, 72:3, 76:3, 77:3, 78:3, 80:3, 81:3, 82:3, 85:3, 87:3, 88:3, 90:3, 93:3, 94:3, 95:3, 97:3, 98:3, 102:3, 103:3, 104:3, 105:3, 106:3, 109:3, 115:3, 117:3, 126:3, 131:3, 135:3, 139:3, 140:3, 142:3, 143:3, 144:3, 159:3, 172:3, 173:3, 174:3, 175:3, 177:3, 179:3, 184:3, 189:3, 190:3, 193:3, 202:3, 208:3, 210:3, 211:3, 212:3, 213:3, 214:3, 1:4, 2:4, 14:4, 72:4, 90:4, 129:4, 142:4, 185:4, 1:5, 2:5, 59:5, 116:5, 134:5, 135:5, 136:5, 50:6

obedience
> 30:P, 32:P, 41:P, 17:1, 19:1, 21:1, 48:1, 3:2, 4:2, 6:2, 7:2, 10:2, 12:2, 13:2, 15:2, 17:2, 28:2, 29:2, 33:2, 34:2, 35:2, 37:2, 38:2, 39:2, 42:2, 51:2, 61:2, 31:3, 67:3, 68:3, 71:3, 75:3, 80:3, 94:3, 118:3, 121:3, 124:3, 126:3, 131:3, 134:3, 135:3, 146:3, 203:3, 208:3, 212:3, 16:4, 18:4, 26:4, 36:4, 41:4, 45:4, 50:4, 56:4, 60:4, 65:4, 67:4, 102:4, 156:4, 180:4, 7:5, 33:5, 35:5, 36:5, 45:5, 46:5, 47:5, 81:5, 84:5, 97:5, 135:5, 18:6, 112:6, 113:6, 115:6

offence
> 73:1

offering. *See* **consecration; sacrifice;** *See* **offerings**

offerings
> those, ordered by Satan are always rejected by God
>> 51:1

oneness. *See also* **unity**
> 6:P, 18:P, 19:P, 12:1, 49:1, 92:1, 23:2, 24:2, 25:2, 27:2, 28:2, 29:2, 48:2, 71:2, 79:2, 170:3, 5:4, 18:4, 31:4, 41:4, 42:4, 43:4, 44:4, 45:4, 47:4, 59:4, 65:5, 94:5, 115:5, 123:5

opposition. *See also* **adversity**
> 35:P, 33:1, 36:1, 54:1, 67:1, 70:1, 19:2, 26:2, 56:2, 117:3, 45:4, 62:4, 10:5, 18:5, 49:5

ordinance
> 6:1, 11:1, 31:1, 51:1, 28:2, 31:2, 34:2, 36:2, 37:2, 38:2, 45:2, 53:2, 56:2, 63:2, 64:2, 67:2, 69:2, 91:2, 4:3, 6:3, 9:3, 10:3, 14:3, 16:3, 20:3, 21:3, 28:3, 29:3, 77:3, 82:3, 84:3, 87:3, 99:3, 105:3, 194:3, 197:3, 205:3, 212:3, 28:4, 43:4, 159:4, 160:4, 161:4, 162:4, 163:4, 25:5, 46:5, 60:5, 91:5, 133:5, 75:6

parent
> 42:1, 46:1, 168:3, 53:4, 147:4, 153:4, 16:5, 62:5, 70:6

patience
> 23:1, 27:1, 73:1, 22:2, 76:2, 85:2, 86:2, 29:3, 97:3, 129:3, 148:3, 149:3, 150:3, 151:3, 155:3, 178:3, 181:3, 99:4, 146:4, 155:4, 178:4, 184:4, 85:5, 15:6, 70:6, 101:6

patriarchal order of the priesthood. *See also* **Melchizedek Priesthood;** *See also* **oath and covenant of the priesthood**

Paul
> 27:P, 39:P, 41:1, 57:1, 59:1, 70:1, 73:1, 88:1, 89:1, 91:1, 103:1, 27:2, 63:2, 64:2, 81:2, 85:2, 31:3, 40:3, 67:3, 90:3, 100:3, 149:3, 163:3, 171:3, 180:3, 189:3, 198:3, 37:4, 99:4, 117:4, 165:4, 166:4, 184:4, 13:5, 15:5, 29:5, 89:5, 119:5, 133:5, 15:6, 35:6, 76:6, 78:6, 94:6, 95:6, 97:6, 106:6

Paymaster
> 8:P, 17:1, 151:3, 70:4, 71:4, 88:4, 90:4, 183:4

Index & Concordance 131

peace
> 2:P, 5:P, 8:P, 12:P, 17:P, 20:P, 26:P, 27:P, 9:1, 15:1, 16:1, 23:1, 25:1, 27:1, 30:1, 46:1, 88:1, 8:2, 24:2, 39:2, 50:2, 51:2, 61:2, 95:2, 5:3, 6:3, 7:3, 8:3, 18:3, 28:3, 29:3, 46:3, 50:3, 66:3, 70:3, 83:3, 114:3, 119:3, 129:3, 140:3, 167:3, 172:3, 173:3, 199:3, 19:4, 22:4, 40:4, 44:4, 46:4, 115:4, 118:4, 119:4, 124:4, 125:4, 137:4, 140:4, 150:4, 151:4, 152:4, 162:4, 171:4, 172:4, 178:4, 27:5, 28:5, 38:5, 44:5, 46:5, 53:5, 55:5, 81:5, 83:5, 92:5, 94:5, 103:5, 104:5, 106:5, 107:5, 122:5, 128:5, 130:5, 132:5, 133:5, 1:6, 2:6, 13:6, 34:6, 37:6, 38:6, 45:6, 60:6, 61:6, 64:6, 97:6, 98:6, 101:6

persecute
> 27:P, 28:P, 30:P, 61:1, 67:1, 85:1, 91:1, 137:3, 152:3, 108:4, 122:4, 123:4, 124:4, 150:4, 42:5, 26:6, 41:6, 42:6, 44:6, 77:6, 112:6, 113:6

plague
> 82:1, 160:3, 124:4, 38:5, 44:6

poor. *See also* **needy**
> a discussion of
>> how we treat the,
>>> 120–137:4

popular
> 14:1, 66:1, 81:1, 83:1, 84:1, 87:1, 25:3, 132:3

possession. *See* **mammon**

praise. *See* **popular**

pray, prayer
> 80:1, 85:1, 98:1, 14:2, 20:2, 55:2, 86:2, 91:2, 92:2, 41:3, 70:3, 154:3, 158:3, 192:3, 197:3, 8:4, 9:4, 45:4, 46:4, 54:4, 60:4, 111:4, 112:4, 140:4, 162:4, 163:4, 181:4, 4:5, 19:5, 42:5, 51:5, 53:5, 67:5, 69:5, 77:5, 78:5, 87:5, 112:5, 114:5, 115:5, 116:5, 120:5, 121:5, 122:5, 123:5, 124:5, 28:6, 29:6, 64:6, 90:6, 104:6

premortal existence
> mature knowledge of gospel from, planted deep in our souls
>> 44:1

pride
> neither rich nor poor exempt from
>> 24:1

priest
> 17:1, 26:1, 84:1, 20:2, 41:2, 94:2, 95:2, 5:3, 6:3, 7:3, 9:3, 29:3, 42:3, 46:3, 65:3, 119:3, 152:3, 190:3, 198:3, 199:3, 88:4, 100:4, 40:5, 63:5, 89:5, 16:6

priestcraft
> 26:1, 51:1, 53:1, 61:1, 68:1, 84:1, 85:1, 145:3, 146:3

priesthood. *See also* **Aaronic Priesthood**; *See also* **Melchizedek Priesthood**; *See also* **oath and covenant of the priesthood**; *See also* **patriarchal order of the priesthood**
> a discussion of
>> Melchizedek
>>> 4–11:3, 182–192:3, 204–210:3

oath and covenant of the
: 39–60:3
restoration of the
: 12–16:3

priesthood society
: 1:P, 3:P, 4:P, 43:P, 3:1, 5:1, 6:1, 7:1, 12:1, 14:1, 46:1, 5:3, 6:3, 12:3, 21:3, 25:3, 28:3, 32:3, 35:3, 61:3, 85:3, 127:3, 206:3, 7:4, 14:4, 15:4, 22:4, 31:4, 74:4, 80:4, 90:5, 98:5, 99:5, 127:5, 87:6, 102:6, 105:6

princess. *See* **queen**

prison
: 88:1, 51:2, 52:2, 54:2, 88:2, 70:3, 100:3, 138:4, 139:4, 151:4, 152:4, 12:5, 29:5, 39:5, 75:5, 63:6, 116:6, 117:6

probation. *See* **mortality**

progress
: perspective of our, compared to steps on an airplane
: 90:5

properties. *See* **property**

property
: converting life into, is Satan's great secret
: 47:6

prophecies
: 93:1, 95:1, 97:1, 98:1, 109:3, 166:3, 4:5, 97:5, 103:5, 118:5, 119:5, 49:6

prosper. *See* **abundance**

publicans
: 80:1

pure in heart. *See also* **Zion**
: 2:P, 17:P, 25:P, 26:P, 38:P, 41:P, 43:P, 2:1, 3:1, 4:1, 6:1, 8:1, 12:1, 15:1, 19:1, 25:1, 33:1, 46:1, 48:1, 18:2, 47:3, 66:3, 71:3, 87:3, 161:3, 172:3, 178:3, 195:3, 207:3, 208:3, 2:4, 15:4, 16:4, 31:4, 73:4, 83:4, 95:4, 104:4, 109:4, 147:4, 1:5, 2:5, 3:5, 4:5, 18:5, 77:5, 78:5, 79:5, 80:5, 81:5, 82:5, 84:5, 87:5, 89:5, 90:5, 91:5, 93:5, 94:5, 95:5, 96:5, 101:5, 109:5, 114:5, 115:5, 116:5, 117:5, 118:5, 119:5, 120:5, 124:5, 125:5, 127:5, 130:5, 133:5, 134:5, 136:5, 9:6, 20:6, 26:6, 75:6, 76:6, 78:6, 116:6

purification
: 14:P, 18:2, 19:2, 20:2, 90:2, 91:2, 66:3, 137:3, 52:4, 162:4, 182:4, 3:5, 25:5, 26:5, 75:5, 79:5, 90:5, 115:5, 116:5, 120:5

queen(s)
: 93:1, 90:2, 93:2, 94:2, 199:3, 8:5

rainbow
: sign of everlasting covenant
: 15:1

redeem, Redeemer, redemption
: noble spirits in premortal life carried out work of
: 45:1

Index & Concordance

repent
> 20:P, 2:1, 10:1, 13:1, 16:1, 24:1, 70:1, 91:1, 98:1, 99:1, 5:2, 7:2, 16:2, 17:2, 19:2, 35:2, 36:2, 96:2, 5:3, 6:3, 19:3, 45:3, 46:3, 70:3, 103:3, 135:3, 153:3, 161:3, 188:3, 205:3, 37:4, 69:4, 84:4, 102:4, 111:4, 112:4, 117:4, 118:4, 121:4, 126:4, 135:4, 136:4, 148:4, 15:5, 46:5, 78:5, 82:5, 105:5, 106:5, 109:5, 2:6, 18:6, 28:6, 29:6, 35:6, 36:6, 39:6, 46:6, 47:6, 59:6, 60:6

resurrected
> 14:P, 13:1, 23:1, 64:1, 86:1, 95:1, 14:2, 26:2, 17:3, 91:3, 202:3, 203:3, 42:4, 13:5, 64:5, 105:5, 108:5, 121:5, 122:5, 132:5

revelation
> is key to magnifying callings and to learning
> > 95:3

riches. *See also* **mammon**; *See also* **materialism**; *See also* **money**; *See also* **wealth**
> 30:P, 32:P, 34:P, 38:P, 17:1, 27:1, 31:1, 33:1, 67:1, 71:1, 72:1, 76:1, 84:1, 86:1, 92:1, 93:1, 95:1, 96:1, 97:1, 99:1, 123:3, 125:3, 126:3, 128:3, 129:3, 130:3, 131:3, 133:3, 141:3, 142:3, 146:3, 167:3, 171:3, 193:3, 8:4, 9:4, 10:4, 26:4, 30:4, 38:4, 40:4, 69:4, 72:4, 83:4, 84:4, 85:4, 87:4, 88:4, 91:4, 93:4, 95:4, 99:4, 100:4, 101:4, 102:4, 103:4, 106:4, 108:4, 109:4, 110:4, 111:4, 113:4, 115:4, 116:4, 117:4, 118:4, 119:4, 120:4, 123:4, 124:4, 126:4, 127:4, 130:4, 132:4, 133:4, 135:4, 140:4, 142:4, 144:4, 148:4, 149:4, 150:4, 152:4, 158:4, 184:4, 44:5, 103:5, 104:5, 4:6, 7:6, 16:6, 17:6, 18:6, 19:6, 22:6, 25:6, 26:6, 28:6, 31:6, 33:6, 34:6, 36:6, 37:6, 38:6, 43:6, 44:6, 46:6, 47:6, 48:6, 51:6, 56:6, 57:6, 58:6, 65:6, 67:6, 72:6, 113:6, 114:6, 115:6

Sabbath
> 42:P, 37:1, 38:2, 39:2, 40:2, 50:2, 51:2, 72:2, 99:4, 53:5, 15:6

sacrament
> 14:P, 23:P, 29:1, 14:2, 20:2, 36:2, 38:2, 39:2, 40:2, 41:2, 60:2, 67:2, 80:2, 81:2, 82:2, 89:2, 9:3, 11:3, 39:3, 42:3, 66:3, 75:3, 93:3, 165:3, 193:3, 210:3, 46:4, 17:5, 18:5, 60:5, 61:5, 62:5, 64:5, 117:5, 121:5

sacrifice. *See also* **consecration**; *See also* **offering**
> a discussion of
> > 3–31:4, 33–52:4, 61–92:4

Salem. *See also* **Jerusalem**
> 3:P, 9:1, 15:1, 16:1, 5:3, 27:3, 29:3, 45:3, 1:6, 2:6

salvation, plan of
> 50:1, 54:2, 25:3, 26:3, 31:3, 36:3, 68:3, 73:3, 12:5, 126:5, 130:5

sanctification
> 14:P, 18:P, 18:2, 20:2, 21:2, 90:2, 91:2, 9:3, 56:3, 66:3, 67:3, 68:3, 69:3, 70:3, 71:3, 74:3, 75:3, 77:3, 84:3, 104:3, 137:3, 210:3, 14:4, 18:4, 21:4, 31:4, 52:4, 182:4, 3:5, 27:5, 47:5, 75:5, 79:5, 90:5, 94:5, 99:5, 115:5, 116:5

sanctified body. *See* **sanctification**

sanctuaries. *See* **mammon**

Satan. *See also* **adversary;** *See also* **devil;** *See also* **hell;** *See also* **Lucifer**
    we must understand, in order to confront him
        55:5

savior
    Adam empowered to become, to his family
        11:1

Savior. *See* **Christ, Jesus;** *See* **Exemplar;** *See* **Jehovah;** *See* **Lamb**

saviors on Mount Zion
    43:1, 32:2, 40:2, 25:3, 35:3, 37:3, 43:3, 66:3, 69:3, 104:3, 156:3, 144:4, 184:4, 64:5, 116:5, 68:6

science
    57:1, 81:1, 83:1, 14:2, 163:3

seal
    26:1, 24:2, 76:2, 79:2, 93:2, 13:3, 16:3, 17:3, 81:3, 84:3, 99:3, 149:3, 168:3, 194:3, 199:3, 209:3, 52:4, 75:4, 108:4, 155:4, 162:4, 38:5, 58:5, 65:5, 67:5, 25:6

secret combinations. *See also* **Gadianton robbers**
    49:1, 60:1, 61:1, 91:1, 97:1, 99:1, 102:5, 103:5, 108:5

selfish
    9:P, 38:P, 58:1, 73:1, 89:1, 91:1, 96:1, 19:2, 32:2, 71:2, 21:3, 74:3, 88:3, 122:3, 124:3, 125:3, 131:3, 137:3, 153:3, 154:3, 157:3, 171:3, 27:4, 55:4, 82:4, 91:4, 97:4, 98:4, 112:4, 117:4, 134:4, 140:4, 141:4, 145:4, 149:4, 152:4, 156:4, 165:4, 169:4, 176:4, 94:5, 11:6, 18:6, 29:6, 30:6, 31:6, 35:6, 37:6, 45:6, 48:6, 58:6, 64:6, 65:6, 66:6, 68:6, 71:6, 72:6, 77:6, 86:6, 88:6, 94:6, 108:6, 115:6

selfless. *See also* **charity**
    1:P, 8:P, 10:P, 12:P, 23:P, 25:P, 31:P, 24:1, 29:1, 5:2, 32:2, 71:2, 21:3, 51:3, 171:3, 109:4, 170:4, 93:5, 100:5, 26:6, 76:6, 87:6

Sermon on the Mount. *See also* **Beatitudes**
    14:P, 16:P, 28:1, 18:2, 82:5, 118:5

servant
    37:P, 16:1, 27:1, 34:2, 61:2, 62:2, 69:2, 87:2, 88:2, 91:2, 92:2, 96:2, 6:3, 30:3, 41:3, 72:3, 82:3, 100:3, 101:3, 103:3, 115:3, 196:3, 211:3, 214:3, 12:4, 49:4, 50:4, 53:4, 74:4, 75:4, 78:4, 79:4, 81:4, 89:4, 183:4, 66:5, 97:5, 110:5

set apart. *See* **consecration**

sex
    57:1, 66:1, 76:1, 154:3, 97:4, 11:6

single women
    64:3

slippery treasures
    110:4, 27:6

snare
    70:1, 73:1, 109:3, 122:3, 124:3, 139:3, 99:4, 103:4, 113:4, 14:5, 15:6, 19:6, 30:6, 108:6

Index & Concordance

Sodom
    1:1, 54:1, 55:1, 56:1, 57:1, 86:1, 94:1, 101:1, 102:1, 103:1, 5:4, 121:4, 23:5, 41:6

sorrow. *See also* **wailing**
    21:P, 34:1, 35:1, 63:1, 93:1, 102:1, 88:2, 51:3, 151:3, 160:3, 19:4, 124:4, 127:4, 136:4, 10:5, 43:5, 44:5, 106:5, 44:6, 48:6, 59:6, 79:6

soul
    11:P, 16:P, 17:P, 23:P, 43:P, 20:1, 21:1, 22:1, 28:1, 60:1, 76:1, 8:2, 19:2, 26:2, 40:2, 41:2, 49:2, 55:2, 59:2, 61:2, 94:2, 7:3, 19:3, 44:3, 47:3, 67:3, 69:3, 83:3, 97:3, 100:3, 102:3, 108:3, 116:3, 119:3, 122:3, 144:3, 151:3, 156:3, 159:3, 165:3, 166:3, 172:3, 175:3, 182:3, 184:3, 189:3, 193:3, 213:3, 2:4, 9:4, 16:4, 20:4, 50:4, 54:4, 56:4, 60:4, 64:4, 65:4, 111:4, 114:4, 115:4, 118:4, 127:4, 140:4, 146:4, 152:4, 155:4, 160:4, 162:4, 164:4, 166:4, 167:4, 171:4, 172:4, 174:4, 175:4, 179:4, 180:4, 182:4, 183:4, 186:4, 2:5, 13:5, 15:5, 17:5, 44:5, 45:5, 49:5, 68:5, 71:5, 74:5, 80:5, 81:5, 84:5, 100:5, 108:5, 122:5, 5:6, 6:6, 29:6, 30:6, 32:6, 33:6, 37:6, 48:6, 50:6, 65:6, 71:6, 85:6, 86:6, 91:6, 95:6, 96:6, 97:6, 98:6, 100:6, 101:6, 102:6, 103:6, 108:6

Spencer W. Kimball
    8:P, 25:P, 33:P, 3:1, 7:1, 37:1, 55:1, 85:1, 21:3, 31:3, 35:3, 118:3, 140:3, 191:3, 7:4, 9:4, 15:4, 17:4, 23:4, 30:4, 31:4, 48:4, 59:4, 83:4, 86:4, 109:4, 134:4, 172:4, 173:4, 177:4, 37:5, 49:5, 92:5, 93:5, 98:5, 100:5, 26:6, 57:6, 76:6, 88:6, 90:6, 98:6, 99:6

stewardship(s)
    in heaven based on stewardships on earth
        50:5

storehouse
    7:P, 36:P, 17:1, 18:1, 64:2, 6:3, 38:4, 39:4, 48:4, 61:4, 71:4, 72:4, 74:4, 75:4, 77:4, 79:4, 83:4, 88:4, 91:4, 96:4, 131:4, 10:6, 51:6, 77:6

submission
    79:1, 118:3, 152:3, 31:5

surplus
    36:P, 18:1, 48:3, 12:4, 24:4, 69:4, 74:4, 75:4, 79:4, 90:4, 91:4, 94:4, 147:4, 9:6, 114:6

telestial
    3:P, 9:P, 10:P, 12:P, 25:P, 26:P, 30:P, 31:P, 32:P, 37:P, 38:P, 3:1, 6:1, 7:1, 8:1, 10:1, 17:1, 29:1, 39:1, 40:1, 47:1, 66:1, 80:1, 103:1, 14:2, 15:2, 23:2, 48:2, 60:2, 68:2, 69:2, 68:3, 80:3, 89:3, 114:3, 117:3, 124:3, 125:3, 140:3, 141:3, 144:3, 164:3, 211:3, 10:4, 15:4, 18:4, 25:4, 34:4, 35:4, 36:4, 64:4, 69:4, 73:4, 82:4, 83:4, 96:4, 101:4, 105:4, 141:4, 147:4, 148:4, 163:4, 185:4, 11:5, 12:5, 19:5, 31:5, 36:5, 70:5, 76:5, 84:5, 85:5, 91:5, 121:5, 126:5, 10:6, 17:6, 21:6, 66:6, 86:6, 105:6, 106:6, 107:6, 110:6, 112:6, 115:6, 116:6

temple
    covenants, necessary to establish Zion/is gathering place for Zion people
        31:1

temptation
    70:1, 133:3, 176:3, 43:4, 97:4, 99:4, 14:5, 120:5, 121:5, 11:6, 15:6

Ten Commandments
>15:2, 100:4, 148:4, 110:5, 16:6

ten virgins
>85:1, 103:1, 87:2, 90:2, 92:2

terrestrial
>testimony, bearing of, purifies heart; bearing of, is an act of love
>>56:3

tithes
>31:P, 34:P, 37:P, 42:P, 17:1, 37:1, 6:3, 8:4, 12:4, 13:4, 30:4, 81:4, 88:4, 89:4, 92:4, 96:4, 147:4, 118:5, 10:6, 12:6, 13:6, 51:6, 114:6, 115:6

tradition
>98:1, 72:2, 73:2, 75:2, 84:2, 7:3, 9:3

treasure. *See* **mammon**

trial(s). *See also* **adversity;** *See also* **opposition**
>29:P, 44:1, 56:2, 58:2, 83:3, 128:3, 148:3, 151:3, 124:4, 23:5, 27:5, 50:5, 58:5, 44:6, 50:6

unite, unity. *See also* **oneness**
>4:P, 6:P, 37:P, 3:1, 9:1, 14:1, 19:1, 68:1, 77:1, 78:1, 92:1, 23:2, 24:2, 25:2, 27:2, 69:2, 93:2, 74:3, 85:3, 114:3, 116:3, 140:3, 147:3, 170:3, 2:4, 19:4, 33:4, 41:4, 42:4, 43:4, 44:4, 45:4, 46:4, 47:4, 48:4, 49:4, 50:4, 51:4, 52:4, 54:4, 55:4, 58:4, 59:4, 60:4, 62:4, 82:4, 156:4, 171:4, 183:4, 185:4, 2:5, 50:5, 73:5, 100:5, 108:5, 97:6

universe
>composition of
>>89:3

vain
>22:P, 28:P, 64:1, 66:1, 69:1, 80:1, 86:1, 97:1, 98:1, 41:2, 45:3, 47:3, 51:3, 92:3, 107:3, 110:3, 114:3, 119:3, 135:3, 146:3, 153:3, 163:3, 164:3, 99:4, 110:4, 111:4, 115:4, 117:4, 118:4, 119:4, 122:4, 124:4, 126:4, 127:4, 133:4, 149:4, 175:4, 181:4, 57:5, 71:5, 95:5, 101:5, 102:5, 104:5, 4:6, 15:6, 28:6, 33:6, 36:6, 38:6, 41:6, 42:6, 44:6, 46:6, 57:6, 79:6, 104:6

veil
>40:1, 55:1, 80:2, 83:2, 84:2, 85:2, 95:2, 26:3, 91:3, 102:3, 178:3, 179:3, 180:3, 181:3, 183:3, 196:3, 209:3, 210:3, 54:4, 12:5, 67:5, 68:5, 79:5, 85:5, 89:5, 109:5, 131:5

violence
>14:1, 36:1, 87:1, 93:1, 95:1, 8:3, 121:3, 108:4, 26:6

wailing. *See also* **sorrow**
>94:1

war
>17:P, 26:P, 42:1, 44:1, 55:1, 62:1, 69:1, 78:1, 80:1, 85:1, 91:1, 102:1, 28:2, 83:3, 108:4, 137:4, 37:5, 102:5, 103:5, 108:5, 26:6, 60:6

warn
>95:1, 113:4, 124:4, 102:5, 103:5, 30:6, 44:6

Index & Concordance

wealth. *See also* **mammon**; *See also* **poor**; *See also* **riches**
    a discussion of
        proper use
            120–151:4
        seeking
            99–137:4

weapon
    29:P, 57:1, 71:1, 55:2, 99:4, 109:4, 132:4, 149:4, 16:6, 26:6, 56:6, 112:6

whore. *See* **Babylon**

wickedness
    today's level of, equals or exceeds times that of Noah's generation
        87:1

widow
    93:1, 7:4, 29:4, 104:4, 109:4, 130:4, 140:4, 146:4, 153:4, 51:5, 70:5, 20:6, 27:6 52:6, 65:6, 70:6

wife. *See also* **marriage**
    45:P, 10:1, 33:1, 62:1, 24:2, 25:2, 58:2, 66:2, 74:2, 76:2, 77:2, 78:2, 79:2, 35:2, 92:2, 94:2, 95:2, 97:2, 13:3, 15:3, 17:3, 23:3, 31:3, 59:3, 82:3, 85:3, 110:3, 112:3, 126:3, 136:3, 183:3, 198:3, 199:3, 207:3, 211:3, 26:4, 41:4, 43:4, 45:4, 52:4, 98:4, 100:4, 156:4, 157:4, 10:5, 20:5, 24:5, 38:5, 42:5, 11:6, 16:6, 106:6, 109:6

wilderness. *See also* **Babylon**
    a discussion of
        our journey through the
            12–41s:5

Wilford Woodruff
    40:1, 55:3, 131:3, 211:3, 148:5

wisdom
    21:P, 32:P, 23:1, 24:1, 26:1, 31:1, 33:1, 39:1, 59:1, 60:1, 64:1, 65:1, 78:1, 84:1, 98:1, 102:1, 45:2, 50:3, 54:3, 71:3, 93:3, 152:3, 161:3, 163:3, 164:3, 165:3, 166:3, 167:3, 168:3, 187:3, 201:3, 208:3, 6:4, 26:4, 27:4, 66:4, 77:4, 100:4, 105:4, 108:4, 109:4, 120:4, 122:4, 137:4, 141:4, 149:4, 152:4, 179:4, 65:5, 3:6, 16:6, 21:6, 25:6, 27:6, 38:6, 42:6, 61:6, 66:6, 82:6, 102:6, 115:6

work. *See also* **labor**
    Christ's, takes priority
        30:1

world, worldly. *See also* **Babylon**
    in, but not of
        74:1

yoke
    17:P, 23:P, 28:P, 62:1, 63:1, 101:1, 92:2, 160:3, 179:4, 68:5, 69:5, 71:5, 102:6

Zion
    an individual with a pure heart
        12:1
    begins in each person's heart
        1:1, 12:1, 13:1
    definition of, is perfection
        12:1
    is a return to the presence of God
        47:1
    is our ideal
        6:1
    principles of
        19:1
    we are
        46:1

Zion people
    characteristics of
        12:1
    temple gathering place for
        14:1

About the Author

Larry Barkdull is a longtime publisher and writer of books, music, art, and magazines. For nine years, he owned Sonos Music Resources and published the Tabernacle Choir Performance Library. He was also the owner and publisher of Keepsake Books. Over the past thirty years, he's published some six hundred products for numerous authors, composers, and artists. He's founded two nonprofit organizations: The Latter-day Foundation for the Arts, Education and Humanity (to promote LDS arts), and Gospel Ideals International (to promote the gospel of Jesus Christ on the Internet).

His books have sold in excess of 300,000 copies, and they have been translated into Japanese, Korean, Italian, and Hebrew. He is the recipient of the American Family Literary Award; the Benjamin Franklin Book Award; and *Foreword Magazine's* GOLD Book of the Year Award for best fiction. His most recent books are *Priesthood Power—Blessing the Sick and the Afflicted*, *Rescuing Wayward Children*, and *The Shepherd Song*.

He and his wife, Elizabeth, have ten children and a growing number of grandchildren. They live in Orem, Utah. Read more of his writings at Meridian Magazine.com.

www.ingramcontent.com/pod-product-compliance
Lightning Source LLC
Chambersburg PA
CBHW080442110426
42743CB00016B/3253